THE ANALYSIS OF DREAMS

MEDARD BOSS, M.D.
*Professor of Psychotherapy at
the University of Zurich*

Translated by
ARNOLD J. POMERANS

NEW YORK
PHILOSOPHICAL LIBRARY

Published, 1958, by the Philosophical Library, Inc.,
15 East 40 Street, New York 16, N. Y.
Copyright 1958 by Medard Boss

All rights reserved

Printed in the United States of America

CONTENTS

Foreword by Dr. E. B. Strauss   Page 7
Preface   9
Introduction   11

PART I
Modern Dream Theories

1. Sigmund Freud's Theory of Dreams   21
2. Critique of the Foundations of Freud's Dream Theory   32
3. Dream Theories of the "Zurich School":   38
    (a) The theory of the "finalist" aspect of the dream
    (b) The theory of the "subjective" meaning of the dream
4. Critique of the Basis of the Dream Theories of the Zurich School   50
5. "Neo-analytical" Dream Theories: 60
    (a) The neo-psychoanalytical dream theory of H. Schultz-Hencke
    (b) The "neo-Freudian" dream theory of E. Fromm
6. The Most Recent Non-analytical Dream Theories   66
7. Previous Attempts at a Phenomenological Interpretation of Dreams   69
    (a) The phenomenological examination of dreams made by R. Bossard
    (b) The phenomenological studies of dreams made by L. Klages

CONTENTS

PART II

The Dream Itself

8   A "Strange Dream of an Urn" — 77

9   Attempt at a Phenomenological Interpretation of the "Strange Dream of an Urn" — 80
Criticism of interpretations in terms of:
  (a) a mere hallucination
  (b) Freud's theory of wish-fulfilment and the instinctual theory of Schultz-Hencke
  (c) hypermnesia
  (d) common ideas about the imagination
  (e) disturbance of the sense of time and space
  (f) "symbolism"

10 The Content of Dreams and Theories of Dream Symbolism — 91
  (a) Dream phenomena and the Freudian theory of symbols
  (b) Dream phenomena and Jung's theory of symbols

11 The Elimination of Dream Interpretation on the Objective and Subjective Level, in the Phenomenological Interpretation of Dreams — 102

12 The Concrete Dream Phenomenon as a Whole and the Derived Conception of the Archetype — 113

13 The Practical Application of a Phenomenological Interpretation of Dreams — 118

PART III

Human Life In Dreams

14 The Dreamer's Possibilities of Existing: — 125
  (a) Being alarmed in shock dreams
  (b) Decisive volitional behaviour in dreams
  (c) Reflective behaviour in dreams

CONTENTS

- (d) Imagination and vision in dreams
- (e) Conscious thought in dreams
- (f) The ability to tell lies in dreams
- (g) Unconscious mistakes in dreams
- (h) Artistic appreciation in dreams
- (i) Moral evaluation in dreams

15 The Relationship to the Divine in Dreams   141

16 Experience of Dreams within Dreams: 151
- (a) Dreaming of existing as a dreamer
- (b) The analysis of dreams within dreams
- (c) The magical dream world
- (d) Being a thing in the dream

17 The Possibilities of "Extra-Sensory" Relationships in Dreams   159
- (a) "Diagnostic" or "Endoscopic" dreams
- (b) "Clairvoyant", "Telepathic", and "Prophetic" dreams

18 "Nonsensical" and "Paradoxical" Dreams   189
- (a) "Nonsensical" time-and-place relationships in dreams
- (b) Dreams about a "paradoxical something"

PART IV

The Dream as a Whole

19 The Problem of the Dream as a Whole   207

Notes   213

Index   220

Foreword

by

E. B. STRAUSS, M.A., D.M., D.Sc., F.R.C.P.
President of the British Psychological Society (1956–57)

This is not an easy book; but any original work on the analysis of dreams, to be of any value, would be difficult reading. The difficulties are even greater for the English reader in view of the unfamiliar framework of Professor Boss's technique: phenomenology never really crossed the Channel sufficiently to make its mark on British psychiatry; and existentialism seems to have as many connotations in the British mind as there are existentialists on the Continent.

However, the reader will miss the meaning and beauty of this book unless he is able to grasp the author's main premises.

A phenomenological psychiatrist is, I suppose, one who is content from the start to regard all human experience as phenomena of a Reality, the nature of which need not concern him. He is prepared, philosophically speaking, to move in and seek to manipulate the world of appearances, leaving the world of ultimate spiritual realities, if they exist, for the consideration of the metaphysician and theologian. An existentialist psychotherapist, in Professor Boss's sense, is one who regards it as important to link up all the psychic phenomena which are his special field of study with the rest of the universe in which they occur as part-phenomena. In that way experience can be made, to a certain extent, to escape from the rigid categories of 'subjective' and 'objective'.

An analysis of the dream-life which uses both phenomenological and ontological instruments is bound to be stimulating, original, exciting—and unfamiliar.

The *interpretation* of all dreams in Freud's over-simplified terms as symbolic expressions of repressed, sex-derived wishes is seen to be unacceptable to an analytical psychotherapist of Professor Boss's approach.

Again, Professor Boss throws considerable doubt on Jung's

attempt to interpret dreams as compensatory mechanisms designed to integrate the various faculties and bring about 'individuation' of the personality through the intervention of 'archetypes' deriving from the non-personal levels of the Unconscious.

Nevertheless, in the last analysis, is there so very much difference between the full experiencing of 'selfhood', which would appear to be the ultimate object of Professor Boss's type of psychotherapy, individuation, the object of Jungian analysis, and the resolution of unconscious, instinct-derived conflicts and the achievement of an appropriate adulthood thereby, which is the desired goal of Freudian analysis?

No one is in a position to state categorically that *his* is the correct or solely possible interpretation of this or that dream. Yet, any psychotherapeutic procedure, including 'faulty' or narrow dream-interpretations, that serves to direct or re-direct a patient's steps on the path which leads to mental health is useful and worthy of respect.

Professor Boss's great merit is that he has enormously widened and deepened our ideas on the meaning of dreams in relation to the rest of life, without demanding our wholesale rejection of the work of other psychologists who have set themselves the same task.

Preface

A psycho-analytical therapist may hear anything between five and twenty dreams daily, and often an even greater number. Thus, at a conservative estimate, during twenty-five years of practice as a psychotherapist I have been told of about 50,000 dreams by at least 500 different people. In any case, thanks to a written record kept during the last five years, I have been able to verify that during that period I have been told of 11,200 dreams by neurotics, by analysts in training, and by normal acquaintances.

I obtained my first insight into the vast realm of dreams, through many years of training in classical psycho-analytical theory and practice, such as is required by the Freudian school. But I increasingly encountered dreams which would yield to the key of the Freudian dream theory only most reluctantly and with the greatest difficulty, so much so that the whole theory appeared to be inadequate. For this reason I examined the scientific works of other dream psychologists. As luck would have it, a psychotherapeutic group was being formed in Zurich under the leadership of C. G. Jung, with the co-operation of A. Maeder, another pioneer amongst dream explorers. During the ten years that this group functioned I had many opportunities of becoming thoroughly conversant with the dream doctrines of both these investigators. The additional therapeutic techniques of dream interpretation which I owe to my association with this group, are a part of the essential tools of my medical activity. However, even here I could not find an adequate elucidation of the dream phenomena themselves, nor did H. Silberer, A. Adler, W. Stekel, and the numerous later studies of other dream psychologists clarify for me the actual essence of these phenomena, valuable as their theoretical conclusions were.

For all of them agreed with Freud's original dream theory in that they replaced the immediate and direct phenomenon by explanations of it. They saw in dreams the expression of something else, something merely assumed to exist behind the phenomena, some mental construct.

There is no doubt that all these dream theories had an important role to play. How else could modern dream investigation have begun tackling this elusive problem at all? It is only thanks to this tremendous preparatory work that today we may ask about the proper and full content of the dream phenomenon. However, this very question forces us to forgo all theories and hypotheses, to concentrate on the dream itself and to see what we can learn from it alone.

This book is thus an attempt to pave the way for the direct study of the dream phenomenon itself, by removing all the disguises and schemata of mental constructs of contemporary dream theories. I was able to undertake this daring task owing to my contact with the existentialist analytical approach of Martin Heidegger. Stimulated by the work of Ludwig Binswanger, I made a thorough study of Heidegger's published, and even of some of his unpublished, writings, and then benefited from Heidegger's unstinted readiness for direct discussion. Whether I have the mind for the strict detail demanded by existentialist analysis and its discussion, can only be decided by this work. I shall not have failed completely in my task, if in this book I succeed in liberating the phenomenon of the dream from the psychological and anthropological point of view, hitherto adopted by those who have been studying dreams, and thus place it in its own light.

Introduction

"Once upon a time I, Chwang-Tse, dreamt I was a butterfly fluttering hither and thither, to all intents and purposes a butterfly. I was aware only of following my fancy as a butterfly, and unconscious of my human individuality. Suddenly I awoke, and there I lay, myself again. Now I do not know whether I was then a man dreaming I was a butterfly, or whether I am now a butterfly dreaming I am a man."

FEW other human phenomena have, in the course of history, been accorded such varied treatment as the dream. Opinions on the dream fluctuate between "its evaluation as a heightening of man's faculties, not infrequently to the point of virtuosity, and the verdict that it represents a decided diminution of spiritual powers, often quite subhumanly so".[1]*

The oldest dream book extant is a papyrus preserved in the British Museum. It belongs to the time of the 12th Egyptian dynasty, to the years 2000–1790 B.C., and comes from Dêr-el-Medineh. A very comprehensive dream guide was discovered in Nineveh. It dates from the seventh century B.C. and was found in the great library of clay tablets of the last great Assyrian king Assurbanipal. The Chaldeans particularly excelled in the art of dream interpretation after they had taken over Assurbanipal's heritage, and when, following their victory over the Assyrians, they had founded the neo-Babylonian Chaldean kingdom. To the same period of ancient history must be ascribed also the dream interpretations of Joseph the son of Jacob, who could interpret not only his own dreams but also those of his fellow prisoners and later those of the Pharaohs.[2] In those ancient days of man's history, dream interpretation was called a divine art because, according to the grandiose, all-embracing, theocentric philosophy of the times, dreams were considered to be immediate revelations of God or of the gods. Thus, as the fourth book of Moses reports, the Lord himself had descended in a pillar of cloud in order to rebuke Aaron

* The references will be found at the end of the book.

and Miriam. "If there be a prophet among you, I the Lord make myself known in a vision, I do speak with him in a dream." We also read in the oldest Egyptian accounts of the dream that Horus expressly attributed his bad dreams to the machinations of evil gods. All he could do was to pray to his mother, the goddess Isis, to save him from the evil consequences of such dreams.

Being visitations from the gods, dreams were not thought to determine the fate of individuals alone. Very often they decided the fate of entire armies and peoples. Thus the Patriarch Jacob took heed of his dream of the heavenly ladder in which the voice of God ordered him to return to his homeland. From clay tablets we may learn that the Assyrian king Assurbanipal undertook his campaign against the King of the Elamites Te-uman as a direct consequence of a dream of one of his seers. In it the goddess Ishtar herself had demanded this campaign, promising protection, fortune and glory. The inscriptions add that the goddess kept to her word given in the dream, and that Assurbanipal conquered the army of the Elamites on the shores of the Eulaeus, captured Te-uman and beheaded him.

The ancients considered not only dreams themselves but even their interpretations as the work of the divine. Joseph the son of Jacob was the first to tell of this. Particularly to his fellow prisoners did he stress the fact that dream interpretation is the direct work of God. He expressly informed Pharaoh that he himself could not interpret dreams. "It is not in me," he said, "God shall give Pharaoh an answer in peace."[3]

When later Nebuchadnezzar ordered Daniel not only to interpret his dream, but also to guess what it was that he had dreamed, Daniel could only accede to this request "because there is a God in heaven who reveals secrets".[4] Even Homer still spoke of the dream as a messenger of the gods. At the very beginning of the *Iliad*, which describes how war and pestilence were decimating the Achaeans, Achilles advises the sons of Atreus to seek the advice of one of the priests, seers or dream-interpreters, "for dreams too are sent by Zeus".[5] In the Second book of the *Iliad*, Zeus deliberately deceives Agamemnon in a false dream, so as to vindicate Achilles and to destroy the Achaeans: "Speed on, false dream," the god orders, "into the huts of Agamemnon son of Atreus, and bid him prepare for battle the armies of the curly-headed Achaeans; for now his chance has come for capturing the spacious city of Troy, for we, the immortal Olympians, are all agreed on it. The pleading of Here has persuaded us, and the Trojans' fate is sealed." On the other hand, in the sixth book of the *Odyssey*, Pallas Athene herself, thinking of the safe return of the noble Odysseus, hastens to the sleeping Nausicaa. Knowing that Odysseus had just landed on the shores of the Phaeacian island Scheria, she appears to the queen's daughter in the guise of a favourite playmate, and admonishes the sleeper to go to this shore and to wash her beautiful clothes there, at the first blush of dawn.

Socrates, too, considered dreams to be divine admonitions that had to be obeyed. It is for this reason that even during his last days in prison he began to write poetry at the god's behest. This at least is what Plato writes in his *Phaedo*:

> "Tell him the truth, Cebes," said Socrates, "that I did not compose them because I wanted to rival him or his works. I knew that that was not easy. I was trying to discover the meaning of some dreams, and I wrote the poems to clear my conscience, in case this was the sort of 'art' that I was told to pursue. It happened like this: the same dream had kept on coming to me from time to time throughout my life, taking different forms at different times, but always saying the same thing: 'Socrates, pursue the arts, and work hard at them.' I had previously supposed that it was urging me to do what I was in fact doing, and trying to encourage me in its performance: that like those who shout encouragement to runners in a race, so the dream, when it urged me to 'pursue the arts', was encouraging me in what I was doing; for philosophy is the greatest of all arts, and that was my pursuit. But then when the trial took place, and the god's festival prevented my execution, I thought that just in case the dream meant, after all, that I should follow this popular kind of 'art', I ought to follow it and not disobey. It seemed safer not to depart before salving my conscience by the composition of poems in obedience to the dream. So I first wrote in honour of the god for whom the ceremonies were being held...."[6]

Thus the ancient Greeks still considered the dream a divine commandment. Because of it many a cult was changed, and new ones were introduced.[7] It was nothing unusual to report dreams in official documents. Even the dreams of women were expressly included in Statutory law.

While this ancient respect for the dream was never lost by the Islamic world,[8] in the West it only rose to prominence many centuries later. No less a person than Bishop Synesius of Cyrene, who lived in the fourth century A.D., wrote the following:

"I am not surprised that some have owed the discovery of treasure to their dreams; that others have gone to bed quite prosaically, and yet awakened as gifted poets after having conversed with the Muses in their dreams. I need hardly speak of those whom the dream warned of impending dangers or of those who dreamt of a remedy that would cure them. What is most wonderful and most mysterious is the fact that sleep opens the soul to the fullest intuitions into the true essence of things, and that it allows it to pass beyond nature and to become as one with that intelligible sphere, from which it has strayed so far that it no longer even knows whence it came. . . . From this we can see that it is always a man who instructs us when we are awake, but that it is God alone who illuminates us when we sleep."[9]

In the thirteenth century the Spanish physician, alchemist, and philosopher Arnald of Villanova was appointed official dream interpreter to the courts of Aragon and Sicily. Because of his skill, his fame had spread far and wide, and gave him a lasting influence on the thought of his contemporaries. In his book on the dream *Expositiones visionum quae sunt in somnia ad utilitatem medicorum non medicam*[10] he writes, for instance, that rain in the dream might well signify enlightenment by God. We find a mystic of the fourteenth century writing as follows: "A sage says that angels appear to man more often in sleep than in waking life, because in sleep man is less distracted by the diversities of external things than in waking." Even at the beginning of the Renaissance all great physicians, theologians, and philosophers were still very much concerned with dreams and their interpretation. The outstanding Milanese doctor Geronimo Cardano admitted that dreams of exceptional brilliance had decided the most important events of his life.[11]

However, between early antiquity and the Middle Ages the dream had for the first time lost its divine nature. Dreams were interpreted by crude rules of thumb. According to Plutarch, already in the fifth century B.C. there were dream books and dream tablets from which one could simply read off prophecies and admonitions. Aristotle and Hippocrates questioned the divine nature of dreams. Aristotle no longer sought the origins of dreams outside man but inside his own nature. Dreams, he said, were the necessary manifestations of this nature. They derived from the experiences and personal attitudes of the dreamer, from his cares, his hopes and also from his biological processes, especially from the coursing and warmth of his blood. In his later writings he even tried to give a psycho-physiological explanation of prophetic dreams. However, the mere fact that he granted the possibility of prophetic dreams clearly proves that he too still based himself on the metaphysical foundations of the ancient Greeks.

Only with Petronius, Nero's counsellor, did the metaphysical foundations of the world of ancient Greece collapse, soon to be followed by the disintegration of this world itself. Arrogantly Petronius declared, "It is neither the gods nor divine commandments that send the dreams down from the heavens, but each one of us makes them for himself." ("*Somnia quae mentes ludunt volantibus umbris non denubra deum, nec ab aethere numina mitunt, sed sibi quisque facit.*")[12] In these sentences we can see the first clear expression of the Rationalism and Enlightenment of the Western World. True, in the second century A.D., Artemidorus of Daldis still felt that he was called to the study of dreams by Apollo himself. It was Apollo who ordered this Lydian to gather all that was known about dreams. On his many journeys he collected from the writings of knowledgeable writers, from traditional folklore and even from the talk of discredited magicians and vagabonds, all that had any possible bearing on the dream. His findings were collated in five large dream books. Artemidorus still admitted that some dreams were of divine origin, as distinct from those dreams that dealt with the activities of the day, and that expressed desires, feelings and bodily processes. Nevertheless, Artemidorus's books are essentially a schematic description of dream images arranged according to groups. Already the interpretations are largely mechanical, and follow rigid methods of deciphering, fixed from ancient times. All the same these dream books of Artemidorus contain many psychological hints that strike one as surprisingly modern,[13] and his work had a decisive influence on all subsequent dream literature. Up to the beginning of modern scientific investigation, very little was written about the dream that was not greatly influenced by Artemidorus. It is for this reason that Philipp Melanchthon himself, the prominent Protestant theologian and friend of Luther, in his preface to the German edition of the five dream books of Artemidorus, expressly pointed to their usefulness in medical science.

Dreams fared no better in the enlightened period of the seventeenth and eighteenth centuries than they did in Nero's times. The precursor of modern positivism, Thomas Hobbes, once more considered dreams to be nothing but the effects of somatic stimuli. Voltaire looked upon the belief that dreams might be predictions or prophecies as nothing but superstitious nonsense. For him dreams were mainly the expression of somatic stimuli, or of excessive passions. Kant still warned us not to underestimate dreams because "in doing so we might well be carelessly overlooking one of nature's great mysteries".[14] He even suspected that ideas in sleep were "clearer and broader than even the clearest in waking life". But he then went on to say that we could have no awareness of these ideas themselves, since during sleep we could not share experience with the body. On no account must the dream, i.e. what one remembers on waking up, be confused with these ideas. For what the sleeper remembers on waking up is altogether something different, and occurs only when he is no longer fully asleep, when he is reasonably perceptive, and when he weaves his mental activity into external sense impressions. It is for this reason that he remembers them afterwards, in part, but finds in them only wild and absurd chimeras.[15] In his anthropological reflections Kant makes the dream appear closely related to superstition, magic and, last but not least, to indigestion.[16]

Then, after the Romantic poets and thinkers had once more honoured the dream with a brief but friendly smile, the once divine art of dream interpretation had to flee before the mechanical materialism of the second half of the nineteenth century, and take refuge in the darkest superstitions and in the practices of unscrupulous charlatans. If technical and scientific knowledge was no longer capable of seeing in even the most intelligent thoughts and noblest feelings of waking life anything but a secret locked in the cells of the brain, a mere epiphenomenon of molecular mechanics, how much less readily could it grant any meaning or sense to that flighty phenomenon which at night so frequently mocks all our rational thoughts. Whenever scientists of the time were at all concerned with the dream, they adopted such ideas as Herbart's. The latter called the dream "a slow process of partial and very anomalous awakening". A similar description is found in Binz's book on the dream which appeared in 1878. In it the transition from dreaming into waking is described in the following words:

"Towards morning the fatiguing bodies contained in the cortical protein are increasingly decomposed and carried away by the purifying blood-stream. Here and there, some cell groups have already woken up while everything around them is still completely inert. At this stage the isolated work of the individual cell groups is perceived by consciousness without the necessary co-ordination of other parts of the brain. It is for this reason that the images produced, corresponding largely to the material impressions of the immediate past, follow upon one another wildly and arbitrarily. As the number of liberated brain cells increases so does the dream become correspondingly less unreasonable."

Binz ends his widely discussed work with the following conclusion:

"All the apparent facts urge us to see the dream as a physical process that is always quite unnecessary, and in many cases almost pathological."

To this devastating judgment of the dream, G. Th. Fechner, in his *Elemente der Psychophysik* (*Elements of Psychophysics*, 1889) makes the following addition:

"In the dream it appears as if the psychological activity had been transferred from the brain of a reasonable person to that of a fool."

Furthermore, Maury believed that waking thought compared with the incoherent jumps of the dream as normal motility compared with certain choreic or paralytic forms of motion. How well these late nineteenth-century opinions agree with the beliefs of another epoch of emancipation, two thousand years before, is best illustrated by a quotation from Cicero: "*Nihil tam praepostere, tam incondite, tam monstruose cogitari potest quod non possimus somniare*" (There is nothing too preposterous, too confused or too monstrous for us to dream about). At the end of his work *De divinatione*, in which he denied the divine character of dreams, Cicero added:

"Now, since the creator of dreams is no longer a god, since nature no longer has any connection with dreams, and since observation does not lead to any knowledge, it is proven that we cannot attach any credibility to dreams."[17]

Natural scientists before the turn of the last century, just as in Cicero's times, at best considered the dream as a phenomenon of so-called physical stimuli. By this they meant that dream images had to be considered as the psychological reflections of sensory experiences occurring during sleep. For instance Jessen wrote in 1856:

"Every dimly heard noise produces corresponding dream pictures. The sound of thunder immediately places us in the midst of battle, the crow of a cock may change into the scream of a panic-stricken man, the creaking of a door may cause a dream of a burglary. If we lose our bed-clothes at night we may dream that we are walking about in the nude or that we have fallen into the water. If we lie across the bed and our feet happen to be sticking out we may dream that we are at the edge of a terrible abyss or that we are falling off a precipitous height."

Twenty years later Maury tried to confirm this theory that the dream arose from illusions due to external sensory impressions. He discovered that a person, whose lip and nose were tickled with a feather while he was asleep, dreamt that he was undergoing the terrible torture of having tar applied to his face, and then having it pulled off so that the skin came off bit by bit. On another occasion somebody sharpened a pair of scissors against a pair of forceps near the ear of the sleeping Maury. In his dream Maury heard first the pealing of bells, then the ringing of the alarm, and he felt himself back in the days of June 1848.

True, not only external sensory stimuli but also internal bodily sensations were considered to be sources of the dream formation. According to Wundt, it was the after-images in the retina which were responsible for dreams of innumerable birds or butterflies. Again, Strümpel explained the typical dream of flying as the image used by the psyche to represent the physical sensation caused by the rise and fall of the dreamer's lung. Finally Krauss believed that he was lending even greater emphasis to this theory of a mere symbolization of bodily sensations, by calling it "substantiation in the dream".[18]

PART I. *Modern Dream Theories*

CHAPTER I

Sigmund Freud's Theory of Dreams

THE modern psychologist hardly understands the scientific short-sightedness of materialist dream interpreters of the second half of the nineteenth century. It has become quite clear since then that a theory holding physical stimuli alone responsible for dreams left the most interesting phenomena out of account: it completely ignored the all-important question why the dream, in its representation of outer or inner sense stimuli, makes use of just one particular picture, out of the many possible ones. It is just this problem which needs emphasizing, as we can see particularly clearly from a dream recounted some time ago by M. Simon.[19] In this dream, the author saw some giant-like creatures sitting at table, and heard clearly the terrible gnashing of their jaws. Waking immediately from this dream, he could hear the hooves of a horse which was just galloping past his window. Simon, a representative investigator of dreams of his day, believed that with the discovery of this auditory stimulus, he had explained his dream satisfactorily. If, however, the noise of hooves produces dream representations reminiscent of Gulliver's Travels, could not the choice of so unusual an association of ideas be explained much more readily by other motivations? Is it not a fact that the intervention of this auditory stimulus played only a very modest role as a source of the dream? Are there not basically quite other factors which determine the choice of memory pictures?

These questions which throw doubt on Simon's interpretation of dreams are to be found on everybody's lips today. The man who raised them for the first time, in examining this very dream of Simon's, half a century ago, was Sigmund Freud. It was he who, in doing so, drew our attention to the tremendous "overvaluation of non-psychic stimuli for the interpretation of dreams".[20] Freud, by raising these problems, radically opposed the psychiatric thinking of his time. He was fully conscious of this fact and even had a foreboding that everything that showed the independence of psychic life from empirically verifiable organic changes, everything that could demonstrate spontaneity in its expression, would terrify the psychiatrists of his day.[21] In this fear Freud was to be proved to have been only too right; his new way of putting questions produced a virtual stone-wall reaction in the scientific world. This is the reason for the appearance in the preface to the second edition of Freud's *Interpretation of Dreams* of the following significant words:

> "The fact that this very difficult book required the publication of a second edition, even before the end of one decade, is by no means thanks to the interest of the specialist circle for whom the book was originally intended. My psychiatric colleagues do not seem to have taken any trouble to overcome the initial suspicions which my new conceptions of the dream produced in them, and the professional philosophers who are, as we know, in the habit of dismissing problems of dream life as mere appendices to conscious states, obviously failed to notice that we have something here from which a number of inferences can be drawn that are bound to transform our psychological theories."

In his introduction to the above work, which is Freud's account of his new dream conception and which appeared in the first year of our century, the proud and significant sentences are to be found:

> "In the following pages I shall attempt to prove that a psychological technique exists which permits the interpretation of dreams and that, by the use of my procedure, every dream will show itself to be a meaningful psychological structure, capable of taking its place among the psychological drives of waking life."

Freud realized that the impression made by the dream on our conscious judgment seems to support the idea that its peculiarities are only due to a psychological deficiency in the state of sleep. The dream, Freud admits, appears to be incoherent, uniting without offence the most crass of contradictions, allowing impossibilities, leaving out of account that knowledge which during the day so influences us, and portraying us as ethically and morally insensitive. We should consider him a madman who, in waking life, behaved as he often appeared to do in his dreams. He who, in waking life, spoke or communicated such things as he appears to do in dreams, would give us the impression of being confused and sick-minded.[22] Nevertheless, it would no longer do to dismiss the problem of the dream simply by assuming it to be a partial state of wakefulness. Already in 1830, the famous neurologist Burdach had remarked that:

> "If we say the dream is a state of partial waking, we neither explain the waking state nor sleep. Nor do we say anything else than that some forces of the psyche are active in the dream, while others are asleep. But this is a state of affairs which exists during the whole of life."

But above all Freud drew our attention to the power of memory in dreams which, very often, far surpasses its waking counterpart. It is just these hypermnesic abilities of the dream consciousness which are the best proof that nothing which has once been present in our minds can be completely lost or, as Delboeuf expresses it, *"que toute impression, même la plus insignificante, laisse une trace inaltérable, indéfiniment susceptible de reparaître au jour"*. Even Maury, to whom, theoretically, the dream meant nothing but *"toute une série de dégradations de faculté pensante et raisonnante"* and who could see in it only one of the famous *"automatismes mentales"* of French psychiatry, related a significant event from his own actual experience. As a child, he writes, he had often come from his home town Meaux to nearby Trilport, where his father had been supervising the construction of a bridge. One night, although a great number of years had passed, he was again transported to Trilport in his dream, and again he was allowed to play in the streets of the town. A man in some sort of uniform approached him. Maury asked his name; the man introduced himself as C——, the bridgekeeper. When he awoke, Maury, still doubting the reality of this memory, asked an old servant who had been with him since childhood, if she could remember a man by this name. "Certainly," was the answer, "he was the keeper of the bridge that your father was building at the time."

Freud concludes from such examples that, if we keep in mind the extraordinary powers of memory in dreams, we shall become aware of the inadequacy of all those theories which see in the absurdity and incoherence of the dream simply a psychical reflection of momentary somatic stimuli, or a partial forgetting of our experiences during the day.

It is for this reason that Freud reminds the one-sided materialist psychiatrist that in the preceding epoch it was philosophy, rather than the exact natural sciences, which governed human thought. Among philosophical thinkers the psychological potentialities of the dream found a readier and warmer acceptance. Thus Gotthilf Heinrich Schubert[23] praised the dream as an emancipation of the spirit from the power of outer nature, and as a liberation of the soul from the shackles of the senses. So also the younger Fichte joined the ranks of those who saw in the dream an upsurge of the spirit to higher levels. Not only the philosophers, however, but also the neurologist Burdach, in the period immediately preceding that in which the intellect was monopolized by technical science, commented in a similar manner on the dream. For him the dream was "the natural activity of the soul, unlimited by the force of individuality, undisturbed by self-consciousness, undirected by the will; in short it is the liveliness of the sensory centres undergoing free play".[24]

This revelling in the free use of one's vitality Burdach imagined as a state of affairs in which the soul refreshes itself in order to gather new energy for its daily work. It is for this reason that he cites and endorses the passage in which the poet Novalis praises the dream world:

> "The dream is a protection against the regularity and the routine of life. It is the release of our much-restricted phantasy, it produces a kaleidoscope of all the pictures of life, and it interrupts, with its happy childishness, our adult seriousness. It is certain that we should age much more readily if there were no dreams, and it is for this reason that we may consider the dream, if not perhaps as given immediately from above, nevertheless as a divine little extra, as a friendly companion on our pilgrimage to the holy grave."[25]

Even more penetratingly does another famous physiologist of the first half of the nineteenth century, Purkinje, praise the refreshing and healing activity of the dream:

> "Especially do creative dreams have this function. They are plays of the imagination which have no connection with the data of daily life. The soul does not want to continue the tensions of waking life, but rather to resolve them, to recuperate from them. First and foremost the dream creates conditions which are the very opposite of waking life—it heals sadness through joy, sorrow through hope and happy distracting pictures, hate through love and friendship, fear through courage and confidence."[26]

Freud points to the writings of F. W. Hildebrandt—*Der Traum und seine Verwertung fürs Leben* as the most significant and at the same time the most formally perfect study of the dream produced at that time.

> "The dream," its author states, "sometimes allows us to look into the depths and folds of our very being—mainly a closed book in states of consciousness. It gives us such valuable insight into ourselves, such instructive revelations of our half-hidden emotional tendencies and powers that, were we awake, we should have good reason to stand in awe of the demon who is apparently peering at our cards with the eyes of a falcon."

Hildebrandt had even recognized the dream as a warning signal. Not only, he writes, can it make us conscious of the hidden shortcomings of our soul, but also, according to the witness of ancient doctors, it can make us aware of unrecognized bodily ills: "The dream warns from within with the voice of a watchman guarding the very centre of our psychic life. It warns us against continuing on the paths which we are treading." In a similar way, but even before Hildebrandt, Herder had greeted the dream as a path into "the depths of the heart and of the spirit".

Special mention must be made of Karl Albrecht Scherner's study of dreams. It was his book *Das Leben des Traumes* which gave Freud the starting point for his own epoch-making dream doctrine four decades later. True, at first even Scherner saw how in the dream "the central force of the ego, its spontaneous energy, becomes paralysed". But he immediately hastened to praise it:

> "The images [of the dream] throw off all the shackles of the ego so that that activity of the soul which we call phantasy is free from all the rules of reason and is also free from all restrictive factors, and thus rises to unlimited heights. True," Scherner continues, "it takes away the last building blocks from waking memory, but from them it creates edifices vastly different from the images of waking life. It shows a bias in favour of the immeasurable, the exaggerated, the grotesque. At the same time, by freeing itself from restrictive thinking, it gains a greater elasticity, a greater adroitness, a greater flexibility. It is extremely sensitive to the most delicate emotional stimuli and it immediately changes the inner life into pictures of the outer

world. The dream phantasy lacks a conceptual language—what it wants to say it must paint perceptually, and since concepts do not intervene here to weaken the picture, it paints in all the fullness, power and splendour of the perceptual form. The clearness of its language, however, is impaired by the fact that it does not represent an object by its proper image. Rather it chooses a strange image, provided that it can express that aspect of the object which the dream chooses to represent. This is the symbolizing activity of phantasy. . . ."

This symbolizing phantasy activity Scherner takes as the central energy of every dream. According to him, it remains the same whether the dream uses its favourite representation of the human body by the symbol of a house or whether it represents the breathing lung by a roaring stove filled with flames, or even when the eroticism of a woman dreamer expresses itself in her being pursued by naked men.

It must be admitted, Freud comments, that in these concepts of Scherner, arbitrariness and lack of concern for all rules of scientific research are only too obvious. However, to reject them without first putting them to any test would be far too high-handed a procedure. For Scherner's doctrine obviously deals with a subject which has rightly occupied and puzzled human beings for thousands of years, yet to the clarification of which strict science, on its own admission, has not contributed anything of value. In contradistinction to the common view, says Freud, science has tried to deprive the dream of content and significance. Even should we reject Scherner's conception as completely unfounded in fact, we must nevertheless consider the possibility that phantasy can take place even in ganglion cells. For instance, Binz's description of the dream work, as a 'passage of the aurora of awakening over the dormant cells of the cortex", and numerous other analogous descriptions by sober and exact natural scientists of that time, were not, Freud continues, much less fanciful and improbable than Scherner's attempts at interpretation.[27]

In order, however, to develop Scherner's theory of dreams more fruitfully, and to derive from it the basis of a new and well-defined psychology, tremendous daring was required. This was achieved by Freud when, with great intellectual courage, he wrote in his *Interpretation of Dreams* that dreams were not simply the meaningless reflections of somatic processes in the brain-cells, but were, in themselves, meaningful psychological structures, which had to be assigned a specific place within the psychic activities of the waking state.

This statement about the dream was, to start with, nothing but an extremely daring assumption. Freud himself was quite clear about this. Therefore he added at once that only its usefulness could determine its validity.[28] It is true that at the outset Freud was entitled to be encouraged in his assumption by two kinds of experiment. In the first place, he recalled Bernheim's investigations at Nancy. Bernheim had been able to prove that people who were allowed to perform certain actions under deep hypnosis, only *appeared* to forget them when awake. By skilful questioning they could all be brought back to memory. From this Freud conjectured that "the dreamer does know what his dream signifies, though he does not know that he knows, and so believes that he does not know".[29] Further, Freud had already performed his own experiments in the study of hysterical symptoms, and the so-called slips of everyday life: forgetting, misplacing, slips of the tongue, and so on. All these symptoms had been as incomprehensible to science before Freud as the dream itself. To Freud's keen perception, however, they appeared as meaningful psychological structures which should have a place in the psychic activity of waking life.

With his basic dream hypothesis Freud, without being quite aware of it himself, had changed from a natural scientist into a scientist of the mind, or, more precisely, into an historian. For if a psychological structure can be meaningfully assigned a specific place in the activities of waking life, man has to be conceived as being an historical, continuous, and purposive entity, embracing both waking and sleeping life in a unity.

How very much Freud considered himself to be an historian appears clearly enough from his comparisons of the psychoanalytical method in general with archaeology, or of dream interpretation in particular, with the deciphering of hieroglyphics. In this he was able to base himself on earlier and similar statements by Gotthilf Heinrich Schubert and Charles Baudelaire. The former, a hundred years before, had already thought of the dream as being the hieroglyphic, original and natural language of the soul. The latter, in a letter to his friend Charles Asselineau, dated 13th March, 1856, begins with these remarkable sentences:

> "My dear friend, since dreams seem to entertain you, I send you one which is certain not to displease you. It is 5 o'clock in the morning and not too warm as yet. Bear in mind that this

is only, so to say, a sample of all the thousands of dreams which seem to besiege me. I hardly need to tell you that the incredible peculiarity of all these dreams and of their whole manner, which is quite strange both to my occupations and to what is dear to my heart, always drives me to the assumption that all of them are but a hieroglyphic language to which I lack the key. . . ."

Freud was so sure of the soundness of the comparison between dream interpretation and the deciphering of hieroglyphics, that he opposed the considered scepticism of the educated of his day (who belittled any possibility of dream interpretation) by pointing to an analogous situation in which the historian found himself when interpreting Babylonian-Assyrian writings. For these, too, there had been a time, Freud wrote, when public opinion regarded the hieroglyphic decipherers as practical dreamers, and the whole research as a swindle. In the year 1857, however, the Royal Asiatic Society put the matter to the test. It asked four of the leading hieroglyphologists to send independent translations of a newly-discovered inscription in closed envelopes, and was able to state, after comparing the four solutions, that their agreement went far enough to justify confidence, both in what had so far been achieved and also in further progress. Since that time, certainty in the reading of hieroglyphic documents has become much greater, and the derision of the learned lay world has slowly come to an end. A comparison of the results of dream interpretation by soundly trained psychoanalysts has already justified the high hopes held in this branch of science.[30]

To the rationalist-positivist thinkers of that time, an enterprise which pretended to have found an historical and meaningful connection between the happenings of the dream and the experiences of waking life appeared to be strange and unscientific in the extreme. The "true" natural scientist was content to describe the different and unrelated, that is to say "meaningless", facts and functions; to register their sequences, to attempt their prediction with the help of causal laws. Hoche, the strictly scientific psychiatrist, for example, was therefore forced to decry Freud's concepts of the dream as being "the fertile ground for every kind of naïve or scientific fancy and for the creation of myths". Even Freud himself found a great deal of difficulty with the historical conception of the dream. He, too, was a child of his times, and immediately after his new thought, the natural scientist broke through, vehemently wrestled with the historian, won the upper hand, and misled his own genius into the acceptance of a natural-scientific dream *theory*. When he returned to this natural-scientific point of view, Freud lost interest in the dream phenomena as such, and in the immediately apprehended "manifest" appearances of dreams. The single concrete phenomenon had to take second place after hypothetical, but generally valid and predictable, forces. The direct manifestations themselves he would have us consider only as symbols of an interplay of forces. By formulating his views in this way, Freud unwittingly characterized natural-scientific thinking in general.[31]

Such forces—or dynamisms—must be posited by the exact scientist in order that those phenomena, which he had previously assumed to be separate and isolated constituents, might be integrated into a whole again. This is why Freud, as soon as he fell back from the role of a historically-minded psychologist into that of a natural scientist, saw the *latent* dream elements, which had been deduced from the *manifest* content, as nothing more than mere constituents of the total dream.

Hence it became his first concern to discover those forces which he could conceive as producing these constituents and holding them together. He was mainly concerned with finding a general source of energy, the activity of which one could imagine as responsible for the entire dream work, for the formation and linking of the latent dream thoughts as the material particles of the dream. Freud soon believed that he had found this generally valid source of energy of the dream, once and for all, in our infantile instinctual wishes. Very dogmatically, therefore, he states that all dreams are wish-fulfilments;[32] the only essential thing about the dream is the dream work which acts on the dream material, the latent dream thought.[33] The actual motive power which produces this work is always an infantile instinctual wish.[34] This infantile wish is therefore behind or under that psychological layer in which the latent dream thoughts are housed. It is found in the realm of the "unconscious" in the narrower sense of the word. For this reason Freud could say that the instinctual energy of the infantile wishes makes use of the latent dream thought. The infantile wish changes the latent dream thoughts for its own purposes into manifest dream images, so that under their cover it can find satisfaction, albeit somewhat cloaked.

How far so technical a point of view had led Freud to a contempt for and abuse of the immediate reality of a given phenomenon, he has shown us in his interpretation of the "Dream of the Run-over Child". One of his agoraphobic women patients had had the following dream:

"Her mother sends the dreamer's little daughter out alone. The dreamer then rides with her mother in the train and sees her little one walking along the rails, so that she is bound to be run over. She hears the bones crack. (At this she has a feeling of discomfort but no real horror.) She then looks out of the carriage window, to see whether the parts cannot be seen behind. Then she reproaches her mother for letting the little one go out alone."

To make the dynamics of this dream appear as an infantile exhibitionist wish, Freud himself changes the text of the dream. "She then looks to see whether the parts cannot be seen behind" becomes "whether she cannot see the parts *from behind*". Thus he can connect this part of the dream with a later idea of the dreamer, namely, that she had once seen her father in the bathroom naked *from behind*. Without any qualms, Freud passes over the fact that quite different conclusions could be drawn from the very content of this dream. For is it not true that we, in looking behind and seeing someone behind us, may be seeing his front, although we ourselves may have to turn back to see anything?[35]

However, in Freud's theory, the dream work of camouflage must have a cause and a motive. Freud believed that the compulsion to disfigure, to hide and to cloak the infantile wishes under cover of the latent dream thought, is caused by a moral factor in the human being. For, in the daylight of consciousness, the ethical values of the dreamer are incompatible with the offensiveness of most infantile wishes. The masking of these offensive dream sources therefore kills two birds with one stone. Not only does the dream wish get its own satisfaction, the ego of the dreamer is no longer disquieted by the urgent character or the moral offensiveness of the wish, which has now been made unrecognizable. Thus the dream also fulfils the important function of the night-watchman, the keeper of sleep.[36]

Freud brought a tremendous measure of diligence, infinite patience, and the entire keenness of his intellect to bear upon his doctrine of the dream censor. He separated the dream work of the assumed instinctual dynamism into four categories. He distinguished:

1. *Condensation* 2. *Displacement*, 3. *Representation* of thoughts by visual pictures, and 4. *Secondary Elaboration.*

By *Condensation*, Freud denotes the fact that the manifest dream always has less content than has the latent dream. In other words, it is a sort of abbreviated translation. This condensation is caused in the first instance by the fact that certain latent elements are left out altogether. Secondly, from many complex parts of the latent dream only a crumb passes over into the manifest one. Thirdly, those latent elements which have something in common are collected together for the purposes of the manifest dream and are fused into one whole.

The second achievement of the dream work, *Displacement*, according to Freud, is entirely the work of the dream censor and can be produced in two different ways. First, the latent element can be replaced, not by one of its own component parts, but by something alien, by way of an allusion. On the other hand, displacement may be due to the fact that the psychic accent passes from one important element to another which is less important, so that the dream seems to be centred elsewhere and appears to be strange.

The third achievement of the dream work, the *Representation of thoughts by visual pictures*, is incomplete. It meets, Freud said, with quite special difficulties, and we should, therefore, not make any great demands on its accuracy of representation. We must just accept that, in those cases where the elements do not easily lend themselves to pictorial representation, the dream work will not stop short of anything, however outrageous. It does not even disdain a complete reversal of the actual dream content, a reversal of the relationship of two people, a reversal in the time sequence and the causal nexus of events, or even transformation of an object into its very opposite.

The fourth achievement of the dream work, so-called *Secondary Elaboration* is, according to Freud, particularly concerned with producing, from the immediate experiences of the dream work, something whole, something more or less coherent. In this way the dream material is often arranged in a way which is easily misunderstood. It may even include further elements, if only, in some small measure, to satisfy the demands of consciousness for logical order.[37]

CHAPTER 2

Critique of the Foundations of Freud's Dream Theory

FREUD, by attributing to the dream work and its processes so great a distortion of "the true meaning of the dream", felt entitled to reconstruct this meaning by an equally great distortion of the manifest dream content. In this reconstruction, therefore, he felt free to interpolate arbitrary elements as a compensation for the possible omission of entire elements during *condensation*. Furthermore, to compensate for the processes of *displacement* he felt justified in shifting the entire psychic centre of a manifest dream. He also balanced those distortions which he expressly ascribed to the dream work of *transforming* abstract thoughts into visual pictures, by simply reversing the character of the relationship between two persons in the dream, and sometimes altering the entire meaning of the dream. Indeed, he could replace the dream content by its very opposite. Finally he could declare whole sections of dreams as mere interpolations due to *Secondary Elaboration*, as not belonging to the actual dream itself but simply producing a certain logical order in the manifest dream. In these reconstructions of latent dream thoughts Freud has without doubt opened wide the doors to arbitrariness and violence to the facts. A manifest dream image can apparently be reconstructed in any way that happens to suit the dream interpreter, and thus, for instance, every dream can be shown to be based on an infantile sexual desire.

For this reason the great number of concrete dream examples with which Freud attempted a "reconstruction of the actual meaning of the dream" does not prove the validity of his theory. Nowhere are we given proof that the processes of distortion which he mentions really do take place, and that he has not rather inserted them for the sake of his theory of wish-fulfilment. Better evidence is essential, particularly since at the conclusion of his work, *The Interpretation of Dreams*, Freud admitted that his theory of wish-fulfilment could not be generally proven but that with it he has stepped beyond the provable.[38]

Freud recognized this demand for a better foundation of his

dream theory, and he called important witnesses in its support. Thus he pointed to the many expressions which clearly bring out the dream's tendency to wish-fulfilment. A Hungarian saying, for instance (Freud wrote), claims that the pig dreams of acorns and the goose of maize; and the answer to the Jewish question, "What does the hen dream of?" is "Of millet." Furthermore, even Aristotle, like Hippocrates before him and Artemidorus after him, had contended that in their dreams the hungry eat and the thirsty drink, just because the dream is a fulfiller of wishes. Perhaps the most pleasant tribute to the dream as a wish-fulfiller *par excellence* was supplied by Herder: Sleep complains to Jupiter of his lowly position amongst his illustrious brothers, the other human faculties. Jupiter consoles him by presenting him with the silver-grey horn of pleasant dreams.

"From it," he says, "spread your poppy seeds and all men, happy and unhappy alike, will desire and love you more than any of your brothers. The hopes, the pleasures and joys which lie therein have been gathered from our most blessed meadows by the charmed hands of your sisters, the Graces. The ethereal dew glistening there will grant the wishes of all those whom you wish to make happy, and since the Goddess of Love herself has sprinkled it with her immortal nectar, its joyous bliss will far exceed what is given to poor mortals by the harsh reality of our earth. Amidst laughter and joy all will hasten into your arms; poets will sing of you, they will try to imitate the charm of your art. Even the most innocent maiden will desire you, and you will be constantly before her as a sweet and rapturous God."

The plaint of Sleep changed into a triumphant thanksgiving, and the most beautiful of the Graces, Pasithea, was married to him.

For his assumption of a dream censor, too, Freud could call on impressive support. Plato himself had written that in each one of us, even the most temperate, there is a violent and bestial nature. The lusts and desires of this nature, however, were subjected to the control and discipline of better and more reasonable instincts, during the waking state. When the reasonable and mild force of the soul was asleep, the wild instincts rebelled and, freed of all shame, they found their satisfaction in the visions of the dream.

Freud, of course, knew that the calling of witnesses could not alone replace a scientific proof. He produced the latter by a mere counter-assertion. When his critics asked why at night our thoughts should suddenly be forced to limit themselves to the creation of wishes, he answered: "I do not know why the dream should not be as varied as thought during the waking state in which we have so many different acts of judging, inferring, refuting, expecting, deciding, etc., I should have nothing against it. For my part it could be so. There is only a trifling obstacle in the way of this more convenient conception of the dream: it does not happen to reflect reality."[39]

Freud had no difficulty in refuting the repeated misrepresentation of his conception of the dream as serving only to satisfy sexual instincts. Such a contention, he wrote, was completely foreign to his theory, and nowhere in all the five editions of his work *The Interpretation of Dreams* could it be found. On the contrary, it was in conflict with all the rest of his work.

> "Above all," Freud continued, "I should not know how to obviate the impression that there are countless dreams which satisfy other than sexual needs such as hunger, thirst, comfort, etc., even if we take the widest possible view of the term 'sexual'."

As an essential proof of the correctness of his derivation of all dream images from instinctual drives, he cited the fact that in free association with the dream contents, instinctual wishes invariably appeared. Yet even if this were generally the case, it would by no means prove the validity of Freud's theory of wish-fulfilment. It would merely indicate that in man instinctual drives are, amongst others, always at work. True, to connect causally the beginning and end points of a free association of ideas fully corresponds to the type of reasoning customary in technical and scientific procedure, since technology can only think in terms of cause and effect. However, there is no safeguard against the possibility that such a causal interpretation of a mere sequence in time of phenomena which are perhaps quite independent does violence to the development of those phenomena which are separated in time, have each a different origin, and cannot be derived from one another.

Finally, Freud believed that he could consolidate his theory of wish-fulfilment by pointing to those dreams which were quite blatantly hallucinatory fulfilments of infantile instinctual desires. Such dreams took place particularly in the case of children. Freud cited the example of a dream of his own daughter. He himself witnessed how at the age of nineteen months she called out in her sleep, "Anna Freud, strawberry, highberry, egg, pap." His daughter had vomited the morning before and had therefore been kept on a fast all day. Freud explained that she used her own name in order to express taking possession, while the subsequent menu comprised everything that must have seemed to her as a desirable meal. The fact that strawberries appeared in two variants was no doubt a protest against the dietary policy of the household, and in particular followed from the fact that the nurse had let her know that her indisposition was due to her having eaten too many strawberries. A similar feat, Freud continued, was achieved in a dream of his grandmother who was then nearly seventy years old. After she had been forced to fast for a whole day owing to floating kidney trouble, she dreamt that she had been invited out for both main meals, and that in each case she was offered the most delicious tit-bits. Just as obvious, Freud wrote, was a dream of his daughter at the age of three and a half years, and inspired by the beauty of the Lake at Au. The little one had crossed the lake for the first time and the voyage had passed far too quickly for her. At the landing-stage she did not want to leave the boat and cried bitterly. The next morning she related, "Last night I crossed the lake again." "Let us hope," her father concluded, "that she was more satisfied with the duration of this dream voyage."

Equally undisguised wish-fulfilment-dreams could also be found in grown-ups, especially when they are exposed to unusually hard conditions of life. Thus, for instance, Otto Nordenskjöld in his book *Antarctic*, writing of his crew who wintered with him, reported that eating and drinking were the central points of most of their dreams. One of us, he wrote, who excelled each night in attending great luncheons, was extremely happy in the morning if he could report that he had eaten a dinner of three courses. The reader will easily understand, the author of *Antarctic* continued, how we longed for sleep since it offered us all that we most lacked. To give another example, Duprel reported that Mungo Park, who nearly died of thirst during his journey through Africa, at that time dreamt continuously of the valleys and meadows of his home which were so rich in water.[40]

Such undisguised dreams, Freud writes, bring out their wishful character so clearly that, in contradistinction to the usual dreams of adults, they are not puzzles at all. For this reason they have no inherent interest but *they are naturally invaluable proofs* that dreams generally and in their deepest essence are wish-fulfilments.[41] But is not this kind of conclusion anything but "natural"? Can it, even by the furthest stretch of the imagination, be considered a proof at all? Why should the structure of a particular type of dream, only because it is easily explicable, become the prototype of dreams in general? Must there not have been some hidden and inadequate assumptions in Freud's ideas which led to his undue emphasis of wish-fulfilment? How else explain the carelessness and obvious bias of a thinker, otherwise so honest and of such integrity?

It is not because Freud's scientific conclusions are based on some preconceptions that we reject them, for all human thought and knowledge involve a pre-scientific ontology. No science can dispense with a pre-scientific tendency of thought. Man never finds himself in a senseless chaos into which only the completely unprejudiced and unbiased scientific investigator can introduce any kind of order. Before there is any science at all there must always be a certain metaphysic, even if completely unconscious; a general notion of the actual nature of things in general, even if it is only vague and uninterpreted. If a primordial understanding of the world did not originally and inevitably belong to the essence of Man, how could scientific knowledge have arisen at all? It is for this reason that all scientific knowledge and achievement are never more than the orderly interpretations and differentiations of a very definite and immediate pre-scientific understanding of the world. Correspondingly all the questions posed by science about its objects are always shaped by a previous conception of the essence of the objects themselves, and methods of investigation are developed accordingly. This ontological approach, which is too often taken for granted, is thus, together with the relevant questions and methods of investigation, the mental tool with which scientific investigators approach reality. Only those things which this tool can grasp, or which can be forced to fit it, are ever considered as real. Everything else is either completely overlooked or dismissed as phantasy.

We cannot therefore object to Freud's particular pre-scientific mental assumptions as such. But for this very reason, his psycho-analytical dream theory, like every other scientific theory, must allow questions to be raised about the special structure of its unconscious ontological approach, and about its relevance to the actual essence of the objects investigated. The mental tool of Freud is that of technological science in general, as it has crystallized slowly but with historical necessity out of Western metaphysics. This has led to the creation of a conceptual world in which everything can be reduced to a predictable interplay of forces, and consequently to cause and effect. With such assumptions no theory other than the Freudian is possible: for only dreams of wish or instinctual fulfilments are susceptible of an immediate and dynamic explanation. Being the only dream phenomena accessible to technological thought, they had to be stamped by the latter as the only basic and real dreams. Because they lent themselves to a facile and shallow mechanistic interpretation they were assigned this predominant position. If, accordingly, they are the only dream structures intelligible to this type of thought, and thus the only ones considered factually possible, then all other dreams can also be nothing but instinctual wish-fulfilment. They have to be reduced to and interpreted in terms of the above hypothesis at any price. Dreams which obstinately refuse to comply with this reductive procedure simply have to be rejected. Indeed, Freud, as we shall see, simply denied them the character of dreams. Nothing that does not suit our particular outlook must be allowed to exist.

Another essential component of every technological dream doctrine is the moralistic dream censor. To every positivist philosophy there belong "ethical values" of one kind or another. They are the relics of a dead god, robbed of their fundamental characteristics and left suspended in mid-air. For this reason there is inevitably some representative of "ethical values" involved in this approach. In Freud's theory we meet him in the form of the moralistic dream censor, as the almost ever-present adversary of the infantile instinctual drives.

CHAPTER 3

Dream Theories of the "Zurich School"

(a) The theory of the "finalist" aspect of the dream
Throughout his life Freud consistently maintained his mechanistic and causal explanation of dreams. He violently opposed all attacks on it. All attempts to undermine his theory by pointing out that there existed dreams of a painful nature, and especially anxiety and punishment dreams, were dismissed long before his critics had any chance even of raising doubts. Already in his first dream investigation we can find the following sentences:

> "If the dream is a wish-fulfilment, then painful feelings should have no place in it. It should always produce pleasure. The question is pleasure to whom? Naturally, to him who has the wish. We know, however, that the dreamer has a very peculiar relationship to his wishes. He rejects them, he censors them, in short he does not like them. The dreamer, therefore, in his relationship to his dream wishes, can only be likened to the fusion of two separate persons who have something in common: instinctual man and moral man. The wish-fulfilment of the one can naturally lead to the displeasure of the other, if the two are at loggerheads. It is for this reason, for instance, that anxiety is produced when the immoral instinctual desires cannot be moulded into sufficiently harmless pictures by the dream work: the moral side of the dreamer is in danger of being overrun by the instincts. Anxiety dreams, therefore, do not change anything in the essence of the dream. At worst we can say that the dream is an attempted wish-fulfilment which miscarried in an anxiety dream."[42]

Freud later expanded his wish-fulfilment theory to include anxiety dreams:

> "While an infantile undisguised dream can be considered an open fulfilment of a permitted wish, an anxiety dream

must be considered as the open fulfilment of a repressed desire."[43]

Nor can Freud allow that the occurrence of punishment dreams argues against his wish-fulfilment theory. In the punishment dream, he says, it is the moral drives that find open satisfaction.

Finally, the fact that latent dream thoughts by no means express only instinctual wishes did not escape Freud. He explicitly admits that in certain circumstances latent dream thoughts could mean something quite other than simple wishes without allowing this to stand in the way of his theory. To him the latent dream thoughts which can be understood and interpreted are by no means the last word in dreams. The essential fact for Freud is the dynamism which he attributes to some drive or urge. So he can counter objections based on latent dream thoughts not due to instinctual wishes, by pointing out that his critics have not been able to follow his change of emphasis from the immediate dream phenomena and the psychical contents emerging from them to the assumed causal instinctual forces behind them. They were therefore guilty of "a simple misunderstanding", a "misunderstanding which confuses the dream with the latent dream thoughts and asserts of the former what belongs to the latter alone". The latent dream thought, Freud writes, could often enough be replaced or represented by an act of decision, a perception, a consideration, a preparation, an attempt at solving a problem, etc. Indeed, it is precisely here that we discover the interesting fact that the unconscious is occupied with such acts. "If you look closely," Freud continues, "you will immediately recognize that all this holds only for the latent dream thought". But this many-sidedness of the dream is

"by no means a part of its essential nature, for if you speak of the dream itself you must mean either the manifest dream, that is, the product of the dream work, or at most, this work itself, i.e. the mental processes which form the manifest dream from the latent dream thought. Every other use of the word is a confusion of ideas which can only create trouble. The latent dream thoughts are the material which the dream work changes into the manifest dream. Why should you confuse the material with the work done on it? A dream may be anything at all when you are considering only the thoughts represented by it; i.e. it may be a perception, an act of decision, a preparation, etc. But besides this the dream is always the wish-fulfilment of an unconscious thought, and if you regard it as the result of the dream work, it is this alone. Its one characteristic, the wish-fulfilment, is constant, the other may vary.[44]

The reproach of "simple misunderstanding" was meant especially for H. Silberer, A. Maeder, A. Adler, W. Stekel and C. G. Jung. They all had objected to the fact that Freud considered the dream, on the one hand, as a kind of hieroglyphic language comparing its symbols with the relics of a "primordial language"[45] and, on the other hand, that he unexpectedly declared the manifest dream phenomenon to be a mere façade. How can there be any talk of a façade in the case of hieroglyphic writing, these critics asked. Is not the idea of a façade a tacit admission of the difficulty which Freud experienced when trying to read the dream writing by means of his causal conception? All of them rejected Freud's conception of what might properly be called a dream, as a mere whim. Whereas Freud's scientific attitude forced him to emphasize again and again that "it is natural to attribute a lesser significance to the manifest dreams",[46] his dissident pupils devoted their entire attention to it. By refusing to reduce the manifest dream pictures to mere instinctual causal forces, they stressed just those purposive aspects which Freud could not admit as appertaining to the dream itself.

However, the Freudian theory of the dream could not dispense entirely with this finalist or purposive method of consideration. Freud, too, unquestionably attributes an aim and a purpose to the dream when he designates as "the meaning of each dream" the hallucinatory fulfilment of an instinctual wish,[47] or when he assigns it the role of keeper of sleep or of night-watchman.[48] According to Maeder, Adler, Stekel and Jung, the finalist significance of dreams, however, goes beyond such assessments. A. Adler saw the dream as "a tentative feeler towards the future". For him the dream "indicated an attempt to face an actual difficulty in the life of the dreamer".[49] According to W. Stekel, too, the dream always seeks a solution of the conflicts of life or of the conflicts of the day. The dream is the "guide to the life conflict of the patient".[50] Even before Adler, Maeder had seen the dream as an "auto-symbolic representation of the current state of the libido transmitted to consciousness",[51] or as "the self-representation of the actual unconscious situation—in symbolic form". He also called the dream "the means by which, during sleep, the unconscious communicates with consciousness as the organ of perception" for purposes of exerting "suggestive and quiet influence" on the conscious ego.[52] Maeder, in 1912, had already attributed to a group of dreams the function of a "preparatory exercise for the ensuing activity of waking life". "They seek and reach attempts at solutions of current conflicts." In so far as these dreams must be considered as attempts at solutions of pending psychic conflicts, they expressed a "prospective function". "The dream offers to the uncertain, disorientated and anxious ego-consciousness, an admonishing, warning, correcting, yet consoling support."[53]

Maeder was practically the first to draw our attention to the possibility of a finalist interpretation of dreams, for which he was severely taken to task by Freud. Since, together with C. G. Jung, he later developed this approach, it is generally known as the "dream doctrine of the Zurich School".

Maeder tried to illustrate his finalist dream conception and his differences with Freud by means of a dream of the poet Peter Rosegger. This example appeared to him as particularly suitable, since Freud himself had discussed it in his *Interpretation of Dreams* and had interpreted it in the usual causal-reductive way. Freud had remarked that this dream put his theory of wish-fulfilment to a severe test. A confrontation of the two interpretations is specially important in view of the fact that we shall have to return to Rosegger's dream when discussing our own work. Rosegger wrote:

"Although I usually sleep very well, I have had many a bad night, since during my modest existence as a student and a writer, I have had to drag along the shadow of a tailor's life as well, without being able to rid myself of it.

I was not then preoccupied with my past. A poet who has emerged out of the skin of a Philistine has better things to do. Nor did I pay much attention to my dreams; it was only much later that I became more reflective. Perhaps only when the Philistine in me came to life again did I notice that when I dreamt at all I was always a tailor's apprentice. In my dreams I worked as such for many years, and without any payment. I would then be sitting next to the master tailor, sewing and ironing, fully conscious that I did not actually belong there. As a city dweller I was interested in quite different things, and I appeared to be permanently on holiday, working as an assistant. I was very often uncomfortable, I regretted the loss of time, for I knew how to occupy myself more usefully. Just as in my youth, I had again to accept many a reprimand from the master who disliked my work and there was never any question of paying me a wage. Often when I sat in the musty workshop, with my back bent, I decided to give notice and to leave. Once I did this, but the master ignored me and next time I was back sewing. How delighted I was to wake up after such boring hours! I decided that should this uninvited dream appear again, I should cast it off with great energy and that I should call out aloud, to conjure it away. I went to bed and to sleep, and there I was again in the tailor's workshop.

This dream recurred for many years with uncanny regularity. Then I dreamt that (at Apfelhofer's where I had begun my actual service) my master became particularly dissatisfied with my work. 'Where on earth are your thoughts?' he demanded threateningly. The most reasonable thing would have been to tell him that I was only doing him a favour by working for him, but I kept silent. I even put up with it when my master took on a new apprentice, and when he ordered me to make room for him on the bench. I moved into the corner and bless me if it wasn't the same workman who had worked for us nineteen years ago and who had fallen into the river on his way home from the inn! When he sat down there was no room. I looked at the master and he said: 'You have no aptitude for tailoring. You can go. Henceforth I know you no longer!' I was so overcome by fear that I woke up. Dawn was streaming through the bright windows of my familiar home. Objects of art surrounded me. In the elegant bookcase eternal Homer awaited me, magnificent Dante, incomparable Shakespeare, glorious Goethe, all of them great and immortal. I could hear the clear voices of my children who were jesting with their mother. I felt as if I had rediscovered this idyllically sweet, this peaceful, poetic and pure spiritual life, in which I had so often felt a moving human happiness. Yet still I was oppressed by the thought that I had not given notice myself before being dismissed!

And strange to say, from that night on, I have been at peace. I no longer dream of my tailoring past which, undemanding and gay as it was, yet threw so long a shadow on to my later years."[54]

In these dreams of the poet who had been a tailor's apprentice in his youth, it is difficult to find "the operation of wish-fulfilment", says Freud, and he continues:

"Whereas his daily life is full of joy, the dream apparently carries the ghostly shadow of an unhappy existence in the past. A number of dreams of a similar kind enable me to give an interpretation. When I was a young doctor I worked for a long time in a chemical institute without making much progress in the skill required there. In the waking state I therefore never think gladly of this barren and humiliating episode. On the other hand, it has become a recurrent dream of mine that I work in an analytical laboratory. These dreams are as uncomfortable as examination dreams and are never very lucid. When interpreting one of these dreams I finally noticed the word "analysis" which was the key to understanding. For I had since become an "analyst"; I make analyses for which I am highly praised, even if they are only psycho-analyses. I now understood that if I had become proud of analyses and congratulated myself on my achievements, the dream confronted me with those past analyses of which I had no reason to be proud. It was a punishment dream of the social climber, just like the dreams of the tailor's apprentice who had become a famous poet. How is it that in the conflict between inordinate pride and self-criticism, the dream happens to serve the latter and thus assumes the nature of reasonable warning in place of an impermissible wish-fulfilment? I have already mentioned that the answer is very difficult. We may conclude that a foolhardy ambitious fantasy forms the original basis of the dream which, however, is replaced in the dream content by moderation and a feeling of shame. It must be remembered that there are masochistic tendencies of the psychic life to which such a reversal may be ascribed. I should not object to these dreams being distinguished from wish-fulfilment dreams as punishment dreams. I should not consider this a limitation of my previous dream theory but rather as a verbal concession to our ideas which find it difficult to comprehend the concurrence of opposites. A detailed examination of some particular dreams of this kind leads to further consequences.

In one of my laboratory dreams I was of the age I had been during the least successful year of my medical career. I had no position as yet and I did not know how to earn a living. But in the dream I suddenly had the choice between a number of women whom I could marry. In other words I was young again and above all *she* was young again who had shared all these difficulties with me. Thus, one of the incessant and nagging wishes of an ageing man betrayed itself as the unconscious cause of the dream. True, the struggle between vanity and self-criticism which was raging in other psychic strata had determined the dream content, but only the deep longing for youth had made the dream possible. Even in waking life one often says: Things are fine with me now, while in the past I had a hard time; but still it was fine then, for I was young."

Maeder thinks that this interpretation is artificial and unconvincing. He objects to Freud's conclusion:

"His [Freud's] theory requires a wish-fulfilment: the wish of every ageing man to become young again is here considered to be the driving force of the dream regardless of the depressed and disturbed state of mind of the dreamer who has been dismissed from his post. His non-acceptance of the manifest dream-content has unexpected repercussions. The liberating effect of the last dream is basically due to the contrast between the unjust and humiliating treatment in the dream, and the idyllic position of Rosegger's real home. If I long intensely for youth in my dreams I cannot see why waking up—the realization of my mature age and my present position—should make me as happy as it did Rosegger. Freud does not explain at all why this dream ceased once and for all. In the interpretation of a dream it is essential to consider possible after-effects on the waking consciousness of the dreamer. Rosegger reports that he had been persecuted by this dream for years. 'I had to accept many a reprimand from the master, just as in youth, receive no weekly wage, etc.' In the very last dream there is the significant culmination: 'you have no aptitude for tailoring', and he is sent away under distressing circumstances. This long-drawn-out unconscious process reaches its nadir and at the same time its end in the humiliation of the dreamer. 'I was so overcome by fear that I woke up.' Rosegger obviously needed this shock in order to correct his ambition and his pride. Only when this happened could the dreaming cease.

Such a dream definitely has the significance of a true inner experience. In this case, the last of a long sequence, it signifies a turning point in the life of the dreamer.

Is it not natural to assume that Rosegger, in the course of his rise from tailor to a highly esteemed writer, had become vain and proud? In his dreams he is subjected to a painful test and correction. The master censures him and will hear no good of him. It is not the past which is pursuing him, but unconscious feelings which oppose the actual orientation of his conscious ego, and which merely make use of pictures from the past for their representation. In the dream the psyche takes stock of the actual situation of the dreamer and takes a critical position in relation to it. This is the Zurich conception of the dream.

In the private correspondence between Rosegger and a literary friend, it is just this question of vanity and ambition which is treated in a highly personal manner which confirms this assumption. This is very well borne out by Rosegger's description of his study. 'In the elegant bookcase eternal Homer awaited me, magnificent Dante, incomparable Shakespeare, glorious Goethe, all of them great and immortal.' These are the true masters of the poet, the mighty of spirit from whom he may learn and through whom he may develop. We must pay attention to the adjectives used: eternal, magnificent, incomparable, glorious. How small and modest must the dreamer appear next to them! The rise of Rosegger had no doubt made him subject to both inferiority and superiority feelings, which made him suffer in the company of his superiors and vain towards his inferiors. After the final humiliation in the last of a long sequence of dreams, there appears a new sense of balance and objective assessment: Rosegger accepts his humble place amongst the mighty of spirit and is happy in his own home and in his family life. Surely we may say that this interpretation of dreams gives us an insight into the development and the maturity of the personality. A process of psychic correction, of balancing and of development takes place in the depth and it has its effect on the total personality, i.e. on the ego-consciousness—a characteristic form of autonomous psychic activity. The dream can convey this to us by its symbolic power of expression.

Freud's approach in this interpretation was decidedly too one-sided and retrospective. The longing for youth of a melancholy and ageing man appeared to him as the decisive feature of this dream. There are such dreams, it is true, but in this case Freud must have been wrong. Probably he projected something personal into it, for he identifies himself formally with his dreams. In fact, in his commentary he speaks of his own dream in which he appears as a chemical analyst, which corresponds to his own past. In his own dreams, the longing for youth was indeed the decisive factor.

If we elevate a point of view to a strict rule, to a kind of dogma, we become blind to everything else. We must reject the rigid formulation of the dream as a wish-fulfilment, and as a mere infantile interpretation of events, and we must recognize that there are dreams (as well as other mental phenomena) in which a progressive movement of the libido produces a picture of a desired end, or even an attempt to realize it. The future, too, can occupy us unconsciously, just as the past."[55]

Maeder's conception was unreservedly accepted by C. G. Jung. Thus Jung writes later:

"The prospective function is an unconscious anticipation of future achievements, like a preliminary exercise or a preliminary sketching of a preconceived plan. It is a pre-combination of probabilities. The fact that it is occasionally superior to conscious pre-combination is not surprising for the dream is due to a fusion of subordinate elements. It combines all those perceptions, thoughts and feelings which have escaped consciousness because of their weak emphasis."[56]

At first, it is true, the "complexity of the material" only led Jung to an extension of Freud's causal ideas, into a "conditional" consideration of psychic phenomena. "For in this realm," wrote Jung, "we are dealing with such a complexity of conditions, that we can assert no *unequivocal* causal connection. A principle of 'conditionalism' is far more relevant." In other words, under given conditions, certain consequences may follow. This idea tries to replace strict causality by the idea of interacting conditions. At the same time he attempts to amplify the one-one cause-effect relationship by introducing the idea of a connection between the effects themselves (inter-effects). Jung adds expressly that this conditionalism does not do away with causality in the old sense. It adapts causality to the complexity of living phenomena.[57] Jung, too, proceeded from the conditional to the "finalist" approach as soon as he became convinced that "every living being strives for wholeness, or at least for the creation of a spiritual equilibrium".[58]

Jung saw in the dream one of the instruments serving this wholeness or spiritual equilibrium. It is in this sense that he ascribes to the dream the special finalist functions of complementariness and particularly of compensation. In the dream, he says, the autonomous, supra-individual, or collective unconscious compensates the conscious ego. The dream confronts and compares these parts of the personality and, in favourable cases, leads to balance or correction. As a compensatory phenomena, the dream sometimes functions as the self-regulator of the mental system. This self-regulating mechanism aims at that self-development and organizing process which Jung has called "unconscious individuation".

(b) The theory of the "subjective" meaning of the dream

Freud himself had already exploded his own purely mechanistic principle of explanation with some attempts at a finalist approach and his remarks on the "sacro egoismo" of the dream and on the "identification of the dreamer with the dream images" point to a further clue, which promises to transcend the horizon of a mere technical understanding.[59]

By the above expressions Freud meant that it was the ego itself that played the main role in dreams, even if it was disguised in other human or animal forms, or in objects. For instance, the dangerous animals which often appear in dreams, were seen by Freud to be symbols of the instinctuality and sensuality of the dreamer. Thus, in interpreting a patient's dream in which a stranger is examined by a Customs officer, Freud explains that the stranger is the dreamer himself who, wishing to hide something from him (Freud), identifies him with the "Customs officer".[60] This merely reiterates an old principle of Hippocratic dream interpretation, which considered the relationship between the dream-content and the dreamer to be self-evident. Even when the images of the dream deal with other things and with other people, wrote Hippocrates, they refer to the dreamer's own self. With this type of interpretation Freud approaches the deep intuition of Novalis and Nietzsche. Novalis knew that "the dream strangely revealed to us the ease with which our soul could enter and change into any object". Nietzsche had said to all who wanted to shirk responsibility for their dreams: "Nothing belongs to you more intimately than your dreams! They alone are your own work! Matter, form, duration, actors, audience—everything in this comedy is only yourself."

The full subjective significance of many dream phenomena was realized by Herbert Silberer in his study of falling asleep and awakening, a decade after Freud's *The Interpretation of Dreams*. He described them at great length as "functional dream phenomena", in which the state or the effectiveness of consciousness and the particular state or functions of the dreaming psyche were depicted. Silberer called these phenomena "functional" because they are not concerned with thought material but only with the functioning of the dream consciousness; that is, whether it functions quickly, slowly, easily, lazily, gladly, successfully, unfruitfully, strenuously, etc. Falling asleep, sinking into sleep, like waking up, could be represented by functional dream pictures. Silberer designated the dream representation of these two processes by the generic name of "threshold symbolism", since they commonly choose the symbol of the threshold for their auto-symbolic dream images. For instance, Silberer, in a dream which occurred shortly before waking, stepped from some open place into an entrance hall and then into the main room. It was on the threshold of the door that he actually awoke. The dream image had represented the threshold between sleep and waking, by the threshold of the door, though it is true that these two processes could have given rise to quite different symbols. Once, when Silberer felt that he was approaching wakefulness, but wanted to remain in a state of twilight sleep, he had the following dream: "I am putting one foot across a river but I pull it back again, and consider staying on this side."

In a similar situation Silberer experienced an equally revealing dream:

> "I tell a lady, ostensibly for gymnastic purposes, to bend her knees. Now, I tell her to get up again. She finds this very difficult. I have to help her and call out: 'Now comes the difficulty of getting up!' (With these words I almost wake up and realize the significance of the dream.) Her getting up is similar both to my emergence from sleep and also to the anticipated getting up from bed."

When waking up it was still quite clear to Silberer that the lady was in fact his own body and his own sleepy soul. His assistance to her, on the other hand, was his will, his impulse, to get up. Again, in the same situation, Silberer once caught the last scrap of his dream just as the alarm went off: a lady had jilted another man in his favour. As an interpretation of this event, Silberer remarked that he had just decided not to sleep on. "The jilting, and this I felt immediately upon waking, referred to my refusal to continue sleeping." It was his own soul which here, in the form of a lady, jilted sleep in favour of waking.[61]

In the further course of his investigation he added the following statement:

"The great effectiveness of this kind of personification clearly points to the fact that I am here projecting to the outside a living part of my own mental life."[62]

Immediately afterwards, and independently of Silberer, Stekel and Maeder drew attention to this very "subjective" significance of many dream phenomena. Maeder's idea of "self-representation in symbolic form" or of "auto-symbolic representation" in dreams has already been mentioned, when discussing the finalist approach. Stekel also recognized that very often an evident meaning of the dream emerges if one interprets one of the sickly, weak, inferior figures of the dream as the "personification of the neurosis in dreams".[63]

By distinguishing between dream interpretations on "subjective" and "objective" levels respectively, Jung brought out very well the possible significance of dream figures as "symbolic representations" or "personifications" of subjective aspects of the personality.[64] We are interpreting on the objective level if we believe that a dream object or a dream person signifies the actual object or person, or at least the dreamer's relationship to it or to him. Interpretation on the subjective level would see in a dream object or person neither the one nor the other, but would merely consider the dream figure as a symbol, as personifying or making concrete the dreamer's own subjectivity. For instance, in subjective interpretation a dream tortoise would signify the tortoise-like and armoured character of the dreamer himself.

CHAPTER 4

Critique of the Basis of the Dream Theories of the Zurich School

ALTHOUGH the additional knowledge gained from dream interpretation on the subjective level is very useful, and despite the possible therapeutic importance of a consideration of possible dream aims and intentions, neither of the theoretical additions of the Zurich School brings us any closer to the actual essence of the dreams themselves. The concepts of finalism and of the subjective significance of the dream content by no means spring from a more basic and essential understanding of man and the world. They are still founded on the old conceptual world with the implicit assumption that all existence, all things, all animals and all men reflect the interplay of cause and effect. In so far as we consider all things to be "caused causes" and the whole world as a mere interplay of forces, or an interconnection between objects, we must needs add finality to causality. For this reason the "causa finalis" is one of the components of Aristotle's original fourfold concept of causality. It is only because of the increasingly one-sided technical approach of Western scientific thought that, together with the "causa materialis" and the "causa efficiens", it is gradually being forgotten. Significantly, only the "causa efficiens" has remained as causality in general.

In his *Critique of Judgment*, Kant still stated with emphasis that without finality not even the simplest manifestations of life could be explained. For only non-living phenomena could be understood in terms of mechanical and causal relations; in an assessment of life, however, teleology became a necessary hypothesis. At the same time Kant did not fail to point out that teleology was not a constitutive but only a regulative principle, a concept which, while indispensable, only regulated the subjective understanding of phenomena, and that causality was merely one category of our reason. It can never be determined whether in nature there is in fact any striving towards an end. Thus Kant regarded both causality and finality as mere mental interpretations of the world which need not be real attributes of the constitution of reality itself.[65] According to Kant's epistemology "nature" is our experiences as organized under the universal laws of an ideal system. We may therefore regard "nature" as having a kind of purposefulness; the "logical purposefulness" of agreement with the subjective conditions of our judgment. But we cannot infer from this any real purposefulness in nature different from this systematic knowing.

Just as ideas of causality require teleology as their necessary complement, so does the idea of the objective world require to be complemented by the idea of a subjective one. Without a subject nothing at all would exist to confront objects and to imagine them as such. True, this implies that every object, everything "objective"—in being merely objectivized by the subject—is the most subjective thing possible. The subject, too, if it is the mere complement to this idea of the object, becomes an objective datum, an object among other objects, and an interaction between the most varied "psychic" objects and data. In this way the totality of the non-bodily manifestations of man is first objectivized in the conception of "the psyche". Since we are aware of part of our mental processes and manage to handle them more or less successfully, and since, conversely, many of our other attitudes to objects and persons are hidden from us and attack us in the form of neurotic symptoms and slips of everyday life, or come to us in the form of creative ideas, the causal, as well as the finalist, approach proceeded to subdivide the psyche further still. The known non-physical aspects of man's life are condensed into the objectivized conceptions of the "ego" and the "super-ego"; those which escape his own perception are mentally precipitated as the unreal abstractions: "the unconscious", "the id", and are assumed to be psychic layers. Some of the other most common psychic representations and abstract notions, to which we shall have to return later, are "the symbol", "the archetype", "the collective unconscious", etc. The degree of objectivization of "the subject" is best illustrated by phrases such as "The psyche is a self-regulating system" (C. G. Jung) or "The human personality is built up of layers which can be compared with geological layers."[66]

Naturally, it did not escape an investigator of the calibre of C. G. Jung that the mere addition of concepts within the same framework of existing ones was not much of a progressive step. To his assertions that the psyche could not be understood causally alone but also required a finalist or teleological approach, he therefore added the remark that only an amalgamation of both points of view (the causal and the finalist) could give a complete understanding of the essence of the dream. He could only foresee such an amalgamation in the future. In any case he admits that "today, because of the enormous theoretical and practical difficulties it has not yet been brought about in a scientifically satisfying manner". But an amalgamation of such concepts as causality and finality, or objective level and subjective level—each complementary to the other—is basically impossible within that conceptual world which, itself, first created, and then separated them.

Furthermore, Jung, as no psychologist before him, clearly recognized the artificiality of the mental separation of human reality into psychic subject and isolated external objects. He saw in this a malignant disease which had attacked all previous psychology in general and the investigation of dreams in particular. He already suspected that there existed a direct relationship between the external world and the perceiving ego. A number of aphorisms in his works bear witness to this turn of his intuition, which far surpasses that of contemporary psychological thought. For instance he writes:

"Originally the psyche is the world."[67] Elsewhere we read: "The self comprises infinitely more than the mere ego, as symbols have shown since time immemorial. It is just as much another or others as it is the ego. Individuation does not exclude the world but includes it."[68]

But Jung did not rest content with such intuitions. He exerted an extraordinary degree of mental effort towards philosophically bridging the gulf between subject and object. This was no doubt tremendously important to Jung, since it was the mental division of subject and object which had led to his distinction between dream interpretation on the subjective and on the objective level. This had brought in its train so much uncertainty about when to apply the one and when the other that it was scientifically untenable.

His attempt to bridge this gulf was bound to fail for the same reasons that had prevented him from uniting causal and finalist concepts. He had at his disposal only the old approach of natural science which never allowed him to free himself from the objectivization of the human being. So, like Freud, he tries to explain the psyche and its functions by first analysing it into its assumed parts. Naturally, to do this he too had to assume forces capable of reuniting these parts. Freud had abstracted his ideas of the instincts from human behaviour. From the fact that in the most varied groups of men the same behaviour, concepts, pictures, myths, dreams and fairy tales were to be found time after time, Jung likewise concluded that there were archetypes which produced these universal phenomena. Just as Freud finally reduced the whole "psyche" to his instinctual concepts, so Jung, in his atomization of the "system of psychic balance", arrived at the "archetypes" as the elements or sources of energy of the latter, and at the idea of the "collective unconscious" as the assembly of all the "archetypes".

However, an archetype deduced from the mere identity of events, i.e. from something logically universal, is no more than a mentally derived hypothesis having an extremely small probability of actual existence. Jung himself therefore has to admit that no one will ever know if there are archetypes at all, when he allows his pupil Jacobi to say that one can never meet an archetype directly.[69] When Jung's followers counter our objections by saying that we meet the same difficulties in the case of the real thoughts and feelings of people, for these also cannot be seen and grasped directly as can external objects, and can only be deduced analogously from language, expression, and gestures, they overlook two factors.

First, unspoken feelings and thoughts are immediately accessible to self-experience, while the latter will never meet archetypes, and secondly the bare thought of another person does not stand in the same relation to his audible speech in the same way as a hypothetical idea is related to a perceptible phenomenon. Human language is not limited to vocal speech, and everyone knows, for instance, of gestures or bodily language. Silent thought about something does not take place in words less distinct than the spoken expression of that thought. It is therefore only right and proper to call it a language that is still tacit. Silent thought and vocal speech are only two subdivisions of the same human language. From this it follows that the one kind of language can never be mentally derived from the other in a way which would be comparable to the derivation of the notion of an archetype. To our basic criticism it is only of secondary importance that recent research into pre-history and modern ethnology have begun to undermine the very empirical foundation on which Jung built his concept of archetype. From innumerable separate investigations these sciences give us an increasingly clear picture of the world-wide ramifications and interconnections between the oldest cultures. Thus the assumption that the similar features in the symbols, myths, dreams and fairy tales of men came about completely independently becomes less and less credible. Their apparent original uniformity, from which Jung abstracted his archetypes, and which at the same time he considered a "proof" of their "empirically demonstrable" reality,[70] has obviously become a purely historical problem.[71]

It is true that he at first emphasized the hypothetical and abstract nature of his concept of archetype, just as Freud originally pointed to the purely hypothetical nature of his theory of instincts. In the entire history of the sciences, there has hardly been one creative investigator who did not mistake some one speculative abstraction in his philosophy for the result of empirical investigations. Freud, for example, suddenly believed in the reality of his instinctual abstractions, just as Jung suddenly considered his idea of the archetype as an actual fact. Jung quite unpredictably thought of these "archetypal dominants", which he had previously considered hypothetical assumptions, as such concrete objects that he called them "regulators" and "stimulators of creative fantasy activity". Just as Freud did in the case of instincts, so does Jung finally call the archetypes the motors of the dream formation.[72] If in the Freudian doctrine the manifest dream images are the products of a latent instinctual drive, so in the dream theory of Jung it is always an archetype which, appearing in the guise of a dream symbol, produces the dream images. Now if we wish to determine the importance and limitations of the Jungian dream theory, we cannot go too deeply into the origins and the characteristics of his concept of archetypes.

Just as Freud traces the origin of the instincts to the erogenous zones of the body, so Jung sees his archetypes originating in organic cortical structures. "They are inherited with the cortical structure, indeed, they are its psychic aspect."[73] Furthermore he considers the archetypes as "the deposits of all human experience from its darkest beginnings".[74] This assumption has already been criticized by the biologist Portmann, who said that great caution was needed before assuming the heredity of acquired psychic structures, and that the very idea of a deposit of human experience was based on Lamarck's outdated biological speculations.[75] Portmann's own criticism, however, is also incomplete. He asserts that the receptor structures in the central nervous system stimulate the archetypal acts of animals which are comparable to the archetypal behaviour of the human being. This is based on completely ill-considered premisses, although it is true that these still pervade the behavioural studies of modern animal psychology. Quite apart from the problems involved in speaking of stimulus-receptors in the central nervous system, we have to go a long and probably impassable way from the experimental models of which Portmann is thinking, to the "proof" of the existence of primary images, arrangements, or structures in the central nervous system.

There is a further close connection with biology in Jung's idea that archetypes are typical patterns of behaviour[76] and above all in his statement that these patterns of behaviour, being systems of "subjective readiness", are closely connected with the concepts of instinct and drive. The archetypes, he even goes on to say, are "nothing but the self-reproduction of the instincts".[77] At the same time they are "identical with instinctual patterns of behaviour".[78] Elsewhere the hypothetical archetype is called "a living organism with powers of reproduction" or "the organ of a pre-rational psyche".[79]

With this last description he ascribes a second function to the archetypes. No longer are they the mere "motors" of psychic life; they have also become primary receptors. "It is well known," Jung writes, "that there is no human experience and none is possible without a subjective readiness. What does this subjective readiness consist of?" In the final analysis, Jung asserts—thus anticipating the models of modern animal psychology—it consists of an inherited psychic structure; or, again, "the forms of the world into which man is born, are already latent in him as virtual images".

The mind confronts external nature with these primordial images, just as the organism confronts light with a new structure: the eye. And just as the eye is attuned to light, so is the primary image attuned to the natural process.[80] These *a priori* categories of the archetype are "naturally of a collective nature and have no individual predestination. So these images must be considered as having no content, and therefore as being unconscious. They only obtain their content, their influence, and finally consciousness, in that they meet with empirical facts which set off the unconscious readiness and awaken it to life."[81] It is in this way that Jung believes that his archetypes can explain the "remarkable correlation between consciousness, on the one hand, and the phenomenal world, i.e. objective processes, on the other". Jacobi added that between the subjective psyche and external phenomena there exists a connection of the order of a pictorial analogy.[82]

But how can all this ever lead to a connection between "unconscious subjective readiness" and natural phenomena in the objective world, let alone to an awakening of the former by the latter? Just as it is not a mere eye but only man himself who perceives light, so it is not a primary image or scheme in the brain or in the psyche that can grasp a process in the dream or in the waking state; even if we granted that the primary image or scheme, just like the eye, was more than a mere hypothetical concept of neo-Kantian thought.

Jung unquestionably felt the inadequacy of this conceptual world more and more clearly, and he realized that this basis of thought, with its unresolved separation of subject and object, could never lead to an understanding of the way in which man meets the physical world. In the past few years he has clearly moved away from biology, on which he had previously leaned so heavily, and has increasingly become concerned with physical hypotheses.

Much earlier, Jung had already compared the psychic economy to an electric generator, and had called the symbol the concrete manifestation of the archetype, a *"psychic energy transformer"*.[83] In his latest work Jung arrives at much more far-reaching physical conclusions. Dissatisfied with the instinctual and psychical nature of the archetype, Jung asks more searchingly about its "true" nature, i.e. its essence. The archetypal images conveyed by the unconscious, especially by means of dream symbols, must never, he says, be confused with the archetype itself. These symbols are

> "highly varied structures which point to an inherently non-perceptual basic form. The archetype itself is a 'psychoid' factor; it is, as it were, the invisible ultra-violet part of the spectrum".[84] "Just as the psychic infra-red, i.e. the biological drive, slowly enters into the physiological processes of life, and thus into a chemical and physical system, so the psychic ultra-violet, i.e. the archetype, signifies a realm which has no physiological properties and which, in the final analysis, can no longer be considered to be psychic. . . . Thus the location of the archetype beyond the psychic realm is analogous to the location of the physiological drive which has its direct root in the physical organism, and which, with its psychoid character, forms the bridge to matter in general."[85]

With these assumptions Jung believes to have taken psychic processes

> "to the point where they become completely obscured and imperceptible, and where they can only be determined by their effects, that is, by their regulating influence on the contents of consciousness. The study of these effects leads to the strange

conclusion that they emanate from an unconscious, i.e. objective, reality which simultaneously behaves like a subjective reality, i.e. consciousness. Thus, the reality behind the effects of the unconscious, also includes the observing subject, and its character is therefore beyond our understanding."[86]

Jung, at this stage, neither clarifies nor substantiates these statements by means of a more exact definition of what is meant by the terms "subjective" and "objective" which he uses in so many different senses. Instead he significantly invokes the aid of modern atomic physics:

> "Although, from purely psychological considerations, I have begun to doubt the purely psychic nature of the archetype, psychology, as the result of physics, is *forced*** to revise its purely psychological premisses. For physics has demonstrated that on the level of atomic orders of magnitude, the observer is an essential condition of objective reality, and only with the acknowledgement of this fact is it possible to produce a satisfactory principle of explanation. This implies, on the one hand, a subjective factor in the physical world picture itself, and, on the other hand, a relation between the psyche and the objective space-time continuum which is essential for an explanation of the psyche. Just as we cannot imagine the physical continuum, so we cannot conceive of its essential psychic aspect. What is of the greatest theoretical importance, however, is the relative or partial identity of psyche and physical continuum, since in bridging the apparent incommensurability between the physical and psychic worlds, it presents us with a tremendous simplification."[87]

Similarly a pupil of Jung, C. A. Meier, had already assumed in 1935 that there was

> "a true and proper complementary relationship between physics and psychology. Both sciences, in their separate spheres, had made observations for many years, and established relevant systems of thought. Both sciences had reached certain limits which were of a similar basic character. The observed material and man, with his sense and perceptive organs and their

* Author's italics.

extensions—measuring instruments and measuring procedures—
—are inseparably interconnected."[88]

It must be admitted that the results of the researches of physicists and the conclusions of Jung's "complex" psychology have an ever-increasing similarity. But is the similarity of results a criterion of their correctness or validity? Is the "pressure" of this convergence truly in the nature of things, or is it not rather the necessary and inevitable consequence of the fact that there never was a clear "division of labour" between the two sciences? Did not both atomic physics and "complex psychology", from their earliest beginnings, have the same philosophical basis? And did not both employ the same method of thought, even if Jung does believe that he has arrived at his results by purely psychological considerations? Similar assumptions and modes of analysis are always bound to come to the same conclusion about reality.

Be that as it may, at the conclusion of his investigations, Jung can nevertheless speak of a bridging of the apparent incommensurability of the physical and psychic worlds. Is it, therefore, not true to say that "complex psychology", together with atomic physics following on their common theoretical paths of natural science, did in fact bridge the radical separation of subject and object, which bridging Jung considered as a prerequisite for a more complete conception of the essence of dreams? But how can there be any talk of bridging when the "identity of psyche and physical continuum", that is, the breaking down of the subject-object division, could only be achieved at the price of the destruction of the spiritual foundations both of physics and of "complex psychology"? For do not both proceed from the basic idea that the whole world is exclusively the interaction between mere physical and psychic objects? Does not physics, in the final analysis, lead to the intellectual difficulty of an unpredictable acausality? And does it not reduce the objects of the world to abstract mathematical formulae? And is there not in the ideas of "complex psychology" a very similar dissolution of basic ideas? In any case, as far as the latter is concerned, all that remains of the entire human reality is the merely inferred, obscure, organizing archetypal forces, till the archetypes themselves become derived postulates "the contents of which, if they are present at all, cannot be imagined".[89]

If, now, the two most prominent dream psychologists of our times, Freud and Jung, can only point to merely "assumed" abstractions, such as unconscious drives and inferred archetypes, as the causes, the basis, or the motors of the dream formation, then one must lose all hope that the methods of natural science will ever lead to a discovery of the actual essence of dreams. In any case it becomes unnecessary to make a detailed analysis of all the countless dream interpretations which keep within the conceptual world of Freud and Jung.[90]

However, more recently, there have been some dream theories which have tried to tackle the dream in original ways.

THE DREAM AS A WHOLE

the waking state, and all our understanding of the dream must fully depend on our particular understanding of waking existence. Now if our ability to be awake is the most essential condition of all our concern with dreams, then dreams themselves force all future investigators to pay heed to the structure of waking life, instead of taking it for granted.

If, on the basis of such a relationship between dreams and waking, we only speak of dreams in waking life, but never let the question of waking life bother us in the dreams themselves, does this not bear witness to the fact that dreaming is a part of waking life? If, then, waking life on its part belongs to our historical continuity, must it not necessarily include the dream also? Perhaps our life history demands both our waking and our dreaming by revealing itself explicitly and factually in the former, whereas it withholds its inherent development in the latter. If this is the case, then our dreaming also, with all its discontinuity and lack of historical development, might well be based on the mystery of the historical continuity of our existence.

CHAPTER 5

"Neo-analytical" Dream Theories

(a) The neo-psychoanalytical dream theory of H. Schultz-Hencke

As a possible new source of a "fuller understanding of the essence of the dream" at which Jung had aimed, H. Schultz-Hencke's textbook of dream interpretation deserves special mention.

The author himself calls his "neo-psychoanalytical" conception of the dream the "extension of the Freudian, Adlerian, and Jungian positions and their amalgamation".[91] He at first attacks the objectivization of man and the hypothetical character of the usual abstract natural-scientific concepts. Obviously he intends to demonstrate that instincts and desires cannot exist independently of a living subject. He says the expression "drive" implies a "towards" and he adds the word "experience". This results in Schultz-Hencke's characteristic concept of "instinctual experiences".[92] However, he fails completely to explain how a subject can experience an instinct. Indeed, he immediately deprives his concept of "experience" of all meaning by returning to Freud's mechanistic philosophy. For within this framework how can one understand a passive process, such as experiencing, considered as an active motor? And yet the author, just as Freud does with his instinctual conception of displaced drives, declares that the "latent drive experience" is the actual motor of dream formation. So the dream "in certain respects represents an attempt to revive the inhibited instinctual world and to reform it".

The "instinctual character" which Schultz-Hencke here ascribes to the dream is underlined by phrases which speak of the instinctual experience as the "nucleus" of the dream,[93] and of its depth as the "latent and inhibited instincts".[94] He further defines the dream as the "interplay between pleasure-seeking instincts and the experience of fear".[95] Thus, just like Freud, he reduces not only the dream itself, but all human experience in general, to instincts and needs, since he expressly calls the latter the "nucleus" of experience.[96] The result is that "the nucleus of his dream-analysis" can only consist of "a supplementation of the dream with real memories of the dreamer's early circumstances of life during which he had inhibited an instinctual experience. The rest is a mere by-product in comparison."[97] "The real memory of the actual incident alone is important. But in it the relevant instinct will frequently not appear undisguised. In its stead we shall find a 'higher' (a sublime) idea."[98]

Schultz-Hencke, like Freud, is quite certain that the inhibited infantile biological impulses are the sources of the dream formation. But he does not reduce his analysis of man to a mere duality of instinctual types, as did Freud. He admits the existence of a great number of different instincts, "ranging from primitive clutching and retention of objects, to the experience of beauty, to pure contemplation and deep religious experience".[99] Acquisitive, retentive and sexual strivings are considered to be especially important. Like Freud, he endeavours to explain the so-called spiritual phenomena of man also by means of these instincts. He writes, for instance: "We may with certainty express the assumption that this simple biological need for a motor discharge is the source of the urge for freedom, which is recognized to be so important."[100] (The reader will note that his "certainty" is tempered by the word "assumption".) But not only this unique spiritual urge, but the "whole existence, and vitality of man, is essentially characterized by this quite specific urge". He actually believes, as emerges also from many of his "existentialist" interpretations of sample dreams, that he can derive total "existence" in general, in Binswanger's sense, from such instinctual experiences.[101] Similarly, he also tries to reduce Jung's idea of the archetype to instinctual experience. For example, he endeavours to reduce the "anima", by which Jung designates the unconscious feminine essence of man, to "the central psychic presence of longing in the most general sense of the word: a universal acquisitive longing".[102] Similarly he believes that the so-called "animus", designating the latent masculinity of woman, can be fully understood if one considers it in terms of an instinctual inhibition during early childhood.

Surprisingly, Schultz-Hencke concludes that "the fact that these 'existentialist', 'psychic', or 'universally human' factors originate in 'biological instincts', *in no way* conflicts with their spiritual character".[103] For particular biological experiences "have a transcending significance which it would be of the greatest importance to recognize and to know precisely". In them we should find "a bridge between character and biological urges".[104] Thanks to this "transcending significance" of the biological instinctual experience, we could, for instance, coin the phrase, "Anal processes too are of philosophical importance".[105] Schultz-Hencke can only arrive at this transcendence, which is possibly meant to replace Freud's "sublimation", by drawing out from elementary biological needs a highly abstract category of human instinctual experiences, which may then appear as "psychological types of instincts".

Although we dare not assert that we can fully understand this last formulation of Schultz-Hencke, we can nevertheless be sure that it, too, is completely within the same philosophic framework within which Freud based his hypotheses. For here as well all human experience and behaviour is reduced to forces, to inhibited or uninhibited instincts, and this is considered to be an adequate explanation. Matters are not improved by Schultz-Hencke's attempts to extend causal to conditional thinking: "Causal thinking is nothing but habit. The basic recognition that only a conditional approach will do justice to the facts has not as yet matured sufficiently."[106]

Just as Schultz-Hencke, with his demand for a conditional approach, merely identifies himself with an old desire of Jung, so ultimately he adopts the idea of the finalist dream aspect of Jung, Maeder and Adler. If the latter see the dream as a self-reproduction, Schultz-Hencke calls it a "mirror" of waking experience.[107] Like them, he too calls the dream an "attempted solution".[108] Nor is Jung's idea of the dream as a compensation lacking either, for Schultz-Hencke not only heads a whole chapter with this idea, but discusses it as follows: "The compensatory nature of the dream is the basic connection between both assertions (between the assertion of the so-called subjective conscious experience of man, and the assertion of man as a dreamer)".[109]

While Schultz-Hencke's *Textbook of Dream Interpretation* gives us many practical hints, it contributes little to our essential understanding of the dream.

(b) The "neo-Freudian" dream theory of E. Fromm

The American author Erich Fromm would like us to see his new approach to the dream as a development of the dream theory of depth psychology. For this reason he expressly emphasizes his agreement with the conceptions of Freud and Jung. For instance, he agrees with Freud that dreaming is a meaningful and significant mental activity under the condition of sleep.[110] He contends, nevertheless, that his dream theory differs greatly from that of Freud in many other respects. Above all, according to Fromm, dreams are not only expressions of the lowest and most irrational psychic functions, as Freud thought they were, but also of the highest and most valuable.

He obviously overlooks the fact that Freud himself had said of the unconscious, as expressed with particular clarity in dreams:

> "Normal man is not only much more immoral than he believes but also very much more moral . . . the nature of man, in good as in evil, far transcends what he believes of himself, that is, what is known to his ego through conscious perception."[111]

Furthermore, in his discussion of punishment dreams, Freud had already admonished us "to observe more carefully the contribution of the super-ego (i.e. of conscience) to the formation of dreams".[112]

Fromm accepts Jung's assertion that we are often cleverer and more honourable during sleep than in our waking life. He also accepts the supplementation of Freud's analytical or introspective dream interpretation given by H. Silberer and Jung in terms of an "anagogic" or "prospective" dream interpretation. But Fromm differs sharply from Jung when the latter assumes a supra-personal and transcendental basis for especially clever and prophetic dreams. In contradistinction to this point of view, Fromm believes that what we think in our sleep is no more than *our own* thinking.[113]

Although Fromm does not deny the origins of his own dream theory, he nevertheless devotes by far the largest chapter of his work to his radical differences with the theories of Freud and Jung. According to Fromm, the unconscious, expressed in dreams, is neither Jung's realm of myth, nor Freud's seat of irrational libidinal forces. It is rather the dreamer's own inner experience that manifests itself by means of a symbolic language. This is brought out by the fact that in the dream "inner experiences, feelings and thoughts are expressed as if they were sensory experiences, events in the outer world".[114] However, what Fromm thus calls his own "art of dream interpretation" is, down to its smallest detail, nothing else than what Silberer and Maeder had called the "auto-symbolic representation of the dreamer", thirty and forty years previously, and what C. G. Jung had designated as "dream interpretation on the subjective level". For instance, Fromm discusses in very great detail two typical dreams, in which the dreamer has to cross a river. According to him this represents the symbol of an important decision and the renunciation of a previous way of life for another. "Crossing the river," he says, "is the decision he must make to cross from the shore of childhood to that of maturity."[115] We can read this very formulation in Jung's interpretation of a similar river dream in 1926:

> "The dream demonstrated to the patient that it was something in herself which prevented her crossing, i.e., her getting from one position or attitude into another ... that the obstacle difficult to overcome and which opposed further progress lay in herself. ... The interpretation of changes of place as changes of attitude is supported by certain modes of speech in some primitive languages...."[116]

With regard to equally typical dreams of nakedness, Fromm also opposes his "own" ideas to the Freudian interpretation of such dreams, as hallucinatory wish-fulfilments of a childish exhibitionism. He says:

> "Freud ignores the fact that nakedness can be a symbol of things other than sexual exhibitionism. Nakedness can, for instance, be a symbol of truthfulness. To be naked can stand for being oneself without pretence...."[117]

Fromm conveniently overlooks the fact that it was just this "inner" interpretation of external nakedness in the dream that had already been a favourite example of Jung's dream interpretations on the subjective level.

Jung even devotes a whole chapter to this interpretation of the symbol of nakedness which he significantly entitles "The Naked Truth". The nakedness of the figure, Jung writes, means symbolically that

> "the situation has thrown off the conventional guise and that it confronts reality, without false veils and without any other means of adornment. Here man emerges such as he is, and exhibits what was previously hidden under the mask of conventionality."[118]

Furthermore, almost ten years previously a pupil of Jung had especially stressed a further possible "inner" aspect of the symbol of nakedness. A. Teillard wrote:

> "From the point of view of depth-psychology it [the dream of nakedness] expresses, by means of a drastic picture, the

complete lack of adaptation of man to his environment, together with feelings of inferiority and shame."[119]

Fromm's approach therefore does not make any new contribution to a better understanding of the dream and, in addition, it deprives the dream doctrines of Freud and Jung of essential parts. It excludes the possibility of supra-personal spheres which is left open in both theories, by simply denying both "the mythological essence of unknown origin" which Freud attributes to the instincts, and also that supra-individual sphere which Jung called the collective unconscious. Fromm could not give any better reasons for limiting the Freudian and Jungian dream doctrines than the statement that dream phenomena are the mere symbolic expression of *our* desires, of *our* thought and of *our* virtues.[120] As if the mere labelling of the being to whom these wishes, virtues and this thought belong, by the pronoun "our", stated anything at all about this possessor and his belongings. Fromm is not even aware of how much he endangers our very humanity by simply suppressing those decisive problems which are inherent in man's ability to say the word "our". By completely ignoring any consideration of the possible basis of the manifestation of human phenomena, he robs our existence of all roots and leaves it suspended in mid-air, together with its ambitions, ethical values and virtues.

CHAPTER 6

The Most Recent Non-analytical Dream Theories

K. LEONARD, in contradistinction to neo-analytical dream theorists, consciously ignores the discoveries of Freud and Jung.[121] He considers their dream interpretation impossible, if only for the reason that both give quite different interpretations of the same dream images. Therefore one of them at least, and probably both, must be wrong. The author does not enter into a discussion of the validity of this criticism. Nevertheless it has often been expressly pointed out, and not least by Jung himself, that the Freudian and Jungian interpretation of the same dream images are not necessarily mutually exclusive, but are rather mutually complementary conceptions. Leonard, all the same, agrees with Freud's "intuition" that the forces of the unconscious are at work in the dream. He also cites dream thoughts and slips of memory which "rather support the interpretation of the dream situation",[122] like Freud in his technique of "secondary elaboration". Leonard also agrees with Freud and Jung in stressing the fact that all those events which had been neglected in waking thought[123] are pictorially represented in the dream. Like Jung, Leonard sees an important purpose of the dream in that it both widens man's horizon, thus preserving him from one-sidedness, and also provides him with insights which he would otherwise lack.[124]

Essentially, however, Leonard tries to interpret dream images as simple pictorial repetitions of external and internal perceptions and feelings of waking life. He claims that the dream-like feeling of suspension in one of his own dreams, in which, supported on the hips of two ladies, he glided easily above the earth, is certainly due to "sensations of suspension within the vestibule [organs of equilibrium] and which can thus produce dream images by itself".[125] Moreover, according to him, anxiety dreams are mainly due to feelings of physical displeasure and therefore approach the fringes of the abnormal.[126] Dream-like distortions and absurdities and the by-passing of factual perception by the dream are due to a breaking up of waking perceptions into their elements, into forms, colours, sensations of tone, and affects, and to the reunifying of these elements into the dream image, according to laws depending on the strength of memory of the individual perceptual qualities. For Leonard, the particular aptitudes for entering into dreams of each individual perceptual element determined by these laws replaces all Freudian answers to the decisive question why just a particular one and not another out of the thousand perceptions of waking life should appear in the dreams. Leonard explains these differences in aptitude of the individual perceptual elements for entering into dreams by going back to an assumption which is highly reminiscent of Binz's description of the "aurora of awakening". Leonard contends that in dreams there occurs a dissociation of sleep and that the "individual sense realms fall apart". "If all man's psychic functions always slept equally deeply, he would never dream at all. We assume that in sleep the activity of the will is weakened more than the imagination." The dream consciousness is so narrow and so short-sighted "that only one concept can emerge clearly in it".[127] Finally, according to Leonard's theory, the chief meaning of the dream is that it is "a carrier and preserver of human memory. Much would be lost prematurely, and there would be no human memory at all, if the dream did not create repeated opportunities for renewal."[128]

All the assumptions in Leonard's dream theory remain completely unexplained. For instance, he fails to tell us how particular sense realms or mental functions can sleep at all, let alone how they can sleep with different degrees of intensity, or how particular organs themselves can produce dream images. The crux of his theory, the dream laws themselves, rests on the assumption that human perception consists of separate sense impressions. How else could they fall apart into their elements during dreams, and be reconstituted into dream images? The untenability of such an atomistic hypothesis of perception has long been demonstrated by modern psychology.

To these basic objections we must add that in our opinion even Leonard's concrete observations require scrutiny. The very first and most important of the so-called dream laws proved not to be the rule when we tested it on ten random dream examples. According to Leonard's laws, form-perceptions of the previous day could never appear in a dream, unless a tacit and undischarged affect had been involved. Four of our ten dreams were clearly inconsistent with this view. As our own experience will show at great length, people dream despite the fact that in their dreams they have intense desires and an unweakened "activity of the will".

Furthermore, there are sufficient dreams which prove that any talk of a narrow and short-sighted dream-consciousness is impermissible. The arbitrary nature of Leonard's dream theory is clearly shown by the fact that it considers the preservation of human memory as the chief meaning of the dream, while very many people who can never, or hardly ever, remember their dreams nevertheless have as good a memory as those who do.

The dream study of G. Siegmund[129] contributes extremely rich, historically valuable and casuistic material. Its determination of the essence of the dream, however, as the author himself admits, is no advance on that of the old past-master of dream interpretation, Sante de Sanctis. Siegmund, too, thinks that the dream is always due to an unresolved tension of feeling.[130] He thinks that this is always the "driving cause" of the dream formation, and the content of every dream must therefore be understood as the hallucinatory solution of a tension.[131]

The latest serious book on dreams that we have seen is one by Hartmann.[132] This work contains extremely interesting dream material. Its author is not, however, concerned with an investigation of dreams themselves, nor with the construction of a dream theory. Dreams merely serve him as clear evidence of the anthroposophic theories of Rudolf Steiner which he presupposes to be true and correct. For this reason he can be of little help in our own deliberations.

If the latest dream theories cannot explain the essence of the dream their very failure is a warning to renounce any future desire for a theoretical structure, and to keep strictly to the dreamer himself and to his dreams.

CHAPTER 7

Previous Attempts at a Phenomenological Interpretation of Dreams

(a) The phenomenological examination of dreams made by R. Bossard

The idea is not new that scientific investigation should restrict itself to the dream phenomena themselves, so that it can discover their own essence without distorting the dream from the start by the alien perspective of theoretical speculations of waking thought.

The most recent of the rare works of those authors who do not reject this idea is that of R. Bossard.[133] He takes a clear stand against the usual approach and says that the nature and structure of dreams

> "cannot be satisfactorily understood through an enumeration of its characteristic differences from waking consciousness. It is not permissible to consider dream consciousness simply as an inferior type of waking consciousness, nor can we accept E. Trömmer's opinion that the dream merely demonstrates the fact that during sleep our inner centres act without co-ordination. What is needed is a phenomenology and an analysis starting from the dream consciousness itself, and thus doing justice to its own laws."[134]

For direct observation shows that "the dream processes have almost the same reality value for the dreamer as the real processes of the external world have in his waking consciousness".

But Bossard also proceeds to place a barrier between himself and dream phenomena. For he judges the "reality-value of the dream processes", which he has just established, from the point of view of waking thought and calls the dream phenomena mere pictures in the usual way. Indeed he sees in them merely ideas produced in the dreamer's brain itself and present nowhere else—"intra-cortical stimuli which the dreamer experiences as sense impressions".[135]

The less critically the author adopts the ideas of the old objective psychology, and the more he succeeds in giving a comprehensive representation of Jung's dream theory, the more certainly also does he wreck his own objective: a phenomenological investigation of the inherent dream laws, the interpretation of dreams by examining their own distinctive phenomena. Thus, for instance, after a short mention of Husserl's highly unsatisfactory definition of consciousness, Bossard immediately introduces the completely unexplained concepts of a waking consciousness and a dream consciousness as objective facts. Then, again, he speaks of a "disturbance of the ego-consciousness" or of "functional remainders" or of a "dissociation of the ego-complex", indeed, even of a physiological defect both of the ego-complex and of the intellectual functions in the dream, owing to the fact that the cortical regions become independent when we fall asleep.[136] Elsewhere he no longer speaks of waking consciousness but of "the existent", which in the dream is confronted with its own being and thus becomes a function, i.e. that of representation. But this assertion, which is obviously borrowed from the "existentialist" investigations of Ludwig Binswanger, remains utterly unintelligible in this connection.

The results of Bossard's own study are limited to the conclusion that the essential structural characteristics of dream consciousness are: objectivity, projection, realization, condensation and metamorphosis.[137] The first characteristic, however, is cancelled out by his remark:

> "The objectivity of the dream, brought about by the more or less complete exclusion of the ego as the highest point of the psychic hierarchy and as a factor which actively intervenes in the stream of consciousness, does not conflict with the fact that, seen from a different point of view, the imaginary world of the dream must be considered as a highly subjective creation."[138]

Finally, Bossard, with admirable scientific integrity, discounts all his discoveries by admitting the failure of his whole undertaking.

> "These concepts ... which served to characterize the structural peculiarities of the dream consciousness, can no doubt be criticized for not completely corresponding to the essence of the dream, for having been discovered and stipulated from the standpoint of the waking consciousness, merely for purposes of dream interpretation."[139]

(b) The phenomenological studies of dreams made by L. Klages

Long before Bossard, and much more incisively, Ludwig Klages pointed to the inadequacy of judging dream phenomena "by the standards of waking thought".[140] By what right, he asked, did we examine dream images on the unproved assumption that the peculiarity of dreams must be understood from premisses of waking consciousness? How did we know that the experiences of waking life determined our dream life, in which there was just as much a rounded world, and indeed "much more so than in waking life, since in any case it had served as the basis of prehistoric life and thought over a period which counted more millennia than so-called world history counts centuries"? According to the evidence of our experience, the dream is no less real than the waking world, even if it is real in a different way. There appear to be two realities of which the one, i.e. that of the dream penetrates the customary world of waking only sometimes, and when it does it shakes its very foundations, by robbing us of the certainty of the delimitation between subject and object.

Klages, too, however, explains the dream world as one of mere images. He considers that waking is a state of sensitive seeing and active thinking about observable physical facts. Dreaming, on the other hand, is a pure seeing of images "which remains after erasing the component of sensation". Everything that is "merely dreamed" is therefore marked by a complete lack of capacity for bodily sensations. One never dreams of physical pains or desires of any kind or degree. This definition, Klages believes, gives us the key to all problems of the dream.

But this key is quite useless when we are dealing with immediate experience. A very educated and enlightened man, for instance, had, since his youth, recurrently and consistently dreamt of a descent to Hell and of the devil. In this he regularly smelled the most intense and horrible odours, which were to him the most unpleasant part of the whole dream. In every new dream he immediately knew what was going to happen, and he therefore became used to holding his nose from the very beginning of this stereotyped dream. Another dreamer discovered that he found the corpse of a child in a cellar, from which there emanated so intense a smell of decay that he had to vomit. This vomiting in the dream was then followed by more pleasant dream experiences. A woman dreamt:

"I am fleeing from a burning hotel. My left hand is completely burned and gives me terrible pains. I run about the town for hours, and in doing so I keep my burnt hand as rigid as possible, for every movement increases my pain. Finally I wake up but continue stretching my hand out as I am still afraid of the pain. It takes nearly five minutes before I notice that I am not actually burnt and that my hand is not sore at all."

The same patient had another dream:

"I am in a low-class public-house. A man cuts off the thumb of my left hand with a jagged and dirty knife. I can feel terrible pains but can do nothing about it. Then the scene changes: I am surrounded by a number of people. A man wants to rape me. I defend myself for a long time, and then wake up with palpitations. For some time after waking I can think of nothing but my painful thumb."

Other dreamers notice colours, which far surpass in their intensity all colour impressions of their waking life. We even know of many people who were throttled in their dreams or whose fingers were bitten or cut, and who had the most clear and localized feelings of pain. These extreme physical sensations did not occur just before waking only, as Klages believes, in which case the feeling of pain might have been due to waking consciousness.

A dream reported by G. Siegmund, who was concerned with this very problem, is as follows:

"I step out from the dark corridor of a house in an old city, into the sunlight. I can see the Karl University in front of me, a fantasy structure of my dream. It is an impressive and imposing baroque building glistening in the morning sun. The idea, arising in the dream itself, that the picture is merely a dream image, is contradicted by my perception that the picture does not have any of the typical dream characteristics, but exhibits so many small details and nuances of light, and is furthermore of such brightness that it could be called photographically true. I say to myself critically, 'If this picture is no mere dream image then I should be able to verify its reality by calling upon another sense.' I excitedly stretch out my hand to test whether the picture will disappear or whether it will resist my touch. I am surprised when I find that it does in fact resist, and conclude that it cannot be a dream-fantasy and must therefore be real."

A similar dream was described by the zoologist Hans Spemann in his *Autobiography*.

"My happiest dreams," he tells us, "dealt with the ownership of animals. Once I dreamt of a trout in a clear river. Suddenly I had the discouraging thought that this was a mere dream, but by touching the trout I convinced myself that I really owned it. This unfortunately did not prevent my waking up and discovering that it had only been a dream."[141]

Rahel Varnhagen relates a dream in which a dearly beloved animal plays a large part.

"I called this favourite 'My Animal', and whenever I got home I asked about it, for it exerted a great force upon me. I do not remember any *sense* experience in my whole waking life which made so great an impression upon me as the mere handshake of this animal."[142]

Finally, Wieland Herzfelde once dreamt that he was flying rather quickly through his open window and diagonally across the street on to some balcony.

"Now I was in doubt if this was not merely a dream. In order to convince myself of the reality of the dream, I passed through the glass door of the balcony into the strange dwelling, apparently into a dining-room. Still in doubt I pulled all sorts of faces in front of the large mirror, and I clicked my finger nails close to my ears. I could hear the noise and therefore was bound to be awake. I was diverted by a plate with delightful sandwiches and without further ado I swallowed a great number of them. This removed my last shred of suspicion that I was only dreaming. I was overjoyed by the realization that I could really fly."[143]

In these dreams, therefore, there can be no talk of merely non-sensory, non-perceptual pictorial phenomena in Klages' sense. There is no more justification for the opinion of A. Teillard, who thinks that "the dematerialization of the perceptual world" is a very striking function of the dream.[144] This author calls upon the ancient Indians in her support, according to whose witness only the Sukshuma aspect of phenomena can be perceived in sleep; only, so to speak, their true essence. Nevertheless we cannot disregard the fact that there occur far too many dream phenomena which possess a physical and perceptible reality and texture which are unknown to the dreamer's waking experience.

Thus the "phenomenological" dream studies of Klages and Bossard provide a fresh and very valuable warning. They help us to be doubly critical of the tendency in our modern technical way of thinking which leads us away from what is directly given towards an objectification of all phenomena. It urges us to make reality unreal by thinking only in terms of mere abstractions and to erect an artificial and calculable "pseudo-reality".

PART II. *The Dream Itself*

CHAPTER 8

A "Strange Dream of an Urn"

A LADY, thirty-two years of age, mentally and physically healthy, had set herself the task of making as complete a record as possible of all her dreams immediately upon waking, even in the middle of the night. She decided to add nothing that she had not actually experienced in the dreams, nor to omit anything simply because it appeared to be too unimportant, too meaningless, too absurd, too far-fetched or too unseemly. This woman had a more than average intelligence and a great natural ability for introspection, and above all an undeviating sense of truthfulness. For economic reasons it had been impossible for her to become a trained psychologist or philosopher. She remembered almost all her dreams very clearly on waking, and therefore considered it impossible for her dream experiences to be falsified subsequently and unwittingly by her waking consciousness. That, at least, is what she replied when I expressed Havelock Ellis's fears in this respect.*

"Tonight I had a strange dream of an urn," this woman reported to me on the 3rd of August, 1950. "At first I dreamt that I was sitting at the dinner table with my husband and children. The table was in our dining-room, which I had made even more cosy by moving the sideboard. I felt safe and peaceful in this room which was so dear to me. On the walls I could see the really good pictures which my husband loved to collect: in the windows I could see flowers, and in front of me the very attractively set table. On it was a lovely beefsteak with roast potatoes and a juicy lettuce. I can still feel the seductive odour of the roast beef pleasantly tickling my nose, and the mere thought of the delicious juiciness of the lettuce still makes my

* Havelock Ellis in *The World of Dreams* contends that there is no proof that the subsequent dream report reproduces the actual events of the dream, since after waking the mind is in quite a different state. The same objection, however, could be made against the recounting of a vivid waking experience, since here too we are no longer in the same situation, when we try to relate the experience afterwards.

mouth water. Greedily I took one bite after another, for I was very hungry. I was fully absorbed in eating, and my husband and my children were tucking in as well. 'Do you remember,' I asked my husband a little while later, 'that we had exactly the same menu on the first day of our honeymoon in Cannes?' He confirmed it with a smile, adding, 'It was exactly a year ago.' In the dream I was not in the least disturbed by this ridiculous assertion, and by the fact that our children, five and six years old, were sitting at the table. We had actually been married for ten years. Indeed I was fully convinced that my husband was right, and I replied, 'I feel as if it had only been yesterday.' I then thought quietly of those happy days. At the same time I was grateful for the happiness of today. I looked at my husband and my children, and I felt extremely fond of them and very near to all of them, especially to my eldest son. While he had originally been sitting in his usual place at the opposite corner of the table he was suddenly and strangely transported right next to me. In the dream it did not appear strange that he had suddenly changed places without any movement on his or anybody else's part. It was quite reasonable. Nor did it strike me as peculiar that while I was sitting so happily amongst my family, there suddenly appeared colourful bridges, reminiscent of very bright rainbows. They extended across the table between me and my family. A large and golden urn hovered on these bridges between us, and particularly near my favourite son.

While I was so absolutely happy, I suddenly thought: 'Who knows how long we shall be together? Who knows what the future will hold? Won't the Russians be here shortly?' I imagined how the Russians might suddenly enter our house one night and kill all of us. But just as quickly I thought of turning our garage into a hiding-place. I did all this in such vivid detail that, in my imagination, I could already see a troop of wildly gesticulating soldiers storming the house. And as so often happens in dreams, it was no longer a matter of imagination, but now I could actually see the Russians approaching. However, I immediately pulled myself together and with great effort of will I dispelled all these dark images. I was determined to feel only the happiness of the present and to leave the future to God. Full of eagerness I again turned to my husband and children and began to devise a plan for a drive in the afternoon.

I then awoke, because the maid had been knocking at the door. But for quite some time I did not know where I was. The luncheon table around which all of us had just been chatting so merrily, had been so real and vivid in all its detail, that it confused me utterly to find myself in bed. At first I could not decide which of the two was real: the luncheon which I had just dreamt of, or my bed."

CHAPTER 9

Attempt at a Phenomenological Interpretation of the "Strange Dream of an Urn"

(a) Criticism of interpretations in terms of a mere hallucination

Naturally our attempts to explain dreams phenomenologically in terms of their own nature and without any previous theoretical suppositions and reductions could equally well have been illustrated by means of another example. All that mattered was to start with some concrete dream phenomenon. This "remarkable dream of an urn" seemed a good starting point, first because it came from a completely normal person, and secondly because it contains so many different events. The first circumstance protects us against the usual objection that the results of modern dream study are only valid for psychologically ill and abnormal persons, and the rich inner content of the dream promises an unusually large number of possible inter-connections.

There is no doubt that in many respects modern dream psychologists of different schools would agree in their interpretation of this dream. They would certainly say, quite generally, that the dream makes a very coherent and well-ordered impression and that only a small part is nonsensical, absurd, etc. True, some portions remind one of the fabulous dreams of the great Swiss poet Gottfried Keller which were considered by his sober friend Wilhelm Schultz to be the poet's subsequent fabrications, much to Keller's annoyance and displeasure.*

The more the experts knew about the character of this dreamer, the more emphatically they would have pointed to the high degree of continuity of the dream experiences and actions with those of her waking life. For as experience shows time and time again, what

---

* See the entry of Gottfried Keller of the 15th of September 1847 in his *Dream Book*: "I shall never relate any more dreams to Schultz during breakfast, because he expressed the suspicion that I fabricate them beforehand. He only knows the simplest of dreams such as: 'today I dreamt of a coffin, etc.'. Since he has no phantasy, either while awake or when asleep, he considers coherent dreams with a beautiful artistic touch as impossible. It is true that dear Schultz's enthusiasms can make him fall into confused dogmatic phrases, but he does not believe in what is nearest and simplest; in a beautiful dream . . . perhaps because he can see no sense in it, at least not for himself."

happened in this dream was above all what should have been perceived or consciously thought or what should have happened in the dreamer's waking life, but which for inner or outer reasons could not sufficiently be realized and unfolded. Thus the dreamer actually felt very hungry before going to bed but was at the time too tired to get some food. She hoped she could "sleep off" her hunger, and while dreaming she more than made up for failing to eat the food. She was furthermore a very maternal woman who would have best preferred to devote herself to her family, but conflicting outer circumstances forced her to work outside her home, so she had to deprive her children and husband of part of her care. In her dream she felt particularly close to her family. Finally in recent months she often had fears of a possible Russian invasion. Evidently she had often thought that preparations should be made against this, but she had always suppressed these thoughts when they arose. In her dream she allowed the possibility to emerge and considered the best way of meeting it. Afterwards in the dream, just as in waking life, she wanted to forget the whole thing.

Furthermore, most dream interpreters would agree that in these nocturnal events and experiences we are dealing with dream images in which certain instinctual drives, strivings, or characteristics of the dreamer find their hallucinatory satisfaction or expression. But does not this unquestioned acceptance of such psychological determination by-pass the phenomena themselves so that they are lost sight of from the very start? Does the viewpoint of psychopathology that dream experiences are a type of hallucination deal with the dream as such, or does it not rather do violence to it from the perspective of waking thought? Who could guarantee that this treatment of dream phenomena is not capricious, or that its validity is proved in the slightest, and that we have not distorted the phenomena, and therefore used quite an inadequate measuring rod? Have we not persuaded ourselves all too readily that the dreamer is no more than a person asleep in whom the dream images can run their course as merely subjective and unreal fantasies or ideas? Can the definition of such a dream as a hallucinatory image mean anything else than the fact that its phenomena are prejudged as mere hallucinations and representations of the corresponding objects of the waking world?

All this tells us nothing about the dream as dream. Indeed, on careful reflection, this definition of dream objects as mere hallucinations is guilty not only of misunderstanding the object to be investigated, but of a double misinterpretation: for, first, to designate the dream object as a hallucination implies that it is a sensory confusion. This is a devaluation of the phenomenon from the standpoint of waking life and does not contribute anything to its elucidation. Secondly, we use this devaluation (which does not even apply to so-called hallucinations) in interpreting the dream. The dream phenomenon itself, however, teaches us unequivocally that the usual talk of unreal hallucinatory dream images by no means does justice to its immediate reality. How often does a dreamer not prize the reality of dream events beyond that of waking experience? The poet Franz Grillparzer, for instance, thought that the waking world compared with a recent dream of his was like a drawing compared with a painting, or a foggy day compared with a sunny one. Our dreamer, too, did not merely see pictures that were only the reproduction of physical reality. Rather she experienced with all her body and soul a world as completely real as she had ever felt during waking life. How else could she have wondered, on waking up, which was the real world: that of the luncheon table in the dream, or her bedroom?

If, then, our dream was no hallucination, neither was it a pure vision of an imperceptible pictorial reality in the sense of Ludwig Klages. Our dreamer was physically and perceptually aware of the glowing green colour of the lettuce, and the odour of the roast tickled her nose most pleasantly.

Even if we accepted Ludwig Binswanger's so-called existential approach to the dream,[145] we should not discover the true facts. It is true that Binswanger, in his phenomenological enquiries, managed to adhere more closely to the dream phenomena themselves than did earlier investigators of the dream. Yet he would certainly have agreed with Szilasi's conviction that the dream images of the fresh green salad and of the splendid urn were the first "beat of the waves of transcendence". Here, just as in the happy mood of the dream, he would see an "embodiment", an "expression" or a "reflection" of the basic pattern of her life: the theme of elevation, the rising phase of the wave of existence. First, however, let us note that his assertions about the dream still involve the old assessment of dream phenomena as mere representations of objects in the waking world. In the second place, his approach is largely indifferent to the inherent characteristics of the dream objects. He says, for instance, that "it is immaterial which particular form impinges on the senses". He attaches decisive importance almost exclusively to an object's direction of movement, since we could equally well dream "of our own body, of one of its limbs, of one of its intrinsic properties, or indeed of anything else with which we exist in the world", as long as these dream phenomena moved in the same direction.[146] Is not such a view necessarily based on yet another mental dissection of the dream phenomena, i.e. a reduction of dream objects to the level of interchangeable objects, endowed with only a direction of movement or significance? Furthermore, we can see that this existentialist dream analysis in Binswanger's sense, with its ideas of "subjective transcendence" and "expression or reflection of existence patterns", is nothing more than a return to a Cartesian point of view. All these conceptions presuppose the belief that the dreamer is inherently involved in dream images in a Cartesian sense, as an object-substance or as a subject-thing. For if man had not originally been assumed to be a thing called "subject" inside himself, he could never be thought capable of passing out of himself into another thing, such as a dream image, nor of being reflected in it and of rising and falling in the direction of the tendency that this image pictorially portrays.

How did our dreamer in fact experience the room, the time, and the objects and persons of her dream environment, before subsequent evaluation on the part of her waking consciousness and without any theoretical reconstruction? Certainly she did not only see images, but lived in so real a world that her surprise on suddenly awaking reminds us of the poser of Chwang-Tse, which serves as the motto of this book. Let us recall her question, "Am I actually the person who is lying in bed and who just dreamt that she had lunched with her family, or did I in fact fall asleep after luncheon and do I now dream that the maid has just woken me up?" At the very beginning of the dream she experienced being in her dining-room so realistically that, just as in waking life, there can be no question of a mere bare, spatial relationship between her body and the space of the room. The room of her dream was from the very beginning the happily attuned space of her whole existence. She had "housed" herself in the room in a pleasant mood, and had "felt at home" in it. How artificial and false, compared with this immediate dream experience, is the usual division of such a relationship into the two parts of an external and an internal world: into a mere external object in space such as the volume of the room on the one hand, and some quite independent psychic experiences, conditions, and behaviour patterns on the other!

Nor was the object "beefsteak" confronted by her as an object encysted in itself. She tells us rather that she was with it body and soul, and that she felt so attracted by it that she became completely absorbed in eating it, that she as a whole human being was no longer anything but this eating-relationship with the meat. How is it then, that in her entire specific behaviour or relationship to the beefsteak and the green salad she existed unequivocally and completely in something "external", and that she no longer had any interest in anything else? We know that she had been hungry before falling asleep and that she had thought of getting some food. Her intense need for sleep had only pushed this thought into the background. For this reason her hunger had to be satisfied in the dream. So we seem to have every right to consider this first action in our "strange dream of an urn", i.e. the eating of the beefsteak, as a typical wish-fulfilment in Freud's sense.

(b) *Criticism of interpretations in terms of Freud's theory of wish-fulfilment and the instinctual theory of Schultz-Hencke*

Even those dream psychologists who do not accept Freud's generalization about this kind of dream, would nevertheless call it a dream of wish-fulfilment. It is precisely because Freud based the general validity of his theory of wish-fulfilment on the existence of such dreams that it is important to determine whether even these phenomena can be considered undisguised wish-fulfilments. If so, we shall notice that Freud was even here forced to admit the presence of at least some displacements or distortions due to the dream work. "An optative thought," he says, "is replaced by a perception."[147] Furthermore, if we keep to the dream phenomenon itself, we shall not be able to observe even the slightest trace of a wish, so its characterization as a dream of wish-fulfilment can only be due to a later and uncritical conclusion of waking life. Our dreamer is supplied with food from the very start of her dream, and therefore does not need to wish it but only to eat it. True, she desired food during the waking state before the dream. But if we derive the events of the dream from these wishes of waking life, then we explain them in terms of, and base them on, an external point of view, probably the highly distorted perspective of waking consciousness. If, on the other hand, we are concerned with the actual essence of such a dream, then we must stop looking for external causes or reasons and try to understand it in terms of itself.

Such an understanding, from the directly given concrete phenomenon, has long been proposed by Schultz-Hencke. But he would certainly see an oral drive or an oral instinctual experience as the nucleus of this part of the dream. Concepts such as drives or instincts, however, are quite unconnected with the concrete phenomena themselves, for the immediate experience of our dreamer was neither a drive nor an instinct. According to her, it was the tastefully laid table which attracted her, and the very pleasing odour of the roast meat and the juicy green salad which enticed her. To turn this feeling of being attracted by an actual something into an inner propensity means falling victim to the customary subjective interpretation of man. Since this kind of interpretation always equates man with his body, it is bound to consider him driven by internal and external forces, just like any other object. Ideas like drives and instincts can only be derived from a feeling of attraction if this feeling is considered in artificial isolation from its essential and primary connections. In these abstractions, however, we are no longer dealing with the phenomenon itself but only with a mere explanation or theory of it. A phenomenon in its actual essence and full content is no better explained by such a procedure than other phenomena are by the concept of forces.

If then the enjoyment of meat and salad in this dream is neither caused by the desire for food, nor due to an oral drive, how else can we understand the dreamer's complete absorption in eating her beefsteak? She herself merely spoke of her complete absorption in the food, of her being nothing but this relationship to the objects of her dream world. How does this very special kind of relationship to her dream beefsteak come about? She admittedly felt hunger before she fell asleep. It is always a person's momentary state of mind which determines the choice and manner of his relationship to things and people. A state of hunger always reveals a world of eatable things. It is these which determine the whole character of the world. Both the active eating in the dream as well as the desire for food beforehand in waking life spring from one and the same source: they are only two different forms of activity of an existence attuned to hunger. Behaviour during waking life remained a mere wish, and we have no right whatever to say that the *wish for food* in waking life caused the *eating of food* in the dream; nor conversely may we attribute to the action of the dream a purpose or finality and maintain that this dream had merely prepared the dreamer for a later meal during waking hours.

This banal beginning to our strange dream tells us most impressively that we exist no less in dreams than we do in waking life. We "exist" in the sense that even in the dream we are always within a world, the reality of which we had best not deny too hastily. The following part of the dream shows, furthermore, that in dreaming we exist in the most *different* ways, "ex-ist" in the literal sense of the word, since in always being "outside", that is, in a particular relationship to objects, we are thus with the objects. Thus our dreamer existed not only in a merely *momentary* perceptive feeling and active relationship to the objects and people of her dream world, she also existed in the manner in which her memory expressed itself and in the way in which she planned her future. She experienced the unity of her past, her present and her future quite clearly. Indeed, the dream plan about a garage hideout proved to be excellent, when she examined it after waking. She not only stuck to it but got her husband's agreement. This dream plan, just like the subsequent very deliberate decision, involving a strong effort of will not to be oppressed by sad thoughts of a possible Russian invasion, is evidence of the possibility of human freedom even during a dreaming existence.

For this reason the dream clearly conflicts with the common belief that the dreaming ego always and completely passively surrenders to images.[148] It is also in conflict with the opinion of Binswanger that dreaming means "I do not know what is happening to me", for which reason the dreamer "never makes life history" in his dreams, but is only a "vital function", and awakens only at that unaccountable moment when he decides to intervene in the real course of events.[149]

(c) Criticism of interpretations in terms of hypermnesia

Our dream also includes effects which have been described as hypermnesia. Our dreamer had remembered the exact menu of her honeymoon dinner in Cannes some ten years previously. Before she fell asleep she had not given it the slightest thought. She had preserved the menu as a souvenir, and thanks to it she could test her "dream memory" and confirm its correctness. But does this justify our explaining our dream as due to a specially heightened faculty of remembering the distant past, in other words as hypermnesia?

How could the eating of this meal ever have got lost in the past, so that only memory could dig it out? It had always been part and parcel of her experiences, and it remains a part of her life history which is herself. It was never irretrievably lost in the past, but since it was part of her own behaviour and experiences it will continue to remain part of her own being. Only for this reason can it freely reappear. It is her mood of happiness which, in the dream, opens up anew and brings into present time that equally happy life and world of the past. Never had this woman been so unreservedly happy as in this dream, except on one single occasion—her honeymoon in Cannes. There as a young lover and now as a dreamer she had been in exactly the same mood, and only because the mood of the dream so completely corresponded to the other mood could she rediscover that world. Good food too belonged to this world of the past, which has yet become so near.

· · · · ·

Comprehensible though large sections of the dream are, and little as they fall short of the possible thought, memory and resolution of our dreamer's waking life, the dream nevertheless contains much nonsense and many absurdities. For instance, it seems absurd that the dreamer, who had merely been thinking about Russians, should suddenly see real Russians attacking her. Quite nonsensical also is the contention of the husband that they had been on honeymoon only a year before, when in fact it was ten years before. This becomes all the more absurd when she agrees with him despite the presence of her five- and six-year-old children which should clearly have demonstrated the error. Even more nonsensical is the fact that her favourite son is suddenly seated at her right side; and the golden urn, hovering above a rainbow stretching out from herself to her family, seems to make no sense at all.

Must we therefore either accept Bossard's contention that the dream is "a disturbance or dissociation of the ego-complex" or else take refuge in one of the many other psychological constructions and suppositions? How else could we explain the origin of such absurdities which seem to do violence to all our reason? Or is it possible that all these dream events cannot be explained from any external point of view whatsoever, and that their true essence will only emerge if we examine what the dream itself has to say?

(d) Criticism of interpretations in terms of common ideas about the imagination

Perhaps the transformation of imagined Russians into physical beings only appears grotesque because we still have a highly artificial view of the human imagination.

In fact, psychologists commonly hold that when we are thinking about something which cannot at the time be perceived by the senses, then a mere copy of a sense perception in the form of a representation passes in the mind or even in the brain. If this were the case it would certainly be absurd for such inner perceptions suddenly to change into external objects in the course of the dream. Our dreamer, however, has something quite different to say about the reality of the dream phenomenon: "When thinking so intensely of a Russian invasion, I was so much with these uncouth fellows in my thoughts, that I could imagine them more and more vividly until they suddenly appeared physically." In fact our dreamer, when she originally thought of these Russians, was not at all just "with herself" or even "within herself", and hundreds of kilometres away from the nearest Russian soldier. By merely imagining a thing or an absent person, in waking life just as in the dream, we are always "outside" and with the thing or person in question. We ex-ist in, and even *as*, our thinking of it or of him. For if man were not so constituted that by merely thinking of an object that cannot be seen by the senses, he could overcome all distance so as to be with it, he would never be able to imagine anything at all, i.e. to come into its immediate presence. For instance, he would not be able to think of an object in his former home now far away, perhaps beyond the seas, as being "much closer" to him than it is to the present tenant, who merely lives there temporarily and without any great interest in it.

Just as our dreamer was with the Russians from the very moment when she first thought of them, and just as she is existentially bound up in her relation to them, so do the Russians exist with her from the start. In waking life too, *this* presence of the Russians, experienced only in thought and not yet as a physical phenomenon, is retained and anchored as such. In the dream, however, our dreamer concentrated her whole being increasingly on this one relation with the Russians, and this resulted in their condensation into physical forms which could be perceived with the senses.

(e) *Criticism of interpretations in terms of disturbance of the sense of time and space*

The apparently senseless confusion of space and time in our dreams is often attributed by psychologists to a disturbance of the sense of time in the sleeper. But closer examination will reveal that the changes in time and space as experienced by our dreamer were by no means accidental and isolated. The considerable contraction of the interval of time between her honeymoon and the present corresponded to the fact that the world of the past had been brought closer owing to her present mood of happiness. This occurred so intensely that she managed to remember every detail of her dinner. She mentioned the "magical" sudden proximity of her favourite son in the same breath as the psychological fact of how close he was to her heart. For the present, however, we merely wish to point out the obvious connection between events in space and time, on the one hand, and the total human condition of our dreamer and her particular momentary relationship to her world, on the other. We wish to indicate that each of these apparently absurd phenomena of space and time in the dream is not necessarily due to a disturbance of the corresponding senses in sleep. Possibly they cannot be measured in terms of the regular passing of time or with the continuous space of daily life, if they are to make sense. We must allow for the possibility that such events in time and space do not constitute a breaking down of time and space, but manifest a quite different and perhaps much more original sense of time and space, possibly hidden in daily life. Since the problems of time and space are overshadowed by the other contents of the dream, we shall defer a thorough discussion till we consider dreams which exhibit phenomena of space and time even more explicitly.

(*f*) *Criticism of interpretations in terms of "symbolism"*

Why did our dreamer see a wonderful golden urn hovering above a colourful and rainbow-like bridge between herself and her family, and particularly near her favourite son? Did the dream urn express symbolically and in vivid imagery her own heart going out to build golden rainbow-bridges between her and her family, as she herself thought afterwards?

Where then was her heart, and where was she herself during this phase of the dream? An observer of the positivist school would consider her to be an independent physical organism with an internal circulatory system and heart, sitting on her chair and separated from her family by a space of two yards. In reality, however, this woman as a human being by no means terminated at the surface of her epidermis, and was by no means enclosed in her own body and chained to her chair. Seldom, as she herself said, had she felt so responsive to objects and fellow human beings as in this dream. Her whole being had become her heart-felt devotion for and her relationship with her family; she was entirely with them and especially with her favourite son.

When Heraclitus distinguishes the condition of waking from that of dreaming by saying that the former has a common world, but that the latter has a world of its own, his judgment too is based on waking life, for man is very rarely alone in his dreams. According to the statistics of C. S. Hall of the Psychological Institute of the

Western Reserve University, eighty-five per cent of dreams are concerned with other people, mainly with strangers, more rarely with friends and acquaintances, and seldom with the dreamer's family.

Now, it could not be said that our dreamer belonged to the shut-in, retiring type of human being. On the contrary, the quintessence of her emotional life was given over to her husband and her children. She told us that at the time of her dream her heart and soul were as open as the mouth of the dream-urn, and that she was as bound by deep affection to her family as the rainbow bridge in the dream had seemed to bind them to one another.

Was she right in fact? Were the dream urn and the dream bridge merely symbols and representations in the form of images of her inner subjective disposition? Could not both urn and bridge be considered as objects in themselves? By what right do dream psychologists, whom this woman is merely copying in her waking judgment about these dream objects, deny the fact that they are objects in themselves, and interpret them as mere symbols projected by the dreamer's psyche? What if there are no dream symbols at all?

CHAPTER 10

The Content of Dreams and Theories of Dream Symbolism

(a) *Dream phenomena and the Freudian theory of symbols*

The opinion that very many and especially the most important dream contents are symbols, is central to all significant contemporary theories of the dream. We must therefore devote particular attention to it.

Freud, for one, would not have doubted that the urn was a symbol of the dreamer's genitalia and that the bridge represented the male genitals. This is what he writes:

> "The female genitalia are symbolically represented by all such objects as share with them the property of enclosing a space or are capable of acting as receptacles: such as pits, hollows and caves and also jars and bottles and boxes, chests, suit-cases, pockets and so forth."[150]

According to Freud, a bridge invariably represents the male genitals connecting the parents in sexual intercourse. True, it may have a further significance arising out of the original one. Since it is because of the male genitals that we are born out of the amniotic fluid, a bridge is the transition from the beyond (of being unborn, of the mother's womb) to the here and now (life). And since man imagines death as a return to the womb (into the fluid) a bridge could also symbolize a movement towards death, and even a change of conditions in general.[151] Freud would thus have considered our dream, and especially that part dealing with the urn and the bridge, as unmistakable proof of unconscious incestuous desires directed particularly at the dreamer's eldest son.

Freud thought he had found an unequivocal proof for this conception in Schrötter's experiment. Schrötter (1912) had ordered his hypnotized subjects to dream of coarse sexual processes during their subsequent hypnotic sleep. In the dreams all those things which Freud designates as sexual symbols appeared in the relevant places. Once, for instance, a woman was ordered during hypnosis to dream of homosexual relations with a girl-friend. In the dream she met this girl-friend carrying a suit-case with the label "For Ladies Only". From this Schrötter and Freud concluded that the suit-case could only be a symbolic representation of the girl-friend's genitals.[152]

However, such a conclusion is very flimsy since it neither explains the full meaning of sexual intercourse nor all the connotations of a suit-case in the actual life of the dreamer. What if sexual intercourse meant more to her than the mere contact of two sexual organs—if, for instance, we agree with Herbert Silberer and Jung, who under certain conditions see in sexual intercourse a symbol of interconnecting and bridging the most different things, even such that do not belong to the sexual sphere at all? Who would, indeed, deny that healthy sexual activity is not a solitary affair, but implies the coming together of two people bound by love; that this, in fact, is of its very essence? Thus the hypnotist by his suggestion of homosexual intercourse had prepared his experimental subject for a loving human relationship, even though he had limited it to a female partner. Possibly for this reason in the dream not only the "symbolic genitals" but an entire person appeared who was nothing else but this very girl-friend and a suit-case. Had the luggage only symbolized her genitals, why then was it a *suit-case* and not, for instance, an evening bag, which would surely have belonged more clearly to an erotic sphere? What inherent connection is there between travelling, which is unmistakably indicated in this dream, and female genitals? Not the slightest. Travelling, however, can bring people closer together and can also separate them. Surely this large suit-case was much more likely to indicate the fact that it contained many other things besides those merely relating to the genital organs: objects of everyday life, perhaps even books, valuable jewellery, and some family keepsakes. These things would not be so closely related to the girl-friend's genitals as to her entire personal history, thoughts and feelings.

In the case of the above unknown dreamer who has not yet, by any means, been sufficiently investigated we shall content ourselves with the preceding remarks. However, just because Freud's symbolic interpretation had always appeared questionable we carried out, some twenty years ago, experiments similar to those of Schrötter. Amongst others, we hypnotized five women of quite different types, whose psychological state we had previously studied for many hours. During hypnosis all five women were given the same suggestion: they were to dream of a certain man well known to them, who loved them, and who approached them with clear sexual intentions and without any clothes. The harmlessness of this experiment seemed to be assured by the fact that these women had all had spontaneous and frequent sexual dreams fairly similar to what was suggested to them in the hypnotic state, or to its expected "symbolic disguise". Three of these women who were not neurotically inhibited, and who were mentally and physically mature, reported dream experiences which followed our suggestion in every detail. Since dreams of this kind were nothing new to them and since they had long had confidence in the investigator, they reported without any prudery that they had had a pleasurable experience, and emphasized the fact that they had felt very happy. They knew nothing of the hypnotic suggestion.

Quite different were the dreams of the two remaining experimental subjects who were neurotic elderly spinsters of forty-four and forty-seven years respectively. Their two dreams were so similar that we need cite one of the examples only. The elder of the two spinsters dreamt, after the same hypnotic suggestion, that she was confronted by an unknown soldier, who was practising with a pistol, and who nearly shot her. This gave her such a fright that she woke up. Significantly, this same spinster had dreamt four nights before that soldiers had been billeted in her village, and that at night when she was returning home from rehearsals of the church choir, three of them had been lying in wait for her and had threatened her with gigantic guns. In panic, she had escaped and had just managed to reach her parental home. This proves that even this experimental subject was not given an undue fright by our suggestion. In order to avoid psychic damage to this woman, all that remained to be done was to be careful not to confront her with a causal interpretation of her dream and to have due regard to the level of development of her waking personality.

The man in the suggested dream remained completely unknown, even after the most searching questions. She could not think of anybody, now or in the past, who resembled the dream figure. The man in the dream had appeared coarse and crude, with a large black moustache, typical of a soldier, and she had never had any dealings with such. Earlier on, while still young, some soldiers billeted in her village had tried to approach her, but she had been so terribly afraid of these people that she had never left her mother's side. She also remembered that she had always been dreadfully frightened of guns. She was afraid of such male objects even from a distance. They could sometimes go off, and she always kept away from them as far as possible.

These ideas and his own symbolic interpretation would have led Freud to see in the uniformed appearance of a man, who according to the previous suggestion should appear as naked, and in the shooting of guns, the unmistakable work of disguise and distortion of the dream censor. Through this symbolic clothing the offensive maleness and nakedness were hidden from the consciousness of the dreamer. While an offending instinctuality could still be expressed, thanks to this distortion, it was also an attempt—unsuccessful in this case—to preserve both the peace of conscience and the sleep of the dreamer. Freud would have found it a little harder to explain why a man, well known to the dreamer, as suggested, had to become transformed into a completely unknown soldier. Perhaps he would have seen in this an attempt to make the whole content seem less indecent, perhaps the results of secondary elaboration. The significance of the pistol, however, would have been beyond doubt. For according to Freud it is one of the most certain symbols of the male genital organ.

What, however, can we learn from the presenting phenomena themselves, without any pre-formed theoretical assumptions? The psychological condition of the three non-neurotic women had been guided by the hypnosis towards loving sexual behaviour towards a known man. Their relationship, in the dream, took the form of a happy sensual relationship with this man, and they allowed him to approach them completely naked. In the case of the neurotic elderly spinsters, however, things were quite different.

Instead of a personal sexual love relationship with a friend, they merely experienced an anxious relationship with a dangerous, anonymous and uniformed man. Obviously the one elderly spinster was quite incapable of opening herself to a mature love relationship embracing all potentialities of life. Because of this limitation of her capacity for love, the man could not reveal himself to her completely. Above all, the possibilities of physical contact with the male had remained completely covered up. The approach of the inexplicable and unfamiliar always occasions anxiety. Great anxiety causes all objects to appear as anonymous and makes us fear everything we meet in the same manner. It is for this reason that the suggested friend appeared to the prude dreamer only as a uniformed anonymous man. The soldier's uniform is not only a definitely male object. It also makes all men equally anonymous and thoroughly covers their natural nakedness. Nevertheless the uniform of our dream is no symbolic covering. On the contrary, it discloses most clearly the childishly narrow, hidden, anxiety-ridden world of the dreamer. Not even the fact that the frightening dream soldier lets off a pistol is "symbolic" camouflage. The dreamer is afraid of pistols even at a distance, so pistols directly and exclusively refer to the danger of a situation that threatens life. If then she can admit a male acquaintance only as one who shoots pistols into her dream world, this clearly shows that out of the male-female love relationship nothing can reveal itself to her but the possibility of being hit and endangered. It is her overpowering anxiety which caused a pistol to appear to the exclusion of everything else.

(b) Dream phenomena and Jung's theory of symbols

Early on, C. G. Jung had questioned Freud's right to call his own dream interpretations "symbolic interpretations" in the literal sense of the word, since he merely attributed to one dream object the significance of another, equally well-known thing. Thus the dream pistol was no more than the token of an equally concrete object, the male genital organ; just as, in waking life, the wheel on the cap of a railway official is no real symbol of a railway, but is merely a sign that he belongs to the railway system. Jung therefore accused Freud of a mere semiotic conception of symbols. A dream object could only be a true and proper symbol if the dreamer could suspect that it had a meaning transcending the "reality" of the perceived object. A symbol is only such as long as this transcendental sense remains incomprehensible, so that the dream object is, at a given moment, the best possible expression of unknown psychic processes, not properly understood.[153]

This was a reiteration of Silberer's description some ten years earlier. Silberer saw the origin of symbols in "man's psychological striving towards something which was still beyond his powers of conception".[154] However, neither Silberer nor Jung has contributed greatly to our understanding of symbols in general, or to symbolic dreams in particular. This is most clearly shown by an example of which Jung himself says that its symbolic character becomes manifest especially clearly and independently of reflection just because the object as a "pure reality" is much too meaningless in itself.[155] He is here thinking of an eye within a triangle representing God in all icons of the Byzantine Church. But the eye within the triangle does not represent something still unknown. It rather denotes knowledge of the mystery of

God as the absolute and final Unknowable. Thus it is based on a particularly deep insight.

What then does Jung mean in his discussion of the definition of symbols when he speaks time after time of "objects as pure facts", to which man subsequently might add symbolic content as a psychic product? This betrays the fact that for Jung as for Freud it is still positivism which yields the decisive criterion. Positivism can conceive as facts only those data that can be explained rationally and causally. It is only because Jung identifies the reality of objects with their complete explicability on rational-causal principles that he can abstract "pure reality" from the "psychological product" of the symbolic meaning. For Jung as for Freud it is always that which is calculable or useful which is the primary measure of reality. Only because this mental reduction of objects had progressed to such an extent in positivism, could Jung speak of the "meaningless" drawing of an eye in a triangle as the purely factual part of this pictorial reference to God. However, in no church and on no icon had the triangle with the eye existed independently, so that an imagined or divined relationship with the mystery of God had subsequently to be superimposed upon it. The full "pure reality" had always been such that the triangle with the eye of God emerged as a token of His immeasurability from the total relationship of faith in the hidden God, and still abides in that relationship. When C. G. Jung, owing to his positivist attitude, reduces all this to the "pure reality" of a mere drawing of an eye bounded by a triangle, he stultifies the entire phenomenon. But Jung was not content with this positivist reduction, and he hung round this "empty shell" of "pure reality" all other originally inherent properties of the object, calling them the "symbolic content".

For this is indeed the invaluable achievement of Freud and Jung, that they were involved in the original exposure of the narrow positivist view. Each in his own way contributed to the view that reality is larger than that conceived by positivism and that it is not exhausted by it. They had the intuition that what had previously been considered the sole reality was only the basis of something far more essential: an entirely new and unpredictable large structure. Their mental tools, however, remained those of positivism, the reality emerging beyond the foundations being directly reduced to equally positivistic facts; for Freud "mystic" drives became a sort of by-product of inner secretions and glandular functions. Jung reduced the "irrational" to psychic "products" of the individual or collective psychic realms. So the single and complete reality of an object was lost sight of as soon as it was divined. In the thought of Freud and Jung it was split into two classes: into the old sensory and so-called "pure facts" and into the more recent psychological "symbolic facts". Freud and Jung could conceive of the relationship between these two classes of objects only by thinking that the latter merely referred to the former. They differed in their evaluation of "symbolic facts" in accordance with the different ways in which they attempted to reduce a reality which cannot be explained by means of a rational causal principle. While Freud sees behind them a clear reference to sexuality, Jung thinks that they point to some psychic structure that has not been fully understood.

This difference does not entitle C. G. Jung to dismiss Freud's symbolic interpretation as merely "semiotic". Jung's dream interpretation, too, is based purely on semiotics, since in it the "pure reality" of the dream is only a token of other objects; psychic products in the sense of symbolic facts. It makes little difference whether what is indicated "symbolically" can be grasped and known or whether it is only dimly suspected. Furthermore, the "symbolic sexual content" of objects in Freud's theory, i.e. the displaced psychic factors, are equally unknown to the dreamer.

Even if C. G. Jung's conception of symbols is not basically new, the fact that he allows a far greater scope to the possible symbolic significance of an object is of the highest importance. Nevertheless, the differences between Freud and Jung are not nearly as significant as their agreement that the symbolic attributes of objects are always due to a human psyche. While Freud is quite definitely of the opinion that it is always the "unconscious" which projects the "psychological symbolic content" on to the object and superimposes it on the latter's "pure reality", Jung similarly thinks that objects become "symbol bearers" if "I project something from my unconscious on to an external object".[156] Thus, for Jung the symbolic value of an object corresponds to the projected unconscious content of the subject.[157] In a more recent formulation Jung designates the symbolic character of an object as the "product of the human spirit": the immediate expression of psychic events or of the immutable structural relationships of the unconscious.[158] Furthermore the symbol may also represent the unconscious which embodies mankind's psychic past.[159] Even when the symbolic content of an object does not merely originate in the unconscious, but "equally in consciousness and in the unconscious",[160] its symbolic value still remains a contribution of the human psyche. Indeed, in Jung's view, the psyche even projects itself on to objects in order to symbolize itself in them. These ideas on symbolism of Freud and Jung are not altered in the least by the fact that C. G. Jung considers symbols as psychic products which arise not only out of the individual unconscious but also out of the so-called "objective" "collective unconscious".

Obviously, when making this sort of positivist reductive approach, even such things as the bridge or the urn of our original dream are torn out of their full context and lose their intrinsic significance. They too are broken down into pure facts or into naked objects, i.e. objects made of a particular material, for a given purpose with a sequence of useful properties. Consequently in this reductive approach to things, the pure fact of the bridge, for instance, is reduced to that of a support with the useful property of connecting two banks. On the other hand, an urn in its "pure reality" is merely something which, constructed of suitable materials, serves the purpose of containing certain objects within its porcelain or metal walls.

Freud, however, discovered that many bridges and many urns, particularly those in dreams, had, apart from their objective and rationally intelligible properties, quite different and irrational contents, and that it was the latter which determined their essential character. A bridge, beyond its useful properties in everyday life, has the symbolic significance of connecting and communicating and an urn that of receiving and of absorbing. Since Freud saw in instinctuality the origin and model of all human life the symbolic content of the bridge and the urn also had to lie within the limits of libidinal significance. Corresponding to their utilitarian properties these objects were endowed respectively with a male or female sexual character. Jung, on the other hand, would rather have us see the original symbolic meaning of these two objects in their general significance of bridging and receptivity. Only secondarily would they, according to the individual's particular disposition, become reduced to the most varying concrete object relations; in certain circumstances, but by no means exclusively, to sexual receptivity and intercourse.

But how do these things, a bridge and an urn for instance, appear to us directly either in our waking or our dreaming world, if we do not previously dissect them into mere objects of utility?

"A bridge swings easily and strongly above the stream. It does more than connect existing banks. Only in the crossing of a bridge do banks emerge as banks. The bridge separates them. It opposes one side to the other. Nor are banks the indifferent boundaries between firm land and stream. The bridge connects river and bank now with one and then with another inland stretch. It brings river, bank, and land into mutual proximity. The bridge *gathers* the land as a landscape around the stream. It thus guides the stream through the fields. Its pillars, resting on the river bed, support the curved arches which leave free path for the waters of the stream. No matter if these waters travel peacefully or in agitation, no matter if heavenly floods during thunderstorms or during the melting of snow rush in great waves about the pillars' arches, the bridge is ready for every kind of weather and for its vagaries. Where the bridge spans the stream it withholds its flow from the heavens by receiving it for a moment under its arches before freeing it once more.

While giving the stream full rein it yet enables us mortals to go on our way from land to land. Bridges guide us in many ways. The town-bridge leads from the castle to the cathedral square; the river bridge outside the town guides carriages and horses to surrounding villages. The modest old stone bridge gives free passage to harvest wagons from meadows and fields, and guides the wooden cart from field path to main road. A highway bridge is an essential part of speedy motor traffic. Always and in different ways the bridge guides the hesitant and hasty steps of men, so that they may reach the other bank and finally, as mortals, the other side. The bridge swings, here with high and there with shallow arches, across rivers and clefts; whether we mortals remember the spanning nature of the bridge or whether we forget it, we are always on our way to the last bridge, for in ever trying to transcend our meanness and our wickedness we are trying to reach the sanctity of the divine. The bridge *gathers* us, and in crossing it we are brought before the divine, whether this fact be especially remembered and we openly offer *thanks* for it as in the figure of the bridge saint, or whether it be concealed or even pushed out of mind."[161]

Now, what is the full and original reality of the thing which we call a golden urn? According to Pindar,[162] in its gold, the most glorious and the mightiest of earthly treasures Theia, the godhead herself, is reflected. It is wide open to the heavens. Its empty shell is ready to receive all that heaven and earth have grown and what has sprung from them. Yet it contains what it has received only in order to bring divine gifts to man, or man's offerings to the gods; it contains our daily bread, or it becomes a sacrificial vessel.

To the undistorted view both urn and bridge reveal all this content and meaning originally and quite by themselves. Only because these things themselves originally comprise all these characteristics, and because bridge and urn are inherently the assembly of heaven and earth, of the divine and the human, can we speak of them as things. For, in contradistinction to the word "object", even today the word which in northern lands etymologically corresponds to "thing", means assembly. In olden times it particularly referred to the courts of justice in which assemblies declared what was right and true.

For this reason the common positivist dismissal of this essence of objects as mere romantic adornments due to muddle-headed and unscientific thinking cannot touch its reality at all. Rather the immediate and full experience of a thing demonstrates how terribly restricted is the positivistic point of view.

· · · ·

A bridge and an urn were our evidence and our justification for considering current concepts of symbolism as illegitimate. They readily showed that all contemporary psychologies get into difficulties when they have recourse to symbols, for they consider the essence of things in themselves as much too impoverished. Only because psychologists lost sight of the primordial and full content and meaning of the bridge and urn, must they take the trouble to fetch the intrinsic characteristics of a thing from outside it. They obtain them by means of "free association" out of the individual dreamer's past, or by means of so-called amplification, that is, by the roundabout path of discovering those characteristics of the respective things known to mythology. By this indirect approach things are bound to become reduced to creations of the human unconscious, which subsequently attributes to them symbolic values or symbolic manifest contents. But any talk of symbols is not only quite unnecessary; it is confusing. Whenever we stress the symbolic significance of a given thing we are tacitly assuming the existence of other, independent and unrelated objects consisting exclusively of an unknown nucleus, endowed with some perceptible properties. In a world not exposed to previous mental dissection, however, all things by themselves appear in manifold meaningful historical connotations and interrelations. The so-called "pure facts" and the "symbolic contents" together, therefore, constitute the total and original essence of things as such. In consequence, there is no need at all for a "symballein", i.e. for a fitting together of what is primordially a unity.

So the theoretical approach which reduces all dream phenomena to mere reproductions of "real objects", the better to endow them immediately with manifold symbolic projections from the dreamer's unconscious, is quite unjustified. The dream things must be accepted as things with their own and full meaning and content, just as they are felt to be within the immediate experiences of the dream. If so, is there any basis for a theory of psychic projection and of the subjective symbolic character of the dream objects? Does not the distinction between dream interpretation on the objective level and on the subjective level become redundant? But how else do things enter our dream world at all?

CHAPTER II

The Elimination of Dream Interpretation on the Objective and Subjective Level, in the Phenomenological Interpretation of Dreams

THE simplest and shortest of the many examples with which Freud tried to explain his dream theory is one in which the dreamer saw his brother enclosed in a box. The first association of the dreamer substituted a cupboard (*Schrank*) for the box. The second association immediately revealed the significance of the dream: the brother is becoming less extravagant (*schränkt sich ein*). It was this thought that the dream image expressed by means of a concrete yet distorting symbolism. According to Freud, both the latent dream thought and the manifest dream image are caused by the hidden desire to see the brother become less extravagant.[163]

In a second example of Freud's, a Munich doctor dreamt that he was cycling down a road in Tubingen. Suddenly a brown dachshund charged after him and bit his heel. A little further on the dreamer dismounted, sat down on a step, and began to thrash the animal, which would not let go. On the opposite side some elderly ladies were mocking him. The dreamer expressly stated that he did not experience the biting as unpleasant or painful. He further stated that he had recently fallen in love with a girl whom he had seen in the street, but whom he had been unable to meet. His best approach would have been the dachshund which this lady always took with her. In order to interpret this or the previous dream on the objective level, i.e. as a pictorial and symbolic representation of an instinctual relationship of the dreamer to a factual external object, Freud had to employ a whole series of mental constructions. First, the dream censor had used the dream work to repress the beloved girl in the manifest dream content, and to disguise her by her very opposite: the mocking elderly ladies, or by her quite unimportant peripheral property, the dachshund. In order to make this work of distortion even more effective the dream work had used the technique of affect-displacement from the girl to the dachshund and had thus recentred the entire meaning of the dream.[164]

It is difficult to understand why the dream censor should have erased the girl or distorted her since the man was fully conscious of his being in love during waking life. Furthermore, the question remains why in this interpretation on the objective level the dog had to bite the dreamer and why he defended himself so much, since the girl (ostensibly symbolized by the dog) had no intention of biting him, nor had he the slightest desire to thrash her. Finally, why did the dreamer have to cycle down the road, rather than up it?

We must, however, resist the temptation to interpret the dreams of people who are completely unknown to us. Freud himself has expressly warned us against this danger, and C. G. Jung has repeated his warning. Both have agreed that the danger of getting lost in wild speculations is far too great. But I myself know of dreams similar in structure related to me by two of my own patients who were well known to me professionally over many years.

One of them dreamt that he was opening a drawer of an old chest. Just as in Freud's example, his brother was found inside. This discovery frightened our dreamer so much that his heart nearly stopped beating. The dreamer saw that his brother was stuffed into the chest like a mummy, and he experienced this so clearly that he could feel his own body being compressed. His brother was in fact a highly vital person and also a highly talented artist. The dreamer, on the other hand, was living the stultifying life of a pedantic bachelor and a subordinate official. Some twenty years ago he had worried about his highly-strung brother and about the latter's extravagance. However, the brothers had lost touch with each other half a generation before and lived in quite different parts of the world. For this reason our patient found it puzzling that he dreamt of his brother at all. Now, anyone who wished to do so could easily interpret this dream in an objective way, following Freud's example. In that case this dream would also lead to a displaced instinctual wish directed at this very concrete and libidinously or aggressively charged external object "brother" and expressing a desire for the brother to become less extravagant. Thus the dream phenomenon would re-emerge as the symbolic representation of this instinctual wish. The dream psychologist interpreting in this way must, however, remember that he would only be dealing with hypothetical mental entities which need not at all correspond to reality. He must remember that in such "translations" of the dream phenomena he ascribes to them something quite alien, i.e. "a latent dream thought" and an unconscious force, without ever being able to justify such interpolations in the light of the reality of the immediate dream phenomena.

A dream corresponding to Freud's second example is that of a thirty-year-old man who came to me because of a slight sexual disturbance. This patient, too, in one of his dreams, cycled straight down a steep road. He was followed not by a dachshund but by a large black Alsatian which bit his calf without the dreamer experiencing any pain. Like Freud's dreamer, our patient thrashed the animal in order to get rid of it. In doing so he saw two well-known ladies walking past him. Instead of helping him both of them merely shook their heads and laughed ironically.

Our dreamer, too, had just fallen in love in waking life. He had even kissed his girl a number of times, but he had been shy and afraid. In his case, however, the girl did not assist the interpretation, because she did not, in fact, own a dog. Furthermore, the ladies walking past neither resembled his girl-friend, nor were they her very opposite. Both were rather vital, mature, happily married women. The dreamer did not manage to produce one single association to elucidate his actual relationship with these two ladies, nor had a similarly unpleasant incident ever occurred to him in waking life.

So the interpretation of this dream on the objective level is much more difficult than in Freud's example. Indeed, the obstacles seem insurmountable. On the other hand, interpretations on the subjective level can explain all the dream phenomena easily, and without the aid of a hypothetical dream censor or the idea of dream work: the dream dog is the symbolic representation of the dreamer's own dark instinctual animality, of that side of his psyche which he still feared and attacked. The vital and mature ladies could be interpreted as symbolizing his awakening mind. They would indicate that the dreamer was no longer so completely afraid of his own sexuality and that he no longer needed to combat and repress it, but that with at least a part of his personality, he could smile at his neurotic fears of sexuality.

Similarly, interpretation on the subjective level would see in the dream brother of the first example the symbolic representation and embodiment of that side of his character which corresponds to him. To the subjective interpretation of the Zurich School, with its finalist and prospective approach, it would further appear as though the unconscious of the dreamer used the brother's cramped position to say: Just look! This is just how you shut up your own vitality! Do free it now!

The interpretations of these two examples on the objective level were in the one case completely useless and in the other case completely unprovable. They were mental conclusions from waking life unrelated to the phenomena themselves. Do interpretations on the subjective level fare any better?

Dream interpretation on the subjective level considers all dream objects including animals and people as the symbolic representations of instinctive drives or other strivings on the part of the psyche, or some other aspect of the personality, or of some psychic functions of the dreaming subject himself. The dreamer projects his psychic content on to the dream images, and thus becomes symbolically personified or made concrete in them.

Is not such an interpretation also mere theory and fundamentally not so far from an interpretation on the so-called objective level? According to the modern point of view objects are perceived by a subject and every perception comes down to the psychic representation of a thing. Such representation of objects must surely be subjective. In particular, Freud himself expressly describes the dream image as the "plastic and concrete representation" of an instinctual wish, i.e. of an obviously subjective psychic aspect of the dreamer himself. The difference between these dream interpretations therefore consists only in the fact that one considers dream images as the representations of definite functions of the dream subject which are tied to very concrete objects, and the other as the symbolic personification of psychic faculties which are as yet without a concrete aim.

Does not therefore the second approach represent just as great a mental outrage to the dream reality as does dream interpretation on the objective level? Is it not also a quite inadequate description of factual phenomena? Is it not forced to by-pass the real phenomena which can never be found where the subjective interpretation presupposes them to be?

All talk of subjective significance of dream phenomena and of projection of the dreamer's psychic content on to them does not consider the dream phenomena as such, for it makes the purely theoretical assumption that dreams take place in the psyche or even in the brain of the subject. It is for this reason alone that such psychic processes can be projected and transferred on to dream images. In support of the hypothesis of the subjective significance of the dream, details are often cited similar, for instance, to the physical response of our first dreamer to the unpleasant confinement of the brother. It is claimed that these dream phenomena, which occur frequently, point clearly to an identification of dreamer and dream image. We must agree that these dreams are indeed often met. Very often this physical sympathy impresses itself most forcefully on the dream.

This happened for instance in the case of a young woman who witnessed a rape in her dream. She saw two young and callous youths and a young girl enter a railway waiting-room in which the dreamer had been sitting for quite some time. In the course of the dream the girl is thrown on a bench about ten yards away from the dreamer, she is undressed and raped by one of the youths. The girl apparently does not resist or participate. The dreamer finds the whole situation quite grotesque and does not know what to think of it. When the girl is raped the dreamer herself, even though she is a mere observer, can feel the pain most acutely in her own genitals. At the same time her whole body itches strongly. This pain and itching even persisted for some time after waking. However, this physical sympathy of the dreamer with one of her dream persons is anything but a justification for the theory of projection or for a subjective interpretation. On the contrary, it is very well suited to showing them to be erroneous.

First, the intense physical experience of the dreamer herself clearly shows that the dream phenomena are neither perceived as images nor as symbols. In our dreams we experience real physical facts: a thing is a real thing, an animal is a real animal, a man is a real man and a ghost is a real ghost. In our dreams we are in just as real a material world as in our waking life and in both cases we express our individuality in our behaviour and relationships with the objects and fellow beings around us.

If, furthermore, our dreamers immediately react with their own bodily sensations when observing that others are being squeezed up or raped, then the dreamers could never have been mere isolated dream subjects subsequently projecting a subjective psychic content on to the other people in the dream. On the contrary, from the very start of their meeting, both the dreamers and their dream partners were so much involved and absorbed in the same behaviour of being squeezed and raped that the dreamers had first to extricate themselves from this togetherness in order to adopt this behaviour as a possibility of their own. Only afterwards, therefore, could the dreamers participate with their own bodily sensations.

The dreamer is not merely involved in his dream brother's constricted posture. It is his brother and no one else who is in the drawer because our dreamer himself is already participating in the brother's vital freedom. True, the dreamer is only potentially and not yet actually uninhibited in life as is his brother. That is why the latter appears asleep like a mummy; but only because the dreamer himself is potentially capable of a freer existence does he meet the brother at all. Once again this is not a case of projection of the dreamer's own behaviour into a dream-picture. It is rather this potential behaviour of his which fetches the brother into the dream world as a human being whose behaviour corresponds perfectly to the dreamer's own potentialities.

In the very perception of their partners our dreamers were already involved in their behaviour and attitudes. While they were merely observing, they did not themselves fulfil them as completely as the dream partners, yet this original involvement with another in meeting him is at the root of man's ability to act like him. For this reason we can always understand ourselves better through others. Although while we are merely observing another man the behaviour that we perceive is still concentrated in the other, yet it would never have become the dreamer's own physical experiences, as it so strikingly did in our two examples, if the dreamers had not themselves been primarily involved in it, in the very act of beholding.

The customary, purely subjective, way of thinking makes it extremely difficult for modern man to pay attention to this phenomenal aspect of human existence, which is decisive in all dream interpretation. Yet it is revealed by dreams of such a great variety, that they are only equalled by the clarity of schizophrenic phenomena and experiences. For this reason a basic understanding of both phenomena—the dream and schizophrenia—can only grow out of true insight into this particular aspect of man's existence.

Thus, a very intelligent man, by no means a psychotic, and unprejudiced by any psychological or philosophical preconceptions, spontaneously reported the following dream, without a single interruption or attempt at influencing him on the part of the investigator.

"The wall of a house was being erected. On looking carefully I could see that three men were working on it. First of all there was an apprentice. He was obstinate, he cursed, he openly rebelled and only pretended to be working. Then there was some kind of foreman who lectured, and pretended to be terribly busy and keen. He reproached the apprentice, and gave him orders, but the apprentice merely continued shamming. The foreman himself also did very little; in his over-zealousness there could be sensed his own resentment and sabotage. Only the third man, an architect, knew at once what was to be done. When he intervened, everything went right. I did not look on the activity of these three men as a mere outsider, as a fourth person. I was not apart from them as a separate physical entity nor did I look at them with physical eyes, and yet I saw everything. Somehow I was within these three men themselves, I was all three at once, and felt myself completely a part of them and of all their actions. Only while I was slowly waking up did I feel myself dissolving out, and becoming quite my own self. For some time I remained an unparticipating observer, looking at the three from a distance."

The first and primary fact of this dream is that of work. The dreamer sees himself doing this through the actions of three people. He himself is from the very beginning so much involved in this house-building that he exists in all three equally, and in their different basic attitudes. Only on waking does he collect himself slowly into his own self, his own physical and separate individuality.

In this dream the primary and everyday structure of human existence, i.e. its absorption in the things and people whom we meet, is so transparent that on waking the dreamer could immediately understand himself in his threefold relation to the world, through the behaviour of the three workers.

Thus neither in the dream nor in waking life is there originally a subject or a person or even a more or less individuated self to which some extra behaviour patterns or properties can be subsequently ascribed. It is rather originally and primarily a human potentiality, an attitude to the world, or a complexity of modes of existence into which a person must develop. To be a person therefore means nothing else than a self-unfolding of human behaviour patterns. It means this so strongly and so exclusively that this unfolding is only called "person" because in it and through it alone do the potentialities of human existence resound (personare) out of their hidden essence.

Thus, both in my dreams and in waking life I am always involved in the behaviour of the people I meet, and I am involved in them even if I do nothing but look on and observe them indifferently, without letting myself be involved deliberately or critically, indeed even if I try to ward them off. If this is true there can no longer be any question of a projection of subjective content, or of a symbolic personification of a part of the dreamer. The phenomenal event itself obviates the idea of projection and symbolization of subjective contents. On careful examination these theories of projection and symbolization prove to be two mental constructions which have resulted from overlooking the essential fact: in my original co-existence with the people I meet, I am always and quite primarily involved in their behaviour.

The view that the dream image of the squeezed-up brother was due to a prospective element in the dreamer's unconscious with an educative purpose involves so hypothetical an idea of the unconscious as a sort of educator, that it cannot possibly have any connection with the dream phenomena themselves.

We do not only speak of behaviour in the case of man but also in the case of animals. Everyday language hardly ever distinguishes between the two. The problem of the essential difference between man's behaviour and that of the animal has hardly been posed at all, let alone answered. Only one thing is certain: an animal only exists insofar as it moves within, and is directed by, its given environment. The animal relationship to its environment, even though the animal cannot express it verbally, has a certain correspondence to human attitudes towards objects and people. For this reason man can somehow experience the animal's relationship to its environment. Indeed an animal can only be thought of as such, and not for instance as a stone, insofar as we have entered into, and participated in, the particular animal's relationship to the environment.

This experiencing of the animal's relationship to its environment is clearly expressed in dreams of the following kind. A middle-aged man dreams that he has to lead a horse into a gorge. He holds it by a rein which is not a real rein, but a kind of umbilical cord coming out of the horse and attached to its breast. After a while it is no longer he who guides the horse, but the horse pulls him towards itself with such force, that he is quite unexpectedly pulled right into the horse and becomes the horse itself. Later on he can again separate himself, once more become a man with his own body, and standing next to the animal he can now observe it from the outside.

In another dream the dreamer saw three dogs rushing about a field and playing about in the water. He could see them in the same way in which the other dreamer perceived his three building workers; at first not as an external human observer. He saw himself as all three of these playful dogs. Suddenly he dissolved out of the animals and stood in his human form at the edge of the pond, looking at the dogs which continued to rush about with great pleasure. Then once more he identified himself with their play so much that he again turned into them. This being pulled into the animal and into its behaviour, and the ability to dissolve out of it again into a mere external observer in human form, alternated a few more times before the dreamer finally awoke.

Dream interpretation on the subjective level completely bypasses the phenomenal events of all those dreams in which it sees one part of the dream subject projected on to the dream image of an animal. The Alsatian of our previous dreamer, too, originally appeared neither as a reproduction nor as a symbol, but was from the very beginning a very real and most lively dog. He could only be perceived as an animal insofar as the dreamer himself had entered into attitudes which somehow corresponded to that of the animal. The dreamer did this because his love for his girl had made him so intensely sensual that he was in a state resembling erotic fascination. His whole existence had become so bound up with this animalistic unfree behaviour, that he was receptive to very little else but the sphere of instinctual sensuality, just as previously when speaking of a hungry person we said that he was receptive only to the perception of foodstuffs. Had our dreamer not been a neurotic and inhibited person, he would probably have been pulled out of this state into a sexual dream of some exciting woman. Because of his attitude to life, however, he was not willing to accept these sensual traits as his own, and condemned them as dog-like behaviour, thinking that he had to ward them off. It would have been very surprising indeed if anything but a vicious dog had been admitted to his dream world.

However, had this dreamer not already been capable of somewhat more mature behaviour he would not have admitted the two vivacious women into his dream at all. But he is still far from achieving a mature sensuality as a possibility of his own. His maturity is still confined to the two women who do not wish to come to his aid. Nevertheless sensuality is real enough for him. So much so that the pain of the involuntary break-up of his anxiety-bound personality structure, caused by the emergence of sensual behaviour characteristic of the dog, is already neutralized by a certain acceptance of more mature attitudes. This resulted in his striking insensibility when he was bitten. Similarly, in the many young women who dream of fleeing from pursuers, the wish to flee from sexuality and sensuality and the simultaneous desire for them, expressed in the strange feeling of being rooted to the spot, cancel each other out.

Our dreamers, however, not only met men and animals but

things as well. One dreamer, for instance, was cycling down a steep road. The other one dreamt of a chest of drawers. How could these objects have entered into the world of dreams at all if we disregard the erroneous assumption of projection and symbolic personification of the dreamers' psychic contents?

Can a man whose whole existence consists of an attitude of being confined, as was the case with one of our dreamers, have eyes and ears for objects other than those which in their essence correspond to confinement? If the existence of a man is so much determined by the idea of being confined then he is only open to the perception of corresponding things. He could only meet just such a chest of drawers which, with its specially thick and massive walls and its heavy locks, so clearly bears all the characteristics of being closed.

The other dreamer neurotically defending himself from, and warding off, all erotic relations, was all the more busily and constantly occupied with them. He was in constant danger of being overrun by them. So every sexual impulse made him anxious and afraid of falling from the lofty heights of free will into the subhuman depths of animal sensuality. Out of all the possible paths such an anxious mood could choose only a steeply descending one, and thus notice only road sections that descended steeply.

There is no longer any need to turn even the fabulous things with which we began, i.e. the rainbow-coloured bridge and the suspended golden urn of our "strange dream", into symbols, by first reducing them mentally to psychic representations of objects and then letting the dreamer place her subjective contents into them. We must rather recognize that these things gracing the dream life of a loving person have a quite original content and intrinsic essence which enable them to unite heaven and earth, human and divine, thus corresponding fully to the happy openness of the dreamer's existence.

The more we divorce the phenomena of the dream from old psychological and anthropological ideas and the more we grant them an essence of their own, the more surprising will it appear that dreamers so frequently perceive only a single person or very few people and only a very limited number of objects whereas our waking world is always conceived of as consisting of thousands of the most different objects. This difference may be due either to a tremendous impoverishment of dream life or else to a tremendous concentration. In his everyday waking life man's attitude of making as much use of as many things as possible is generally a lazy one, and things appear to him as mere useful contrivances. It is due to this indifference and "objectivity" that man in his everyday world meets a thousand and one things all of which appear in so impoverished a form, and so poor a context, that they become reduced to an empty shell. The dreamer, on the other hand, is frequently, and intensely in a very definite mood. Corresponding to this unequivocal mood, only those objects and people are allowed to enter the respective dream world whose essence and being correspond exactly to the behaviour patterns in which the dreamer himself happens to be moving. Only for the perception of things and gestures appertaining to such a sphere is the dreamer himself open. Corresponding to his concentrated mood the dreamer can enter into these realms of existence and behaviour all the more vividly. It is for this reason that he feels closer to their things and people, and that they can all be united in a single dream world of the moment, however far removed in time and space they may be in his waking life. The unequivocal mood of the dream often manages to bring forth things and people whom the dreamer had long "forgotten" and whose spiritual or physical appearance he would have been quite unable to describe in waking life. They attain full corporeal reality in the dream world, and appear as if they had happened only yesterday.

But this roll-call of all sorts of things and people to a renewed and explicit presence in one and the same momentary dream world, this repetition of the entire past of the dreamer, could never have happened, even in the dream, if any detail of the real past, however small, were ever truly lost. In fact no action, no experience, no event is ever lost. The entire past persists as a part of man's existence even if, under certain circumstances, it appears in a disguised and forgotten form. Occasionally a dreamer will meet things and people who combine the most different traits and properties and who represent mixed figures. Freud interprets this phenomenon as a product of the distorting dream work. He speaks of the deformation technique of "condensation". In reality such a condensation is anything but a disguise and distortion—the mixed figures of the dream show an especially complete aggregation of those ways of existing in which the dreamer is involved and in which he moves with correspondingly great concentration.

CHAPTER 12

The Concrete Dream Phenomenon as a Whole and the Derived Conception of the Archetype

I BELIEVE that, in a series of 823 dreams, I have the most impressive evidence for the inseparable belongingness of the things, animals and people encountered by the dreamer to the total pattern of relationships in which he moves and has his being. So much so that he exists *in* and *as* his relationship to them. These 823 dreams all emerged during the three-year psychoanalysis of an engineer in his forties, who came to me for psychotherapy because of deep depressions and complete sexual impotence. During the different stages of treatment he hardly ever dreamt of the same figures, and whenever he occasionally did do so, it was only of those things or beings which had determined his previous phases. But the people who characterized the dreams of his final period were not even present by way of indication in the dreams of the earlier periods. He maintained that with one single exception he had never dreamt at all in his life before treatment. This dream occurred two days before the first consultation.

In this first remembered dream of his life the dreamer was in a dungeon, dimly lit by a very small barred window beyond his reach. The bars of this window attracted his special attention. They consisted of wrought-iron work, the artistry of which was in pronounced contrast to the extreme poverty of the dungeon itself. On closer observation the dreamer noticed that all the bars were mathematical signs and numbers: square roots, integrals, indeed entire mathematical formulae. Soon after the beginning of treatment he brought fresh dreams to almost every consultation. During the first six and a half months he dreamt exclusively of turbines, cyclotrons, automobiles and aeroplanes. Within the last three weeks of this first period there were three occasions on which he wanted to cross a bridge over a frontier river in one of his technical machines. But on every occasion the bridge was broken and only a fragment of the bridge would stick out from the banks of the river. Then, for the first time, he dreamt of the presence of a living thing: a potted plant. During the very same week he could dream of green pine trees and red roses, though the roots of the roses appeared to be worm-infested, their buds sickly and their leaves withered.

Four months elapsed before his next dream. Now he no longer met animals in the form of unseen subterranean creatures, such as worms. Yet his dreams were still only about dangerous and harmful insects. Dreams about insects occurred during the subsequent half year 105 times; naturally not without occasional interruptions by old dreams of machines and plants. Then there followed a period of half a year in which he dreamt of toads, frogs and snakes. Originally both animals and machinery had always been of a vague grey colour. One night, however, he was frightened by a bright red snake of tremendous thickness and length. The first mammal he encountered in his dreams was a mouse. He could barely see it disappearing down a mousehole. A little later on, there followed a dream in which a rabbit was being swallowed by a wild pig. From then on pigs began to play a very great role in his dreams and this continued for some weeks; so much so that the patient finally got cross and asked if this piggery would never come to an end. In time however the pigs gave place to lions and horses. The first dream about a human being occurred two years after the beginning of psychoanalysis. It was a dream of an unconscious woman of more than life size in a long blood red dress, swimming in a large pond far below a vitreous cover of ice. He was terribly frightened at this discovery and ran for help. Half a year later he dreamt that he was dancing at a peasant fête with a woman similarly dressed in blood-red, who was now fully awake and very passionate, and that he fell deeply in love with her. In his waking state, feelings of the complete meaninglessness of life had already begun to disappear at the time he could admit plant-life into his dream world. His sexual potency improved considerably, and finally gave rise to a full love life at the time that he dared to begin to dream of lions and horses.

In his dream of the mathematical prison bars he became aware how much he had been a prisoner of his life-denying mathematical thought, and how exclusively intellectual all his attitudes had been. In these dreams he became aware of his imprisonment with a clarity which far surpassed that of waking life. During the following period, in which he dreamt of dead, grey machinery, his waking world too was one in which all things had become reduced to mere useful objects. He himself was essentially no more than a useful cog in an industrial machine. It was only because of his highly developed intellect that his ability to step up mass production from year to year was unimpaired. However, he had ceased to function as a full human being, and his intoxication with excessive work was meant to cover up his terrible boredom. Something had constantly to be going on outside and, since nothing went on inside him, he became an excitable busybody. His own life history had come to a full stop. It was because of this mutilated existence of his, because he himself was nothing but a useful automaton, because his own development was broken, that he could only dream of dead machinery and broken bridges, leading him nowhere.

But did not his waking life contradict his poverty-stricken dreams? Was he not in fact carried safely across the river four or five times a day by a bridge, when driving between his business and his home? Was he not aware of plants and animals? Did he not meet dozens of people in the factory and did not his wife await him every night? Or was the dream perhaps more truly indicative of his real way of existing, because in it he was more awake than during the day? A closer examination revealed that he was in fact so asleep during the day, so enmeshed in abstract technical thought, that he was unaware of the full reality of things, plants, animals, people in the street or in business, or even of his wife. In the course of treatment he became more and more aware of the fact that his whole world had long appeared grey and as though peopled by nothing but marionettes and ghosts. In fact not even the bridge of his waking world was as firm and safe as he persuaded himself and others it was. There had been quite a few occasions when he had a suspicion of the true nature of his daily reality. Whenever he crossed the bridge he suffered from what is clinically known as agoraphobia. More and more frequently he was seized by an inexplicable panicky fear that it might collapse at any moment. It was only by a trick that he managed to let his driver proceed across the river: he shut his eyes tightly while they were on the bridge.

During his psychoanalytic treatment, however, he regained his full human potentiality and his world again became wider. In his first dream relationships with plants and lower animals he had already been able to re-experience instinctual possibilities of living corresponding to the nature of these creatures. Finally, when he had developed into a mature human being, he could meet a dream sweetheart, and in his love towards her accomplish to the full all that is richest in man.

C. G. Jung was the first to draw attention to such a "phylogenetic development" of dream phenomena: to serial dreams which take place during especially intense periods of maturing in the life of the dreamer. But Jung immediately explained these phenomena as the products of archetypes which, as we learnt during our critique of the dream theory of the Zurich School, he imagined as autonomous beings similar to organisms, and with a creative force of their own. Whenever a particular archetype was "constellated" it would, according to Jung, appear symbolically disguised as one of the dream phenomena. Thus Jung would have considered all the innumerable animal figures of the earlier dreams of our patient as symbolic of the animal archetype, and the women dressed in red of the dreamer's anima-archetype. He would certainly have interpreted the preponderance and great number of markedly maternal women, who made their appearance between the two dreams of women dressed in blood red, as emanations of the mother archetype. In fact these maternal figures varied between anonymous everyday mothers promenading with their prams in the city gardens, and scenes in which our patient's own grandmother gave him the milk bottle and afterwards powdered his bottom.

Later the dreamer even committed incest with his own mother, and still later he dreamt of maternal angels safeguarding the Christ child. Once in a dream of a deep forest gorge, he met a gigantic good fairy with flowing blonde tresses, and mighty breasts from which there sprang waterfalls of milk. In this dream he himself was as large as the fairy's toe. Significantly his behaviour in waking life had changed most strikingly during the time of his maternal dreams. Whereas previously he had been a sober, matter-of-fact, calculating, distant and "schizoid" person, he now behaved almost childishly. His wife, against whose interference he had previously defended himself most violently, was now expected to be tender in the extreme, and he even wanted her to put him to bed for some time. His secretary, whom before he had hardly so much as greeted, now became his confidante, to whom he complained bitterly that people were cruel towards him. He greedily looked for compliments from his employers, and for his Christmas present desired nothing so much as frequent invitations to their homes. His subordinates laughed at him behind his back, since he had started to lisp in an affected manner. During analytical sessions he wanted the analyst to carry him in his arms. Once he even said that the analyst looked much more feminine than before, and that he could almost swear he had noticed a strong tendency to female breast formations.

From these transference phenomena on the analyst and from his waking behaviour towards his fellows, it was clear that he was being a child. External circumstances had prevented him from abreacting his childishness during his early youth, and this delayed acting out of his childhood so affected his entire existence, and held him so much in its grip, that people seriously began to doubt his sanity. It was this utter surrender of his whole existence to being a child, even during his dreams, which made him exclusively aware of earthly or divine mothers.

In waking life, as in the dream, every kind of childish attitude spontaneously calls for maternal forms, because childish existence *is* intrinsically the relationship to maternal beings. It is for this reason that maternal phenomena are inherent in all childish attitudes. The unusual complexity of the patterns in which our patient embodied his childishness at that time leads to a particularly clear understanding of the origins and true nature of the idea of archetypes: to obtain the notion of the mother-archetype from the concrete phenomenon itself, the original unity of childish relationship and the objects belonging to it must be destroyed and the objects separated and isolated. These are the different mother figures of waking or dreaming life. From the great number of such isolated objects a subsequent operation of thought then abstracts a hypothetical but universally valid generic idea. This abstraction is then personified into an autonomous entity possessing its own creative and motive powers. Only then does the mother-archetype show itself in its most common contemporary form, viz. as a hypostasized abstraction from the concrete objects which belong to the original unity of a human relationship with things and fellow men.

All the other archetypes are of the same character and origin. Just as the idea of a mother-archetype is due to a mental isolation and a hypothetical abstraction from the total childish attitude to life, so the idea of a father-archetype turns out to be a corresponding derivation from the total phenomenon of a filial attitude to life.

"Animal dominants" and "shadow archetypes" are mental constructions out of our animal-like instinctive dispositions. "Animus" and "anima" are artificial mental abstractions of all those forms which appear in feminine or masculine intellectual ways of living. Again, the "wise old man" archetype is an hypostasized abstraction of the dream phenomena in which there appear the dreamer's most mature potentialities as yet unrealized in his daily life.*

We shall see later that very definite modes of existence also underlie the magical nature and essential character of dream forms like the large milk-giving fairy of our dreamer. There is, therefore, not the slightest support for the hypothesis of an archetype. We shall be able to illustrate this by the example of dreams in which the magic phenomena and the numinous effects supposed to be characteristic of archetypes will emerge even more strikingly than in the dream of the fairy.

* The true nature of this archetype is above all shown by those dreams in which the recurring wise old man or woman can always be recognized as the dreamer at the end of his or her own life. (*See* dream on page 174.)

CHAPTER 13

The Practical Application of a Phenomenological Interpretation of Dreams

STARTING with two examples of Freud's we tried to replace dream *interpretations* which use such ideas as symbols and archetypes by a phenomenological *analysis*. Our reflections on the actual nature of reductive interpretation led to a recognition that dream interpretations, both at the subjective and also at the objective level, first reduced the actual dream phenomena to rationally explicable objects and then endowed them with an abstract significance. The phenomenological approach, on the other hand, does not consider dream phenomena as mere symbols requiring a subsequent metaphysical transformation from the sensible to the supra-sensible. It examines the dream phenomena in their own full content, and interprets them as such.

Modern man, however, thinks little of mere contemplation or of a "purposeless" search for a truth that seeks "no more" than to clarify the nature of phenomena. Those who can only understand the world in terms of cause and effect are condemned by their very philosophy to evaluate all objects in terms of their utility and efficiency. Even the most disinterested scientific investigation is only countenanced as long as it keeps within the sphere of activities which have a practical interest. Therefore it was inevitable that the modern monomania for efficiency and results seized upon "existential" analysis from its very inception. The battle-cry went up: Psychoanalysis! Existential analysis! and both were thrown together into the arena of the struggle against man's neurotic ills, so that their results could be compared. It is because both are called "analyses" that this mistaken idea is spreading rapidly.

The error of such an approach must be obvious to anyone who understands anything at all of psychoanalysis or of existential analysis. The word psychoanalysis, according to the explicit intention of its original users, means two quite different things. On the one hand, it is merely a particular psychotherapeutic technique; and, on the other, it means a whole system of psychology offering a theoretical understanding of man. This second meaning of psychoanalysis as psychoanalytical theory was considered of secondary importance by Freud himself, who saw in it no more than a changeable theoretical superstructure.

However, existential analysis is only comparable with psychoanalysis in this secondary sense. For existential analysis as such is indifferent both to psychotherapeutic techniques and to practical consequences and aims.

Like Martin Heidegger's fundamental ontology, it "only" enquires into the nature of being and particularly the being of man. Even when existential analysis is modified and limited, as it is with Ludwig Binswanger's purely anthropological approach, it is only concerned with phenomenological study and clarification of the essence of healthy and sick human existence. The crucial question, whether this anthropological restriction is possible or permissible, need not concern us here.

Why then is it that so many depth-psychological therapists of all schools are so disturbed by existential analysis? It is probably because no psychotherapy can exist at all without the idea of an essential human norm, whether the psychotherapist is aware of what this norm means to him or not. Every form of psychotherapy deserving of the name strives only towards bringing out the patient's intrinsic nature and norm and must therefore be based on some idea of such a norm. This holds so much for psychoanalysis as a psychotherapeutic procedure that Freud had very early expressly pointed to the fact that the patient's insight into his own condition, and his simultaneous improvement, were characteristic of this kind of treatment, but this did not hold for physical treatment. For this very reason so much depends on a therapist's own evaluation of what is human. If, for instance, he thinks of man as a libidinal apparatus striving towards pleasurable discharge of impulses, as psychoanalytic theory conceives him to be, then he will be well satisfied with a cure which enables his patients to adjust to their customary environment, and to find their pleasures in it. On the other hand, if the psychotherapist conceives of man's essence as existence in Martin Heidegger's sense, then he will speak of a complete cure only when his patients can see themselves, so to speak, as a light emanating from the mystery of existence, in whose rays all things and fellow-beings are allowed to appear and to develop according to their own nature.

But there is no need for this new goal to stop the psychotherapist from keeping as closely as possible to Freud's practical indications, as developed in his papers "Zur Technik". In this he may even be more strict than those psychoanalysts who still believe implicity in the picture of man suggested by orthodox psychoanalytical theory. He for one will lend his ear more readily to experience—which, in a great number of cases, proves the superiority of Freud's technical rules over the "improvements" of his successors.

This apparent paradox is probably based on the fact that the deeper and existential meaning of Freud's technical rules emerges only under the scrutiny of existential analysis. Their full significance is not apparent in psychoanalytic theory. How else explain the fact that although Freud discovered the "basic rules" of psychoanalytical practice intuitively, he could only account for them by means of surprisingly superficial and untenable arguments? The same holds for his method of so-called free association; for his advice that the analyst should sit behind the patient so that the latter cannot see him; that he should be silent and reserved and that he should have a "freely floating attention"; and finally, for the demand that he should tackle that human relationship between doctor and patient which Freud called transference and resistance symptoms.[165]

Now if a phenomenological approach cannot escape the modern fate of the West, and if it is pulled head over heels into a competitive struggle, then its value will need to be judged by its therapeutic efficacy. As an argument against its "correctness", and against its criticism of interpretations both on the objective level and on the subjective level, we are often told that most previous kinds of dream interpretation were therapeutically successful.

Indeed, the experiences of therapeutic practice leave no doubt about this. Over and above this they show clearly that dream interpretations on the objective level are more effective than interpretations on the subjective level for persons who are in philosophic agreement with the assumptions underlying the objective interpretation. On the other hand, dream interpretation on the subjective level leads to better therapeutic results when the patients themselves have an "auto-symbolic" understanding, and in consequence understand this kind of subjective interpretation more easily. But is this any objection at all to the truth value of phenomenological dream interpretation? In no psychotherapeutic situation is there ever a question of applying methods to matter equally responsive to them all. This would overlook completely the doctor-patient relationship, in which the patient comes to the doctor with his own particular level of understanding. Thus it is a basic assumption of every psychotherapeutic intervention that the doctor must first find a common level of communication with his patient if he is to help him at all. For this reason no psychotherapist, however skilled in existential analysis, would ever frighten his patients with the insights which the dream yields to the investigator. No therapist can escape the fact that, because of generally held attitudes, he will have to begin either with interpretations on the objective level or with explanations on the subjective level, or yet with quite superficial pre-analytical hints, if he wishes to be understood by his patients and be effective at all.

Nevertheless, the therapeutic efficacy of a particular interpretation can never be a criterion of the correct evaluation of the nature of dream phenomena. Not even the greatest achievements of technology prove to us that technical thought gives us essential insight into the true nature of things. On the contrary, it is just the complete irrelevance of all our tremendous technological knowledge and power to fulfilment and a happy life which should lead us to suspect that nature only reveals its least essential aspect to the methods of technological investigation.

On the other hand, although interpretations on the objective and subjective levels have undoubted therapeutic effects despite their lack of understanding of the dream, we can expect a cure in a much deeper sense from an understanding of the full meaning of the dream world. For if, in spite of all the rationalist depreciations of waking thought, man learns to respect dream phenomena in their own full reality, then the complete and inherent content of his dream world may reveal to him the actual measure of his life accomplishments. This happens to a far greater extent and much more deeply than is the case when he considers these dream phenomena as mere reproductions of symbols, projections or other "psychic realities" on the part of a subject, or even of a psyche, however highly individuated. Such a cure is dependent on the fact that the analysand either accepts or learns to accept phenomenological dream interpretations, and that existential analysis does not remain a mere intellectual pastime of his but that through it he is enlightened and completely transformed. We can only say that a sufferer has the roots of his suffering torn out when he has proceeded beyond a merely "psychological" or anthropological attitude to things, fellow-beings and to himself, and has been led to the healing experience of belongingness to man and to a new and true relationship with the essence of all things.

Our attempt to preserve dreams as much as possible in their full phenomenal state and to demonstrate them as such has led to the most important recognition that dreams cannot be divorced from man as mere objects, in order to be compared with other man-made objects. We learnt that man when dreaming, no less than when awake, always exists in his relationships with things and with people. We have learnt, indeed, that these relationships go to make up his entire existence. We also learnt that man can realize his existence in dreams, just as in waking life, through the most varied relationships and attitudes.

Are there more possibilities of being related to things and people in the dream than in waking life? Or are there certain possibilities of living which occur exclusively in dreams? In other words, is it the number of possible attitudes which is the essential and not yet adequately formulated difference between waking and dreaming existence? Or could both forms of existence only be distinguished by particular modes of behaviour which are exclusively their own? The answer to these questions will emerge from an examination of all those dreams that we have studied in which a particular relationship between the dreamer and his dream world appears with special clarity.

PART III. *Human Life in Dreams*

CHAPTER 14

The Dreamer's Possibilies of Existing

(a) Being alarmed in shock dreams
IN the strange dream of an urn we saw the existence of a dreamer in her very varied relationships to the things and people of the dream world. Originally our dreamer was completely absorbed in a contented relationship with her pleasant dining-room, and later in the act of eating her beefsteak. Finally, even in the dream, her existence appeared as the recollection, the realization, the imagination of, and the active intervention in, the things of her world. All these life-possibilities of the dream were potentially hers in the waking state as well.

Now there is a certain class of dreams which are distinguished by the fact that the events in them are nothing but exact repetitions of unpleasant events experienced in waking life. These are the traumatic or shock dreams.

The fitting of such dreams into Freud's theory of wish-fulfilment was particularly difficult. Their occurrence even forced him to admit that, according to his theory of the function of dreams, such a repetition of unpleasant events should not occur at all. "What wishes," Freud asks, "could be satisfied by a repetition of this highly painful traumatic experience?" He had to resign himself to the answer that it is hard to guess and he could only get over the difficulty by blaming the recalcitrant object itself, and not his dream theory. The dream was not up to its task, he says, and it is the dream work which here fails in its attempt to change a painful memory into a wish-fulfilment.[166]

But what do the shock dreams themselves have to show? We know of a young graduate who, during a climbing tour, fell off a small ridge. This caused a heavy concussion and a serious spinal injury. He could not remember hitting the ground after his fall, but in his dreams during the first nights after the accident he was always physically involved in the events to the extent that he could remember them during waking life. In his dreams he kept on slipping off the ridge time after time, just as had happened on the day of the accident, and he even noticed a solitary small plant on the rock which he recalled in his waking experience also. Whenever he started slipping in the dream, he felt the self-same fear that he had experienced at this phase of the real accident.

During the Second World War, I was an eye-witness of an accident in which twenty-three soldiers, driving in a lorry through an Alpine pass, dropped thirty feet down a cliff. Miraculously, most of them were unhurt and even afterwards remained free of any physical or psychological disturbances. A non-commissioned officer, however, died immediately, because just before the lorry had raced over the edge of the road he had jumped off and had been thrown against a wall. He lay dead at the edge of the road, his skull broken. Two of the soldiers dreamt of this catastrophe every night after the accident. Both experienced it exactly as they had experienced it in waking life. Indeed they contended that they noticed details in the dream that they would never have been able to remember in waking life.

In both cases the dream experience started with the drive in the lorry carrying them to the barracks where they were to obtain their week-end passes. In all the dreams they felt uncomfortable from the very start, because the lorry was driving at such an unusual speed. They suspected that something was wrong. This uncomfortable feeling agreed exactly with their waking experience. Then, continuing and repeating the events of the real catastrophe in every detail, they and their comrades became aware that the lorry driver was having difficulties with his brakes. Their fear increased and thoughts about the possibility of jumping off at speed alternated rapidly with inhibiting fears about the dangers of doing so. In their dreams they could see the sharp bend and the lorry overshooting the edge of the road between a small chapel and a little transformer hut. Between these there was just enough space for a lorry to pass. They could still hear the crackling of the bushes at the road's edge as they were being uprooted. In great panic they experienced the fall into the depths. At that very moment of the dream both soldiers regularly woke up with a scream. Immediately before the dream fall one of them could see the non-commissioned officer jumping off and lying inert on the road as the lorry rushed past him. This was just what had happened, although consciously the dreamer had not taken it in. The other soldier dreamt vividly and clearly of the two buildings on the side of the road: the small chapel with its open arch and gate in front, and the little transformer hut with the large insulators on top of one another. These dream details, while corresponding exactly to the objects between which the lorry had rushed into the depths, were recalled to mind through this traumatic dream alone. Thus while some events in both these shock dreams went unnoticed in the waking state, all of them could in fact be verified in daily life, and none of them was distorted.

Many, if not all, shocks and catastrophes are repeated in dreams just as vividly and realistically as in our two examples. How are we to understand this absolute congruence between dream events and daily reality? Perhaps we shall come a little closer to answering this question when we learn that of the twenty-three soldiers, all riding and crashing in the same lorry, twenty-one did not have shock dreams. Obviously they had "their feet so firmly planted on the ground" that they could immediately get up on them. However, "having one's feet firmly on the ground" usually means casting away all silly thoughts and fears of danger and death, when all has gone off well. This, at least, is what the soldiers themselves told me. They all reacted in the same way. All of them continued as if nothing had happened. Thus, immediately after the catastrophe, we had the grotesque picture of all those soldiers who were not seriously injured scrambling madly out of the gorge just like excited ants. Completely indifferent to all that had just happened, their one desire was to rush to the train that was to carry them to their week-end destination. The regimental doctor had the greatest difficulty in keeping even a few back for a check-up. Here there was no question of their urgency being due to a wish to rush back to a protective mother. Most of them were hurrying to distractions of quite a different kind.

We know of only two of these twenty-one soldiers who neither had shock dreams nor tried to cover their deadly fright by an escape into everyday activity. One of these exceptions was a deeply religious man. He had no need to flinch at the certainty of death, because he was safe in his faith. The other throughout years of philosophic reflection had looked at the problem of life and death so often and so closely that he had learnt to cope consciously with this fear. The two soldiers who afterwards suffered from shock dreams were people who stood midway between our two exceptions and the "healthy everyday people". They could no longer manage to flee the fear of death by a mere return to everyday life, and had not yet accepted the fact that the certainty of death was an inescapable factor of their lives, or learned to look at death as a part of their life history. It is for this reason that the tremendous suddenness of the fall, tearing all veils from them and forcing on them the knowledge of the transience of their existence, produced an even greater fear. Their fright was so dreadful that it literally shocked them *out* of their own selves, and *threw* them into a panic fear. Since they were thus shaken out of themselves and in extreme anxiety, everyday objects and people only just enabled them to keep a hold on themselves so long as they were awake. Their dreams, however, betrayed that in fact they were not at all "themselves", but beyond themselves with panic. As victims of this state of panic it was only the world of the threatening and all-engulfing gorge that could reveal itself to them.

While these two soldiers needed outside help to find their way back to themselves, the dreams of our young graduate show that he had already begun defending himself against becoming a victim to the events he had experienced in waking life. In the first shock dreams he had already made an effort towards a renewed self-discovery and self-determination. Whenever he began slipping over the ridge and feeling afraid, he said to himself that the accident had not yet quite happened and that it could still be prevented. For this reason he exerted all his will-power to delay the moment of beginning the dream mountain climb, and to seek desperately for an alternative that would not lead to an accident. This slowing up of time was clearly connected with the idea of putting back the hands of his watch. His dream exertions, so expressly directed at erasing this feeling of being a victim to the disastrous event, and at finding a way to a new self-determination, were soon crowned with success. Very shortly afterwards this shock dream ceased spontaneously, admittedly only to be replaced by shock dreams of a very much lighter kind. In these he recurrently slipped on an orange peel. In waking life he had stepped on one by accident just as he was leaving hospital for the first time. This had frightened him considerably since he was still in plaster and a fall might easily have had very serious consequences. This dream repetition of the minor accident regularly took place with the same precision as had the more serious one. If these shock dreams of slipping still show a rather involuntary and anxious feeling of being a victim to life-destructive external circumstances, the final phase of his original shock dream yet points to quite an opposite mode of behaviour. In it the dreamer is capable of a very energetic willing for a given end.

(*b*) *Decisive volitional behaviour in dreams*

Like the volitional behaviour in the traumatic dream of the young graduate, the equally unequivocal act of willing of the dreamer in the "strange dream of an urn" is difficult to explain by customary methods of dream interpretation. Most dream psychologists agree with the statements of L. Binswanger which we mentioned previously. Here dreaming is still considered to be a passive surrender to a stream of images, and the dreamer a mere unwitting plaything of life, a mere life function without spirit or spiritual history.[167] E. Fromm, following Bergson, considers that dreaming is the condition of man in which he wills nothing, whereas waking and willing are one and the same thing.[168] Even in popular language a dreamer is somebody who lets life slip by in brief snatches. However, if we are unprejudiced we shall see that these assertions prove to be generalizations derived from one kind of dream only. Time after time we find that dreamers decide to intervene in the course of events and that they carry out their decisions most consistently.

For instance a twenty-five-year-old student related the following dream:

"I am in our former home with my governess, who acted as my mother. I can see a stream flowing round and round in our garden. By merely exerting all my will power, and without any physical actions on my part, I manage to lead the stream out of its old bed, and so to bend its course that it can flow away from the garden. I have to exert my will to the utmost and constantly. As soon as I stop willing, the stream tries to return to its old bed."

This was the dream of a young man, who had been suffering from increasingly severe neurasthenia over many years. Although he looked the picture of health and possessed great will-power, yet even the smallest physical or mental exertion produced such fatigue that insomnia, colitis and exhaustion appeared with great intensity. In spite of his more than average intelligence he was therefore forced to postpone taking his long overdue university examinations. This brought the extremely ambitious patient close to despair and suicide. However, shortly after this dream had revealed his real state to him, he managed to pass his examinations with distinction and without any special effort. The dream had been able to teach him, and he was struck by it as if by lightning, that he had been utterly and completely arrested at his childhood stage of life and that he was always going round in circles. He saw that all his energy had been consumed by his incessant attempts to oppose the pull of these infantile life attitudes and to direct the current of his energies towards the outer world. So he had no strength left for acting and thinking in the world at large.

There is no doubt that this dream phenomenon once again confronts psychological thought with the threefold danger of which we have spoken so often before. But we wish to point it out once more, and thus save ourselves the trouble of distinguishing our approach from that of all other dream psychologists on each of the many occasions we shall have of discussing other dreams in this part of the book, which is after all only concerned with the different possibilities of man's life in dreams.

This dream could easily have misled us into an interpretation on the objective level, in which the circular stream enclosing the dreamer would have become the "symbol" of the mother's womb. Just as easily it could have lent itself to an interpretation on the subjective level, which would have contended that the inner psychological stagnation of the dreamer had here been projected into the "symbol" of the unalterable path of the stream coursing around the parental garden, guarded by the governess. Finally we might have interpreted it, just as erroneously, by the approach of L. Binswanger, who would have seen in the circular stream an expression or reflection of the circuitous direction of meaning in which the dreamer's existence was involved.

In reality the dream phenomenon itself neither justifies the assumption of any symbolization of an external object, nor that of a projection of subjective inner conditions, nor yet of an expression or a reflection of an existential direction. It rather discloses to us "no more" than the fact that the patient's whole dream existence was one of stern resolve to lead the river out of its usual circular path. His entire existence was nothing other than this special relationship towards the dream thing. In the light of his infantile disposition this world could show itself as a world stamped by no other dream thing than the parental home and the governess. From this resolute endeavour to make the river flow along a straight path he could understand his own debilitating striving towards progress in life. Since, however, his efforts were only of a volitional, ambitious and over-compensating nature, they were bound to be wrecked on the rocks of his fundamental childishness.

In dreams people sometimes show an astonishing resolution, though during the day they do not quite know what is happening to them since they allow themselves to drift into and fall prey to their respective moods. Thus a woman who in waking life was completely irresolute, nevertheless in one of her dreams managed to jump from the roof of a house, in order to throw a woollen blanket over her husband whose clothes were ablaze. Even in the dream itself she was surprised at her own courage and her unusual resolution. While jumping she realized that in her whole waking life she had never acted so bravely.

(c) Reflective behaviour in dreams

The possibility of reflecting about oneself in dreams, of contemplating, retrospecting and recollecting, of which we obtained a glimpse in this dream of jumping, completely contradicts the usual idea that in his dreams man is a mere puppet and completely passive. For instance our dreamer, in another dream, reflected on her freedom of will. She dreamt:

> "It is a moonlit night. I am in a courtyard in the middle of which there is a stable. I am disguised as a Turkish woman and my belt and shoes are adorned with rich jewellery. I carry a golden chain in my hand and I descend the steps from the stable to the courtyard where I have a rendezvous with some man. I know it is a man who looks coarse, strong, and Russian. I don't actually like anything about him, but he attracts me irresistibly and magically. While I descend the steps and look at the golden chain on my arm I think: 'Perhaps my husband is right when he says there is no freedom of will, everything is fate; one is forced to act in a certain way and in that way only, even if it is against one's own will.' Then I ask myself if I am perhaps like this because my own will and my own resolution were broken during early childhood by my wilful mother. By collecting all my physical strength I suddenly pull myself together and exert my will to turn back and to leave this man to his fate."

The dreamer added: "Just think of it, Doctor, that I should say 'No' to a man who fascinates me erotically; I have never managed to do this all my life."

(d) Imagination and vision in dreams

Just as the customary approach denies the possibility of a resolute intervention in the events of the dream, so does it deny the possibility of imagination in the dream. It is alleged that the dream immediately changes thoughts into visual pictures. This assertion has already been shown to be inconsistent with our "strange dream of an urn" in which the dreamer vividly imagined a Russian invasion. Existing as imagining oneself with things and people, that is, in imaginary memories, realizations, and predictions, is illustrated by the following dreams. A middle-aged man was concerned in waking life with advancing far beyond the level he had attained. In his dream he was admiring the view of a snow-covered mountain from the bottom of a valley.

"There were," he reports, "about ten of us and a mountain guide. We were talking of climbing the snow-capped mountain which lay behind, a very difficult mountain indeed. In the dream I recalled that I had climbed the smaller mountain previously. I could remember this climb almost step by step and very vividly. I could imagine each foothold and each pass on the way. I then asked myself if I was up to climbing the more difficult mountain with its much greater dangers. I thought of all the pros and cons and could not make up my mind. Then the guide began to talk enthusiastically about the climb. I myself began to feel very keen, I took in every word of the guide, and in my imagination I was already in the future, and felt what it would be like to climb the mountain myself."

Another dreamer was informed in his dream that a friend, who was believed to be lost, had returned from Russia. The dreamer remembered that he had instilled false hopes into the parents of this friend for many years, and had told them with a bad conscience that their son was still alive. He himself had no longer believed in his story.

"Now I saw that I had been justified," the dream report continues, "but then I imagined the future and how my friend would outshine me in knowledge once he had made up for his loss. In my dream imagination I could already see how we were beginning a life-long competitive struggle."

Then again, a young colleague who had never experienced anything similar in his waking life, had a true vision in one of his dreams. This happened when, in the course of his training analysis, previously disguised and vaguely feminine attitudes and behaviour patterns emerged. In his dream he was with his sister, who had died some years before. Now she was not only his sister, but his sweetheart also. Standing close to her he suddenly noticed a black hole in the air, at eye level and fairly near to him. This hole was not merely empty. Its blackness began to move, to boil and to rotate. Had he continued looking, the dreamer added, he would have become quite frightened, for the hole seemed to suck him into itself. Whereas his sister and the other dream things were experienced as physical and corporeal realities, he was aware throughout the dream that the hole was a vision or an illusion. Although he saw it with his own eyes, he was convinced that he would not be able to touch it. This distinction and the description of the phenomenon are all the more reliable since this dreamer was a highly skilled psychiatric colleague.

(e) Conscious thought in dreams

Both the dream about the possibility of rebuilding a garage to serve as a hiding place from the Russians, and the self-reflection of the dreamer who thought about freedom of will, demonstrate that in the life of our dreams we are able to exist in the way of being with things and people in thought. There is evidence for the view that this distinctive mode of living occasionally surpasses that of waking thought. We know for instance that the philosopher Karl Leonard Reinholdt freely admitted that the chief idea of a deduction came to him quite clearly in a dream, after he had wrestled with the concept for many weeks, and had unsuccessfully tried to modify it.[169]

Herbert Silberer tells of a thirteen-year-old pupil who had been given a very difficult geometry problem by his teacher. The pupil went home, drew, constructed, and thought for a long time without achieving anything. Even after dinner and in bed he was still thinking about it, until he was finally overcome by sleep. He then had a dream and on the following morning he reported:

> "I slept badly because I was still thinking of this problem, until I suddenly managed to make a construction in which, by drawing parallels to the hypotenuse of each triangle, I obtained three parallelograms, in which the diagonal of one was part of the solution. Now—still in my dream—I drew another diagonal and the proof easily followed from a theorem I had learnt previously. I know that after this I managed to sleep peacefully. When I was awakened in the morning I could see the whole drawing before my eyes. I jumped up quickly and before getting dressed I drew it all in one go."[170]

Even better known is the experience of the chemist Kekulé who attributed his discovery of the ring structure of benzene to a dream fantasy. This is how he describes it:

"Again the atoms were juggling before my eyes . . . my mind's eye, sharpened by repeated sights of a similar kind, could now distinguish larger structures of different forms and in long chains, many of them close together; everything was moving in a snake-like and twisting manner. Suddenly, what was this? One of the snakes got hold of its own tail and the whole structure was mockingly twisting in front of my eyes. As if struck by lightning I awoke. . . ."

It is for this reason that Kekülé concluded his report to the Benzole Convention (1890) with the following words: "Let us learn to dream, gentlemen, and then we may perhaps find the truth."[171] Another witness, whose reliability is beyond the slightest doubt, told us that twice in his life he had built in his dreams a new kind of cigarette machine, such as he had never seen in waking life. He noticed everything so clearly that he even observed the small oil drops on the bearings. He examined the mechanism very carefully so as to remember every detail. On both occasions he went to his office straight after waking up to make as exact a drawing of the machine as possible. Both machines had proved to be very useful inventions.

A German-Swiss woman, who could not speak much French, once dreamt of a collision with a French motor-cyclist. While she was parking, he damaged her front mudguard. She wanted to take him to task for his clumsiness, but even in the dream she found it extremely difficult, since she could not think of suitable French expressions nor arrange them into more or less grammatically correct sentences. In reporting this dream, she complained quite spontaneously of the great effort of thought she had needed to remonstrate with him. Naturally, her bad temper towards this clumsy Frenchman had its good and sufficient reasons. But we need not discuss this here, for this dream is only cited as a further illustration of the possibility of mental reflection in dreams.

A woman of thirty years dreamt that a Franciscan monk, who had travelled all over the world as a wandering preacher and who had learnt everything there was to know, had returned to his monastery because his days on earth were numbered.

"I was in this monastery nursing him. He lay in his bed and he had a very spiritual face. The room was friendly. It was lit by the golden glow of the evening sun and I asked the monk to tell me the true relationship between man, truth and God. I told him that I knew of his omniscience, and that I felt he could tell me. He answered that what we men saw and imagined as reality and truth was a mere fabrication of our own desires and instincts. It was a stage prop, hiding, distorting and diminishing the divine truth within us. After he said this, he died."

At the time of this dream this woman had been spiritually and emotionally blind in everyday life. Her interests were limited to what was of practical use. In her dream, however, she had the great clarity and richness of thought usually found only in the case of a much-travelled spiritual man at the end of his life, as the essence of his life-long reflection about truth. Only because she had already participated in this while dreaming could the monk appear in her dream world at all. Here she anticipated the experience of her whole life, and thus only dimly suspected the truth contained in the dream after waking into her much less receptive daily existence.

The effort to reflect about dream objects occasionally leads to outcomes and illumination, the immense significance of which are fully realized in the dream itself. It is true that after waking these dream discoveries very frequently disappoint us, and may appear to be quite extraordinarily trivial. Many people see here a specially cogent proof that the dreamer's powers of thought and judgment are weakened. Nevertheless it pays to examine very carefully this alleged *"abaissement du niveau mental"*, and not to make do with a mere external appearance. Ever since the very beginning of our detailed study of dreams we have never met a single case in which the dream judgment of what is good and correct did not prove to be fully justified. Admittedly one must try to understand the things discovered or created in the dream in their full essence, and to beware of the customary unwitting process while awake of reducing them to mere useful objects. For instance, a thirty-six-year-old woman dreamt that the father of a scientist was visiting her.

"This man," the dreamer said, "was a well-known professor of physics who had become completely stiff, a real cripple. In addition he was very old. In the dream he could only hobble backwards as if he were suffering from advanced Parkinsonism, and he kept on falling over. He was still very clever and critical. Until last year his lectures had been excellent but none of the students had ever turned up, for his lectures had long been printed and he repeated them every year without changing one word in them. His lectures were outstanding but they were always the same. During every physics lesson he always repeated the strange sentence: 'If there were a door here I should go out into the open.' "

This sentence appeared to the dreamer to be of world-shaking significance. But after waking up it appeared to her as entirely meaningless, stupid and irrelevant.

During her waking life this dreamer was an intellectual blue-stocking. She was far superior to all her colleagues and she was very proud of her knowledge and of her technical ability. She had reduced her life to this one possibility of scientific reflection about things. During waking life she had no idea of the crippling effects of such an existence. She considered this relationship to the world as the only possible and right one. In her dream she learnt the truth from the professor. In co-existing with this dried-up scientist she was still within her purely rational and intellectual world, but from the old man she learnt that her attitude was one that was doomed to failure; that it was without hope and restrictive, and led not to real but only to intellectual freedom. All the same, the fact that she did become aware of the door was of vital and staggering importance for her. On this awareness there depended her choice between serious neurosis and cure. True, if the dream door is considered as a mere isolated object having given properties, then the professor's statement is bound to appear as meaningless and insignificant. The real door of the dream, however, the door in the wall of the lecture theatre, to which the physics professor alluded in an apparently idiotic sentence, is endowed with very rich meanings. One of its sides points to the lecture theatre, and thus to the entire previously inert, indeed malignant, distortion of the dreamer's own life. It was in the lecture theatre that her entire past existence had unfolded, and had been a part of this sphere of purely intellectual relationships. But a door is not there merely to be shut, it also invites us to open it. In the latter case it becomes the "between", it becomes a threshold and a transition into another world. It invites us to go out into the street where we can meet things and people in quite other and fuller ways than in a lecture theatre.

In her dream this woman became aware of her particular philosophy long before she did so in waking life. In waking life she naturally considered herself to be a completely emancipated young woman. However, she once dreamt that she was living in an age in which sexuality had not yet been invented. Only the upper strata of society knew of it although some books on the subject had already appeared. The lower classes only sensed something vaguely without actually knowing anything about it. She saw a young man of the people sexually excited and unaware of what was happening to him. He only felt very hazily that something had changed.

In her dreams she already understood herself, if only through other people and things, as a woman who had only a most superficial knowledge of sensual and instinctive relationships between people. Deep down, she dimly suspected what was happening when her sexuality was aroused. Even this ability to suspect, she had only been able to gain through long analytical work. It was due only to the analysis that she gained the vague knowledge in waking life that she herself had already changed a great deal.

(f) *The ability to tell lies in dreams*

A man can hide the truth from himself and from others in his dreams. He may then make mistakes or be acutely aware throughout the dream that he is lying. For example, a young woman dreamt that she was having an argument with her husband because he reproached her with coming home too late. She defended herself by telling him in great detail what she and her girl-friend had done the previous night, and that the film had been so interesting that they had felt they just had to go into a café to discuss it afterwards. This whole story was invented from beginning to end. In her dream she was fully conscious (which by no means corresponded to the reality of waking life) that she had not gone out with her girl-friend but that she had had a date with a boy-friend. In the dream she managed to lie so well that she even cried, and thus convinced her husband. Quite satisfied with the success of her deceit, she woke up and could still find a few of her crocodile tears on her cheeks.

(g) *Unconscious mistakes in dreams*

Apart from conscious lies man can also commit unconscious mistakes in the Freudian sense. Thus a man dreamt that he was spending his holidays on a farm, far from his home. Everything there was unusual. People and animals were of exceptional vitality. It was the dreamer's greatest delight simply to be allowed to be there. Then, however, the holidays were over, and he was in the train that was to carry him home. He was unhappy about returning. In his dream, corresponding to the reality of his waking world at the time, his relationship with his wife had become completely cool. At home the two married partners had been utterly bored with each other. As the train was approaching his home town the dreamer was overcome by irresistible fatigue and a feeling of tiredness. "All I need now," he said to himself in his dream, "is to fall asleep by mistake and to miss W———" (the railway station of his home-town).

After a while he discovered to his great annoyance that he had indeed fallen asleep in the train, for on opening his eyes (still in the dream) he found that the train was going through a completely strange part, probably well beyond his home-town. In the dream he was immediately aware of the great trouble it would be to find his way back home.

(*h*) *Artistic appreciation in dreams*

It is not only by way of intellectual reflection and by scientific and philosophical evaluation of objects that we can exist in our dreams. We can also exist as artistically appreciative and creative people. When, for instance, Ludwig Tieck became acquainted with Correggio's paintings he could not understand why people praised them so much and he tried very hard to understand them. Then he dreamt that he was in a gallery and that the master himself came close to him and spoke to him in the following words: "Aren't you a stupid man not to recognize what is excellent?" Thereupon he led him to one of his paintings and revealed its beauty to him. Tieck awoke and, full of these thoughts, he could hardly wait till the gallery opened. He immediately went up to one of Correggio's paintings which dazzled him with its brilliance. His eyes had opened and from that time on he was Correggio's greatest admirer.[172]

The composer Giuseppe Tartini said that his Devil Sonata was a weak reflection of a melody which he had heard Satan play in a dream.

(*i*) *Moral evaluation in dreams*

We usually think even more highly of man's moral decisions than of his intellectual and artistic achievements. Moral problems too are not at all alien to dreaming man. Thus a middle-aged woman had the following dream:

> "I have to guard seven gigantic carnivorous animals in a room: tigers and panthers. All of them have magnificent white teeth. At first a very large but young panther attacks me from behind and bites my legs as if jokingly. At the same time I have to concentrate on the largest tigers by looking them straight in

the eye in order to root them to the spot. I am not so much afraid of the animals themselves, but fear that I shall not be able to keep concentrating, that my will-power will weaken if I have to keep the animals in check the whole day long. I may not lower my gaze for one single second for then I should no longer be able to force my will upon them. I feel a great moral responsibility, for if I let the animals escape they will not only eat me up, but also the many visitors to the zoo who are standing outside."

This woman was a temperamental southern European whose instincts were in fact similar to those of a voracious animal. After her marriage she tried in every way to lead a more moral life and to become a good Swiss housewife. In her waking life, just as in her dreams, she was afraid of what would happen to her family if she gave free rein to her instincts. Furthermore she felt a true moral obligation to control herself for the sake of her family. Therefore, in waking as in dreaming, her existence consisted largely in morally defending herself from and banishing the bestial in her.

A psychotherapist once dreamt:

"I have just learnt that Stalin has given his troops marching orders for an invasion of Europe. At the same time this Stalin happens to be my patient, just lying in front of me on the analyst's couch. He does not look exactly like Stalin. Only his build is characteristic of Stalin. I just know that he is Stalin. Yet his face has, apart from Stalin's moustache, the unmistakable expression of the present Pope, and my patient's somewhat rasping voice reminds me only too well of a brutal teacher who had made my first school years so bitter and unbearable. As this dangerous Stalin is now lying before me, I suddenly realize that I have a unique chance of preventing the terrible suffering which an invasion of Europe would bring in its train; that I could prevent it all by simply throwing myself on the prostrate Stalin and stabbing him to death. I can quite clearly see a strong dagger in the bottom drawer of my desk. But my conscience is beginning to prick me. I ask myself whether it would be right for me to prevent a misfortune and a crime by becoming guilty of a crime myself, even if only the murder of a great criminal. This moral problem tortures me for some time. I am most strongly conscious of my tremendous responsibility and I suffer the sharpest qualms of conscience. I become so excited that I wake up in a sweat and with violent palpitations."

This dream meeting with Stalin has the character of a most vehement moral argument. The whole existence of the dreamer is completely concentrated in the relation that a dictator has to those oppressed. Because of this all the oppressors of his past are fused in the dream world into one figure. The Pope is a part of it because this dreamer in his youth was bitterly tormented by a pathologically sadistic priest. That is why until the time of this dream he did not wish to recognize any distinction between Catholicism and communist methods.

CHAPTER 15

The Relationship to the Divine in Dreams

DREAMS also offer the further possibility of living in relation to a Being whom we call God or gods. The more this religious relationship is destroyed in waking life, the more significant a role it plays in the dream life of modern man. Very frequently in our analytical practice we meet a sudden relationship with heaven and with the Divine in people who in waking life are utterly materialistic. This happens quite spontaneously and without a single word about religion on the part of the analyst.

Thus a first indication of a religious relationship is found in the dream of a woman of thirty-four years.

"I am at a garden party. I have moved away from the other guests and have turned my back on them. While the others are admiring some fireworks, I stand in front of a little pagoda in the park. Inside the pagoda there is a small pond. On the water there float two lotus leaves. A small bridge connects one leaf with the other. Next to the pond there is a clay figure of a kind of garden god. It has fallen down. To my horror I find that it is not the god who is supporting the little bridge, which is merely resting on the two floating leaves. I immediately realize that the whole garden, in which this party is taking place, is similarly floating on the water, while everybody is mistaken in thinking that the garden god is the protector of the party and the support of everything. I quickly imagine the panic should the guests notice that everything was floating on the water, and was supported merely by two weak and fragile leaves. It is for this reason that I quickly pick up the small clay figure before any of the guests can notice that it had fallen down."

In waking life this dreamer was a lady of "good society". Her whole life, when she did not happen to be rushing from one Grand Hotel to the next, was one of garden, cocktail and other parties. She was so intoxicated by her mad rush that she did not have a single minute to reflect on the meaning of her life, let alone on anything divine. The fact that such a shallow and superficial life did not agree with her real self was betrayed by severe and chronic intestinal complaints which had for years stubbornly resisted the treatment given by her physician. It was because of these complaints that she finally consulted a psychotherapist. Corresponding to her starved religious feelings, the divine element in her first "religious" dreams could only appear in the form of a fallen idol. Yet only half a year after the beginning of her psychotherapeutic treatment she is no longer completely absorbed in the fireworks of social intercourse. She has already separated herself from it and has turned her back on it, if only for a short while. Only because of this could she become aware of a pagoda at all: a place which recalled her to essential things. What she then discovered was terrifying.

She became aware of the fact that her existence had no real basis and that everything might collapse and sink at any moment. Not even the figure of clay, the idol to which her social circles had reduced the divine, could any longer offer support. It had fallen. Once again she deceived herself and the others, ran away from the fear that her life had no foundation, and covered up the truth. Quickly she re-erected the clay god so that nobody should notice anything, in order to avoid panic, and to enable her to return to her old ways of living. Half a year later the same patient had the following dream:

"I am in the very elegant Grand Hotel of a very fashionable spa. I am walking past the mineral springs. I can see the glasses of the guests arranged in numbered compartments on the wall, and I say to somebody that there is something reminiscent of funeral urns about these compartments. My companion does not want to hear anything about it. On the contrary he gets enthusiastic about the excellence of the springs and their architectural beauty. For my part, I find the springs and the park empty and very boring. On the other hand, I am enchanted by the sight of the sky. The snow-white clouds had so arranged themselves that they clearly looked like Greek temples and columns, almost like an entire city of temples. Fantastic in its beauty there appeared a relief hewn out of white marble and representing a hunting scene of Artemis. There were many foaming horses and barking dogs. I draw everybody's attention to this, and tell them that this is far more important than the mineral spring. Everybody is now admiring the sky."

In her dreams this woman has gone a good deal further than in her waking life. The world of Grand Hotels has ceased to interest her, and appears empty and boring. Her old attitude, still expressed in words of praise by her companion, is no longer her own. Indeed everything in the spa appears to be as funereal as the urn-like arrangement of the glasses. In fact, for her it had been a true cemetery in which she had buried all her human potentialities. But she is beginning to reach out towards heaven. Corresponding to her own sensual inclinations, it is not a heaven peopled by Christian figures. The latter, her education had taught her, were mere ascetics damning all earthly joys. It is the gods of the Greeks who originally appear to her. Not even these are real as yet, but merely a cloud formation. However, her discovery of the heavens is already more important to her than the goings-on on earth.

From another woman, well in her fifties, we have the following report:

"I dreamt that I was visited by a beautiful young steer. The steer came into my bed in order to sleep with me. I could distinctly feel his animal bones on my thighs. At the same time I knew that it was Zeus who was visiting me in the form of a young steer. As if to convince me that it was really the god who was with me in the form of this animal, his front and hind hooves suddenly turned into slim and strong human hands and feet, more beautiful than any I had ever seen. In the certain consciousness of divine proximity, I now sank into an infinite depth, no longer surrounded by any concrete objects. All outlines had become superfluous and would only have appeared as narrowing and restricting. It was a complete surrender, an infinite confidence of being safe in the divine Zeus. This was an experience far greater than even the most intense love relationship and the most satisfying orgasm with a man. Furthermore it took place on a much higher and supernatural level. It was the immediate experience of the proximity of God, the unification with God, indeed a truly numinous experience!"

So went the dream of a very healthy and "down to earth" woman whose life was largely devoted to the care of a large family. Her spiritual and artistic interests, extremely keen during her school years, had largely been forced into the background under the pressure of everyday work. In accordance with her scientific upbringing, her waking thought was strictly rational and logical. She had been almost completely closed to all religious experience. She even felt a definite inner barrier against Christian ideas of religion because her educators had represented Christ almost exclusively as the tortured sufferer. This masochistic piety, she said, had always been utterly repulsive to her.

In contrast to the black Alsatian in the dream of our cyclist, the animal of this dreamer did not deliver her into the bottomless pit of a world of fear. The steer presented her rather with a world of such vastness that heaven and earth, earthly animal and immortal god, became as one. It was a world of universal divine love transcending all space and time, the "realm beyond all forms".

A Christian dream was once dreamt by a business man who, though of Protestant family, had in his own waking life long been a marked and cynical atheist. His instincts were so strong that since his puberty he had been exclusively interested in women; not as human partners but merely as sexual objects. A daily "consumption" of two to three women had been his rule for years. If nevertheless he was very successful in business this was not due to his exertions, but rather to his excellent intelligence and his natural loquacity. In his forty-second year this man had suddenly become sexually impotent. Life then lost all its meaning for him. He became subject to the deepest depressions and had to call on a psychotherapist. In the sixth month of treatment he had the following dream:

"I enter a monastery built high above a river. In the valley below, I can see a power-station or factory, in which the workers are rushing about busily like ants. While talking to a high Catholic priest, I think of buying this monastery from him in order to turn it into a week-end villa. But I can see that it is far too high above the river. Finally the priest takes his leave of me, because he has to say mass in the church which stands still higher up the mountain. During the farewells the priest's face becomes thin and parched and then shrinks. All the more clearly can I now see his robes, which are glowing with indescribable beauty. As he leaves, the priest tells me that he will come back."

Before this man thought of coming for treatment his fate had beckoned to him with the unmistakable hint of his neurotic impotence. It had signified that he owed life something more than the animality of sexual behaviour, and told him that he had been blind to all that was "higher". In this dream, however, the higher regions appeared with great clarity. Although he is already high above the valley, above mere technological processes, he wants to return, to change the monastery into a week-end villa. For him a week-end villa meant sexual orgies. Yet he renounces this desire. The position of the monastery is no longer suitable. He has risen too high. Just as in the dream he has to forgo changing the monastery into a week-end villa, so in waking life he is no longer allowed to return from his monastic abstinence and enforced impotence to his old life of naked instinctuality. New possibilities of being have opened up to him. Into the dream world of this atheist there is suddenly admitted a high Catholic priest. With the appearance of this priest a door to the religious sphere is opened for the dreamer. True, in the dream he is left behind by the priest when the latter has to climb up to celebrate mass. But to his horror he can see in the fading of the physical face of the priest how transitory is the purely fleshly side of man's life and how quickly man's time on earth is up. At the same time the priest's glowing robes indicate the world of the highest spiritual possibilities. After this dream he could surrender to real love for the first time. He fell deeply in love with a young woman and while he loved her his impotence suddenly and completely went.

A dream of a similar kind was reported to me by a middle-aged woman who, before psycho-analytical treatment, could only fight her deep and dangerous depressions through compulsive mountaineering, and then merely with somewhat transitory success. From childhood on this woman had had all religious ideas destroyed by her father. He, in his own youth, had had religion forced upon him to such an extent while a boarder in a Protestant institution that, in protest, he had adopted a wholly materialistic and rational philosophy. He would not even let his daughter be confirmed. After the analysis had proceeded for quite some time, but without any mention of God, religion or heaven on the part of the analyst, this woman had the following dream:

"I am discussing tomorrow's mountain climb with Rezaniv, the well-known guide. I do not wish to go on the climb as I think that it is too strenuous for me. But the guide persuades me to go all the same. He says it is only a Dolomite tower and that it is certainly not going to be too difficult for me. I still hesitate. Suddenly the scene changes. I now find myself alone in a real tower. I am suddenly face to face with an unknown man with whom I fall in love and for whose embrace I long. He pulls me through a big oak door to a white marble terrace and wants to embrace me there. But the terrace has no railings and as it is full moon, I am afraid that my husband might see us. I certainly did not want to hurt him in this way, so I pull myself away against my will. I know that a high church dignitary lives on the top of the tower. I feel I must look for him. I climb up the winding staircase. On the first floor I find some clothing of this Prince of the Church. It must be a ceremonial robe, I think, for it is wonderfully embroidered in gold and silver. I climb further up and on the next floor I find other valuable church robes. Finally, I meet the old gentleman himself, wearing only a white loincloth, as I know it from pictures of Gandhi. From there on the dream becomes quite hazy. I believe that he wears some pointed headgear of gold, perhaps it is a bishop's or a Pope's tiara. Possibly he is walking on crutches between two boys. All I know for certain is that he approaches me and that he speaks to me. He fills me with great reverence. He tells me that I can only serve God by leaving everything behind. He adds that he has always been expecting me."

On the first stage of her ascent this dreamer is assailed by powerful feelings of erotic love. But she manages to withstand them. First of all the terrace has no railings. The dreamer knows the dangerous depths she might fall into if she surrenders to such temptation. Above all she renounces her erotic longing for the sake of her love for her husband. By overcoming *eros* in favour of *caritas* she has already climbed higher. On every one of the subsequent floors she steps over bits of ceremonial robes and, leaving more and more church clothes behind her, she finally meets the holy man himself. He is almost without covering, with only a remnant of Indo-Catholic attributes. Thus the church dignitary with his fragile figure in this dream, too, points to the impermanence of all physical existence lasting only, as it does, for the short span between youth and old age. All the more does his spiritual power affect the dreamer. From it she hears the call to unstinted religious service, a call which had long been waiting to be heard. Hitherto she had constantly kept it at bay, through earthly possessions and through the loud noise of social intercourse.

But why should a climb to the church tower have followed the planning of a climb of the Dolomite tower? Many similar transformations in dream scenes leave no doubt that the secular sport of mountaineering is merely a rehearsal for divine service. It is only because of our dreamer's atheistic attitude that for her religious service is exclusively conducted by secular mountain-guides. They merely help her physical body to overcome its downward pull. This is surely why mountaineering served her as a useful if transitory means of fighting her depressions. As soon as even the slightest perceptible approach to the divine through a spiritual attitude had been revealed to her mountaineering lost its compulsive character.

We know many dreams of similar structure; of people who had to buy aeroplanes and become keen aviators in order to oppose the downward pull of their depression. In his dream one such man flew directly into heaven and landed at St. Peter's feet. Peter would not let him in and sent him back to earth. Aeroplanes, he told the dreamer, were not a suitable means of transport in heavenly space. They belonged to the devil, since their wings had not sprung directly from their own hearts.

A woman of fifty years, who had once been healthy, vivacious and efficient, had, through the emptiness of thirty years of marriage with a completely heartless and purely materialistic industrial leader, fallen more and more into a deep and stultifying depression. At that time she repeatedly dreamt of travelling without plan or purpose through endless and unavoidable marshes and flooded areas covered by fog. She always thought that she would drown the very next moment. Such was her dream world. It was also the world which in waking life she could see behind the façade of the thousand and one objects and pleasures of everyday life. She herself said that these distracting everyday objects emerged only vaguely out of her own grey, marshy and foggy waking world, and that they were nothing but a vague lie. With this the patient merely wanted to say that in her dreams her real and undisguised world was revealed to her with greater purity and emphasis than would have been possible in waking life.

When in the course of long treatment she finally had the courage to come to herself, all her dreams changed. Now, for instance, she dreamt:

"I am walking along a narrow path in a dark and sombre forest. It has been a rainy day. All the leaves of the trees are dripping. There are many children with me, and on the trees we can see bees, glittering with all the colours of the rainbow. One by one they leave the trees and, fluttering like butterflies, they hover over us. The children want to catch them. At first I forbid them to do so because the bees might be dangerous. But they are good bees and accompany us like little spirits. Suddenly the path becomes steep. On the edge of the forest we can see a forsythia blossoming in golden colours. I part its branches. It covers a milestone on which I can see that a cross has been engraved. Below there is the inscription I.N.R.I. On the right we can suddenly see an Indian temple. I wake up and I can still hear myself say the words: 'This is where the architect found his design.'"

The mood of this woman is beginning to get better, and accordingly her dreams also reveal nature in a different mood. True, the forest still has a certain darkness and the rain has only just stopped. But young life is already surrounding her, and the rainbow-coloured little spirits, even if she dare not quite trust them yet, bring a colourful note into her world. Her elevated mood furthermore leads her to see a steeply ascending path. A golden forsythia illuminates her world with even more brightly glowing colours and helps her to the discovery of the Christian cross and of its prototype, the Indian temple.

In her new elation of spirit she has renewed access to the heavens. This sphere appears even brighter and warmer in one of her dreams a few weeks later.

"A soft mountain landscape in the evening at dusk. I can see a dark cross against the warm colours of the sky. One point of the cross is highly luminous. In astonishment I first approach the luminous spot and I can see that the cross is a crucifix. The nail at the foot of Christ is a gigantic diamond and it was from it that the radiation emanated."

How much she had become a victim of her fate is betrayed by the following dream. Her fate would not release her, in spite of all resistance to and limitations of secular forms of love, until divine love also was revealed in the light of her existence.

"I reach a mountain pass. In front of me, but with their backs to me, I can see a youth and a prostitute. I try to follow them because I have a compulsive urge to see the girl's face. Alas, I can never pass this woman to get a glimpse of her for even one moment.

It is a journey lasting a lifetime, and never ending. In time the girl changes into a Red Cross nurse. I have almost overtaken her when a frontier guard stops me and bars entry into the foreign land. He explains that only those who are marked may enter the Holy Land. I tell him that I must follow this girl at all costs since this is my fate. Thereupon the guard takes a knife and cuts a cross on my forehead. Now I can suddenly see her emerging from a large crowd in a church square. She is wearing one of those lovely blue cloaks reminiscent of women in Renaissance paintings. She enters the cathedral. I follow her. As I enter the church I am in absolute darkness and can only feel my way with great difficulty. Suddenly a warm and ethereally beautiful light breaks through the wonderful stained glass windows in the cathedral wall, illuminating the gigantic cathedral with all the colours of the rainbow. I have reached my goal and I awake in the happiness of peace."

In this dream the woman had concluded her life's journey. She had brought it to a good end and had fulfilled her purpose. Even more clearly than in the case of the mountain climber of the previous dream, did she have an immediate experience of divine love, after having passed both *eros* and *caritas* and everything secular. Her fortune or misfortune, her illness or health, now depended on whether she could repeat the fullness of her life as consistently in the waking state.[173]

The content of all these "religious dreams", and the manner in which they are reported by the dreamers, leave no doubt that they are experiences of an expressly numinous kind. The dreamer about Zeus had used these very words in order to describe adequately the unusual note of her experience. In the descriptions of the other dreamers, who were not familiar with this word "numinous", we heard expressions such as "I was deeply moved by the events" or "A holy shiver ran through me". There is not the slightest reason to deprive the content of these phenomena of the character of immediate data or to overlook it completely. If we grant it its full reality, each one of these experiences will appear as a real "numen", i.e. a real hint of the Divine. If we avoid arbitrary constructions and simply keep to the facts in the dreams, then in all their phenomena—in the Zeus-steer, the clay god of the garden party, the Artemis of the cloud formation, the colourful ceremonial cloak of the Catholic priest, the stone cross with the initials of Christ, the Indian temple, the saint resembling Gandhi and the crucifix with the diamond nail, the ethereally beautiful light of the cathedral and the angel mothers of a previous dream—we shall simply see them as such and not as anything else. For only then do we allow them to be what they really are: direct appearances of the Divine revealed in the light of the dreamer's existence.

In the very numinous character of such dreams many modern psychologists would find a special justification for reducing them to mental archetypes; or at least for seeing their causes and possibility of existence in such archetypes. It is said that the awe inspired by such dreams suggests that the underlying archetype is quite near; furthermore, the fact that such numinous dream phenomena had found similar expression in the most different people in the most different ages, and in all parts of the world, were additional reasons for assuming the presence of an archetype. Phenomenological interpretation must defend itself with all its might against such assertions. For, quite apart from the reasons already adduced against these arguments (*see* page 53), we can also see that the concordance in these divine manifestations, and their independence of place, time and race, insofar as these are exactly verifiable at all, radiate from the possibilities of relationships common to all men. Similarly searchlights of a particular colour directed at something will always reveal this thing, but how it is seen will depend on the particular intensity of the light and the brightness of the colour. We compared this with the relationship of a light to that which it illuminates, since in the existence of dreaming man, too, the essence of things is revealed according to his radiance.

In any event the numinous phenomena themselves neither justify nor demand ideas like archetypes as motive power or as originators. These dreams are rather an admonition to modern man to stop his constant attempts at explaining the mysterious background of all existing things in terms of familiar ideas borrowed from the world of technology, and instead to respect it in all its mystery and inexplicability. If we do so, not only does the notion of archetype become superfluous in these dreams but, over and above this, we shall see what havoc is wrought by the modern psychological attempt to look at all phenomena as the effects or signs of an underlying entity, and then to explain and derive them causally from this entity. For if we do not listen to what the dreams themselves have to tell us, we debar ourselves from every possibility of even suspecting their true nature.

CHAPTER 16

Experience of Dreams within Dreams

(a) Dreaming of existing as a dreamer
WHILE we are dreaming, we can know that we are dreaming. We can also dream within a dream and relate the dreams we have dreamt within a dream. We may even give an interpretation of the dreams we have just dreamt in terms of depth-psychology. Not infrequently we confirm the fact of dreaming in the dream, for instance by the reassuring remark, "Thank goodness, it is only a dream!" I should like to cite the example of a medical student who jotted down the following report:

"I had worked for my examinations throughout the day. Dead tired I went to bed at ten o'clock, but my head was so full of this swotting, that in spite of being terribly tired I could not fall asleep for a long time. When I finally did fall asleep I continued to worry about penicillin, on which I had read up some pages just before going to bed. I dreamt that I was sitting in a clinical laboratory and that I was growing a large culture of fungi from which I was to extract the penicillin. Throughout a whole dream day I had had to rush about the laboratory and I had become terribly tired. I was grateful when evening drew near. Now I was at home, and so exhausted that I dropped into my bed and fell asleep with all my clothes on. But my dream-sleep was disturbed from the very beginning of this well-deserved night's rest by an unpleasant dream: The fungi had followed me from the laboratory, had taken root in my blankets, were growing into giant mushrooms and were threatening to stifle me. I could hardly breathe. I said to myself that it was quite useless to stay in bed and, quickly throwing back the blankets covered with fungi, I jumped out of bed and returned to the laboratory.

My chief received me very crossly. 'Get the devil out of here,' he said, 'and see that you get to bed. Blind ambition can only do harm!' I was so frightened by this unexpected reproof that I really woke up. I could see from my watch that only two hours had passed since I fell asleep, while in the dream I had worked throughout the whole day and deep into the night."

We can see that this man had the most varied relationships to the same external thing. Immediately before going to bed he is concerned with his reading about the theory of penicillin. He is thinking about the fungi. In the dream which follows he is absorbed in the practical handling of penicillin and in carrying out the corresponding laboratory work. Soon, however, in the dream within the dream, the role is reversed and it is now the penicillin that stifles him and overpowers him. To rational and logical thought these events seem to get increasingly absurd as they proceed from reading during waking life, to the behaviour of the dreamer in the ordinary dream, then to the event of the dream within the dream, and then on to the student being overpowered by the moulds. In reality, however, it is just this apparently ridiculous absurdity of the dream which demonstrates the dreamer's disposition most clearly. For in being overpowered by the penicillin mould, we can see his real and unhealthy surrender to the objects of his studies, whether the mere reading of his scientific books, or the mad rushing about in the dream itself, where it is still experienced as an apparently free decision and capacity for independent action. Nevertheless, in the world of the dreamer there have remained some remnants of intelligent insight. Otherwise he would not have been able to hear the reproof of his chief warning him to behave reasonably.

A young woman used a dream, which she remembered as a dream within a dream, as a diagnostic proof. At the same time in the dream memory, she obtained a first inkling of her true relationship with the person of whom she had dreamt. The dream was as follows:

"I am on the Jungfraujoch. My father returns from a hunt and says that he is giddy. His face is quite blue. The animals, and especially the cows, get into a panic. I am afraid and I tell him that it is imperative to go down this very night because I fear for his heart. My father laughs at my anxiety and boasts that there is nothing wrong with his heart. I tell him quite frankly that I think his condition is very serious. As proof of the truth of what I say I tell him of a dream that I had dreamt the previous night, which I could remember very clearly in my dream. In this dream, remembered in my dream, my father had been my lover but he had been marked by death and, just as now, the animals had noticed it and had got into a panic about it."

I have to add that this woman could only remember in her dream that she had had such a dream during the previous night. She was not aware of it the day before or the day after.

As her subsequent psychoanalysis repeatedly confirmed, the only true human love relationship that this woman had been capable of until the time of this dream had been directed at her father, notwithstanding the fact that he had died ten years previously. This daughter-father love relationship was of such an exclusiveness and intensity that it had prevented her from having any other, more tenable, relationships. True, she had only allowed this "incestuous fixation" to exist in the spiritual, spinster-like attitude of abstract thought about her father. At this giddy height and icy distance even this love relationship threatened to go on the rocks. It was high time that she made room for accepting deeper, warmer and more vital attitudes. She lived exclusively in her ties with her father. For this reason the threatened loss shook her to the very core, to the vital basis of her life. This showed itself clearly enough in the panic of the cows.

(b) *The analysis of dreams within dreams*

Another woman of approximately the same age told of her dream within a dream which led to so-called hypermnesia:

"In my dream I am walking with a companion through the empty streets of Berlin, and I tell him that last night I dreamt that I was sweeping away the autumn leaves in a street in front of a block of flats where I had lived as a child. I entered the flat itself to make sure that it was in fact the block in which I had previously lived. So much for my recounting the dream in the dream. Then I continue down the street with my companion and I meet our old charwoman, Miss S., who had in fact worked for us at the time when we were living in these flats. I greet her with great joy and I draw my companion's attention to the odd coincidence between my dream and the meeting with our old charwoman whose name I should normally not have been able to remember at any price. Still dreaming I realize, after my meeting with the charwoman, that I had dreamt of the house and of my sweeping and had remembered her name only because all those things belonged to the world of cleaning and because I myself am so immersed in the analytic cleansing of my soul."

(c) The magical dream world

In the penicillin dream an external thing attained an importance which things in the waking life of present-day adult, cultured people rarely do. In dreams, things may become so overpowering that their power seems like that of a magical spell. A thirty-two-year-old artist dreams that she is being drawn irresistibly towards a man hiding in a strange country. After a long journey she reaches a door on which there is written in large letters: "Beware! Danger! High Tension! Mana Charge!" The man's attraction is, however, so irresistibly great that she ignores the warning and enters. Now the man stands before her. She knows immediately that he is no ordinary mortal. She cannot make up her mind whether he is an evil magician or a divine being. He casts a yellow light that might be a kind of aura. His face is that of an evil dwarf. His hands, too, have something claw-like about them. The dreamer thinks, "He must be a devil, for everything has a sulphurous smell." Nevertheless, she lets him carry her away. A thought quickly enters her mind, "If my mother knew of this she would call me a slut." Soon she and her uncanny companion enter a dark ravine. The dream continues:

> "Because of the weak, pale and iridescent moonlight I can recognize only some of the outlines. I can dimly see that on the floor masses of slimy toads are crawling about with dogs' faces. Horrible creatures with large bats' wings hover in the air. They constantly cuff me and pinch my arms and legs. Even more horrible is the fact that the trees and stones are moving as well. Their forms change as if they are made of gelatine; they flow into each other and reach out towards me as if wanting to suck me in. In doing so they whisper to me incomprehensible magic words. I feel that the mana forces of which the doorplate had warned me are at work not only in the man who had carried me away but even in the stones. The magic spell emanating from all these things forces me to throw myself on the ground. I feel myself turning into a snake and have difficulty in moving without arms and legs. The magician skips behind me, giggling and gloating at the fact that I had become a helpless victim of the forces of his domain. He then starts spitting fire at me from his horrible mouth. Soon I am burning brightly; I have been turned into a stake. This is the most terrible thing of all because

now I am completely defenceless. The entire hellish brood now starts yelling gleefully. I can feel it in the very marrow of my bones and am frightened out of my sleep."

Our dreamer thus found herself in a world not normally encountered except in the fairy stories of children and so-called primitive people. She had fallen victim to a magical way of living. Magical life, however, is one in which we perceive the overpowering force of things and our own helpless surrender to them. In this form of being, in this surrender to the overpowering force of things, we can also conceive of ourselves in terms of objects only. It is only thus that we may experience such things as a mana substance or a mana force, and that our dreamer felt compelled by the mana force to throw herself at the magician like a wicked slut. In other words she was not in control of her natural sensual forces, as she mistakenly believed during waking life, but she was impotently delivered up to animalistic behaviour.

Dream figures capable of affecting the dreamer magically were hitherto considered dream phenomena of a numinous kind, as the particular and direct manifestations of an archetype. Thus the magician of this dream would no doubt be considered by many as the corporeal manifestation of the magician archetype. He would even be cited as empirical proof of the reality of such an archetype. In fact, however, the male cannot appear to our dreamer in any other form than that of a demoniacal magician, since her sensual relationship corresponds to that of a child helplessly delivered to some superior force. So the magical character of her meeting with him is not due to the effect on her of an archetypal and independent demoniacal being, but to her special existential structure in the light of which all natural sensuality must appear as a magical and demoniacal force in her dream. This magical dream thus gives us yet another hint about the true nature of the idea of the archetype (*see* page 117).

The mode of this mana-like magic and mythical life, this being a victim to things, as shown by the above dream, is the very opposite of the mode of existence of the dreamer of our "strange dream of an urn". The latter could, of her own free will, force herself out of her impending bad mood.

(*d*) *Being a thing in the dream*

The worst thing that happened to our dreamer of the magical dream was her transformation into a snake and above all into a thing, a burning stake. As such a thing she felt herself to be a particularly helpless victim of external forces. As a mere thing she felt deprived of any possibility of intervening in the course of events. Our dreamer was no more capable than an inert stake when it came to taking her fate into her own hands, and preventing herself being burned up and consumed in the fire of her own instinctuality. This experience cannot be brushed aside as that of an inherently wicked person, and thus of no concern to "normal" people, for this woman was completely curable by psychotherapy. Furthermore it is not at all uncommon for a dreamer herself to become a thing or to begin to experience herself as such from the very start.

Thus, one of our patients once dreamt that she was a duster on the floor, and was having great difficulty in crawling over the doorstep. Another woman of thirty years experienced herself as a toy balloon ascending to the ceiling and hovering there. The same patient, in another dream, dreamt that a hangman cut off her arms and legs and then cut the rest of her body into strips to make a wickerwork basket for gathering offal. The dreamer asked this horrible man if he ever prayed. He answered cynically, "No, only sometimes in the summer." A happy bride dreamt of herself as a birch gently quivering in a spring breeze. Finally, a young married woman dreamt:

> "I saw a dark brown fertile field in which a plough was cutting large furrows. Suddenly I myself became the field and the sharp steel plough went easily through the length of my body and cut me into two halves. Although it hurt, it was indescribably beautiful. I experienced myself as the ploughed-up field, and the furrow as my own flesh, but it was not bleeding."

But can we, in fact, in the case of these dreams, speak of dreamers turning into things? Certainly not if we consider things merely as substances with given properties. Not even if those things which the dreamers feel themselves to be are regarded in their full historical context as capable of giving character to their world. They would still be "dead", while the things which our dreamers themselves have become are things which *ex-ist*, which stand in direct relationship to their environment.

A close scrutiny of our dreamers brought the unanimous report that in being these things, they were nevertheless still human, and living in a very human way. They could look at the things they happened to be, just as during waking life we can contemplate our own body.

So, for instance, in the example of the dream about the duster, the dreamer's whole horror and despair at this event was due to the feeling "that her entire body had been misshapen into an ugly thing". But it was only the corporeal reality of these dreamers which had assumed the forms of things. The dreamer's life was merely corporealized more palpably and intensely. Psychosomatic medicine analogously shows that if a man is constantly under pressure this will eventually express itself somatically in high blood pressure. The dream things, however, are always the whole body of the dreamer. For this reason they are not a mere "symbol" of something nor yet the partial embodiment of some possible attitude of a particular person. Since the thing concerned is the dreamer's entire body, he lives his whole being in this way.

In the burning stake, a person was embodied whose whole being was in actual fact given over to scorching fires of sensual passion. The duster, on the other hand, embodied a dream life that was in fact completely prostrate because of a deep depression and in which progress was only possible with the greatest effort. Again, the toy balloon ascending to the ceiling embodied a woman who lived exclusively in very childish, airy-fairy and playful attitudes to the things and people of her world. The reverse side of this escape from maturity was experienced in the dream in which the dreamer was being woven into a wicker basket for offal. For, as so often happens to people who float on air without substance or foundation, this woman, time after time, was actually used by all and sundry as a rubbish heap, on to which people used to throw the dirt of their most primitive instincts. According to this special experience of being mistreated, her dream body turned into the rubbish-bin of the dream. In waking life she usually attributed her misfortunes to deliberate persecution by a horrible and cynical fate. In her dream, however, she was shown her own misguided attitudes by the blaspheming hangman. Again, a bridal existence, full of virginal expectations and yet anxiously looking into the future as the bride feels the awful awakening and quickening of life, could hardly have found a more characteristic bodily form than that of a birch quivering in a spring breeze. Finally, the young woman who saw her body as a field through which a plough was cutting a furrow had, a few days previously and for the first time, unreservedly surrendered to the love of a man. She experienced this event itself as a "natural event". She had just become pregnant, without being aware of it at the time of that dream. These two events had so intensely attuned her whole existence, that it seemed to overflow her human body, and corresponded to Mother Earth herself, to a field ripe for sowing.

Freud would have considered the furrow and the plough of this dream as symbols and symbolic disguises of the female and male genitalia. He would no doubt have reduced the dream to much too low a level. The injustice which such an interpretation would perpetrate on the dreams emerges clearly enough from the fact that our dreamer was by no means a prude. In many previous dreams she had found no need for the "symbolic distortion" of genitals. She had often enough dreamt of "very natural" sexual experiences. This occurred while she had known merely the physical stimulation of the sexual act and not as yet love in all its richness. However, once she had experienced this love, the openness and fertility of her whole being became embodied in a freshly ploughed field, the full essence of which corresponded most completely to her new attitude towards heaven and earth.

CHAPTER 18

The Possibilities of "Extra-sensory" Relationships in Dreams

ALL the dream phenomena that we have so far been able to interpret lead us to the certain conviction that we can exist in our dreams. In dreams, too, we are always involved with the things, animals, plants and people of our dream world, involved in all the different forms of behaviour towards them that make up our waking existence. Is it not possible that in our dreams we see the world even more clearly than in the waking state? Since ancient times people have believed that there are diagnostic, telepathic and prophetic dreams in which the dreamer can discover more than he can in waking life. There is no reason why we should not examine these rumours of extra-sensory dreams, which even strict science has not been able to silence.

(a) "Diagnostic" or "Endoscopic" dreams

It is held that the so-called diagnostic dreams warn the dreamer directly, or under the cloak of a symbolic guise, of the beginning of an illness which had either escaped his waking perception, or which he could not possibly have suspected at the time. The ancients attached far more importance to this aspect of the dream than do modern doctors. Hippocrates, Artemidorus and their Roman successor Galen drew our attention to them repeatedly and with emphasis. Arnald of Villanova, a doctor in the Middle Ages, even compared diagnostic dreams to lenses. Like magnifying glasses, he said, these dreams could perceive the first symptoms of physical diseases and report them to the dream consciousness long before the waking mind could notice that anything was amiss. He cited the example of a patient who dreamt on two successive occasions that his ear was being beaten with a stone. Shortly afterwards the man contracted a serious inflammation of the ear on the side on which he had been beaten in the dream.

One of our own patients rang up her doctor on two successive nights, simply because she had had a recurrent dream that made her terribly anxious. Every time she was frightened out of her sleep by this dream, only to start dreaming it again as soon as she had fallen asleep. This made her so nervous that she could not stand it any longer. In these dreams a Balinese demon of disease would appear to her and force her to sit on an overheated central-heating pipe. She experienced an insupportable burning pain between her legs. It was this pain which always woke her. However, after waking she no longer felt the slightest bit of pain. On the third night she once more began with the same stereotyped dream. Again the pain woke her at about three o'clock in the morning. On this occasion, however, the pain persisted after waking. At the same time she was suffering from ague. The doctor could now diagnose acute cystitis.

The overworked young doctor had been so cross at having his sleep disturbed because of such stupid dreams that he had omitted to test the patient's urine. It would appear as if this dream had occurred for the express purpose of drawing the attention of both patient and doctor to the beginning of the cystitis. Could this disease be better "symbolized" than by the picture of an overheated pipe? And yet, if this dream in fact had a purpose and especially a diagnostic one, why did it have to be so obscure as to elude both patient and doctor, and thus fail in its goal? Why did it oppose a clear explanation of the dreamer's true physical condition and not allow her to dream directly and undisguisedly of cystitis? Here there could not have been any moral or narcissitic motive for displacement to cause distortion. The patient dreamt about the central-heating pipe and the demon, and not directly about her physical symptoms. It is a purely hypothetical assumption to describe such phenomena as diagnostic dreams, and to suppose that they show the purposive qualities of a special human diagnostic faculty. By merely speaking of a diagnostic dream we have already prejudged the dream content itself, and reduced it to an isolated symptom of an equally hypothetical physical state of the dreamer. It is an explanation read into the dream phenomenon from the waking state. In reality such a relationship of dream content to a physical state does not exist. The fact that the dreamer felt ill is by no means an isolated physical symptom.

Thus, in fact, the dreamer's whole essence was tuned to being hot. Out of such a disposition of the whole existence the corresponding things reveal themselves. Above all, those things which we ordinarily understand in being hot can then make their appearance: among them the central heating which has an important place in our modern world. Man always finds it much more natural to experience and understand his own state from external things and from his relationship to them, than as an isolated bodily state. Our dreamer clearly understood from the Balinese demon of disease that it was not an ordinary feeling of heat, but rather that her whole existence was in the throes of disease. We cannot speak of a diagnostic dream symbol without doing violence to the dream phenomenon itself.

So-called diagnostic dreams may occur, not only before the onset of physical diseases, but also before that of psychological disorders. The oldest example is probably the experience of Nebuchadnezzar. His dream took place in the sixth century before Christ. It is given to us in Daniel, Chapter iv. When the Babylonian king was still at the height of his power, when he was "at rest in mine house and flourishing in my palace", he felt compelled to let Daniel interpret the following dream:

"I saw and behold a tree in the midst of the earth, and the height thereof was great. The tree grew, and was strong, and the height thereof reached unto heaven, and the sight thereof to the end of all the earth: the leaves thereof were fair, and the fruit thereof much, and in it was meat for all: the beasts of the field had shadow under it, and the fowls of the heaven dwelt in the boughs thereof, and all flesh was fed of it. I saw in the visions of my head upon my bed, and, behold, a watcher and an holy one came down from heaven. He cried aloud and said thus: Hew down this tree and cut off his branches, shake off his leaves and scatter his fruit: let the beasts get away from under it and the fowls from his branches. Nevertheless leave the stump of his roots in the earth, even with a band of iron and brass, in the tender grass of the field; and let it be wet with the dew of heaven, and let his portion be with the beasts in the grass of the earth: Let his heart be changed from man's, and let a beast's heart be given unto him; and let seven times pass over him."

The king was a victim to the things of his world; his existence can therefore only be understood from what happens to them, in that they can be interpreted as predicting the disease soon to overtake him. This is how Daniel understood the dream. But because Nebuchadnezzar did not heed Daniel's warnings, the word was fulfilled twelve months afterwards. The Bible says "he was driven from men and did eat grass as an ox and his body was wet with the dew of heaven till his hairs were grown like eagle's feathers and his nails like birds' claws".

Dreams no less clairvoyant are reported by the mentally ill of our time; dreams in which the threat to existence occurred when the sick person did not even suspect the tragedy about to overtake him in waking life. From a collection of many hundreds of such dreams, belonging to people who have since become psychotic, and all dreamt before the psychosis had appeared, we should like to mention two examples. A woman of hardly thirty years dreamt, at a time when she still felt completely healthy, that she was a fire in the stables. Around her, the fire, an ever larger crust of lava was forming. Half from the outside and half from inside her own body she could see how the fire was slowly becoming choked by this crust. Suddenly she was entirely outside this fire and, as if possessed, she beat the fire with a club to break the crust and to let some air in. But the dreamer soon got tired and slowly she (the fire) became extinguished. Four days after this dream she began to suffer from acute schizophrenia. In the details of the dream the dreamer had exactly predicted the special course of her psychosis. She became rigid at first and, in effect, encysted. Six weeks afterwards she defended herself once more with all her might against the choking of her life's fire, until finally she became completely extinguished both spiritually and mentally. Now, for some years, she has been like a burnt-out crater.

Another patient, a girl of twenty-five years, dreamt that she had cooked dinner for her family of five. She had just served it and she now called her parents and her brothers and sisters to dinner. Nobody replied. Only her voice returned as if it were an echo from a deep cave. She found the sudden emptiness of the house uncanny. She rushed upstairs to look for her family. In the first bedroom she could see her two sisters sitting on two beds. In spite of her impatient calls they remained in an unnaturally rigid position and did not even answer her. She went up to her sisters and wanted to shake them. Suddenly she noticed that they were stone statues. She escaped in horror and rushed into her mother's room. Her mother too had turned into stone and was sitting inertly in her armchair staring into the air with glazed eyes. The dreamer escaped into the room of her father. He stood in the middle of it. In her despair she rushed up to him and, desiring his protection, she threw her arms round his neck. But he too was made of stone and, to her utter horror, he turned into sand when she embraced him. She awoke in absolute terror, and was so stunned by the dream experience that she could not move for some minutes. This same horrible dream was dreamt by the patient on four successive occasions within a few days. At that time she was apparently the picture of mental and physical health. Her parents used to call her the sunshine of the whole family. Ten days after the fourth repetition of the dream, the patient was taken ill with an acute form of schizophrenia displaying severe catatonic symptoms. She fell into a state which was remarkably similar to the physical petrification of her family that she had dreamt about. She was now overpowered in waking life by behaviour patterns that in her dreams she had merely observed in other persons.

In the two following dreams of another patient, the course of her whole life was observed in so pregnant a manner that they became indispensable for the extremely difficult diagnosis of her disease. The first dream began with a very harmonious and genial mood in the music-room of her parents' house in which she had spent the early years of her life.

"I sat at the piano with my brother. He was playing and I was turning the pages. Suddenly I heard heavy steps on the staircase leading from the bedrooms to the lower floor. I was frightened because I thought that I had closed the back door. My brother went up the stairs to see who the intruder might be. From the piano I could look into another dark room on the same floor. I suddenly noticed a dark wild man, hairy and gorilla-like. The whites of his eyes were flashing out of the darkness. He stood quite still and in fact did not seem to frighten me but seemed to be possessed of a natural goodness. I thought that it must have been something else that frightened me. I therefore went up to the other floor myself. I could see that a kind of skeleton was moving with a sort of clattering noise. It became more and more inhuman and finally turned into a broomstick with a rather large and oval white disc. I knew at once that it was this that had terrified me. What was horrible was the fact that it was so inhuman and shapeless, that it was flat and had no face at all. In panic I fell down the staircase and into the void. Somewhere I was caught by Mr. S. He carried me away in his arms and all my panic was suddenly gone."

At the start of this dream the dreamer could feel the harmonious world of her childhood attuned to her loving closeness to her family. She had always been extremely fond of her brother. Then something terrible happened, something which shocked her out of her harmonious self. She made sure that it was not the wild "gorilla" which frightened her. Only hysterics are frightened to death by animals. It was the skeleton that terrified her in her highest sphere, in her spirituality. And the real horror was that this human being had become a mere spiritless ghostly monster of wood and cardboard. About her there was nothing but a bottomless void, into which she was bound to fall without hope of rescue. Her whole world had become this empty void. It was not a mere "expression" of self-disintegration any more than a psychotic's experience of the destruction of the world could be described in this way. Binswanger and Szilasi subjectively misrepresent the essence of human existence as a reflection of the external world.[174] Indeed, from the very start, existence is rather the "ecstatic" relationship, a true "being" with the things of the world, a constant revelation, and a continual opening of doors. Therefore, the destruction of the whole world so often experienced by psychotics, whether dreaming or waking, does not merely "express" their own disintegration but is rather an interference with their own relationships with the world. It is an immediate cessation, that is, of their being in and of the world around them; that is of their existing any longer as human beings.

But our dreamer's fall into the absolute void, her inability to continue existing, was halted for a little while. She fell into the arms of a friend and all her fears were gone immediately. Shortly afterwards the patient went into a decline in her waking life. She became cold, psychotically detached, and devoid of desire, like an automaton. She said that her world was only a hazy picture. Suddenly, however, she was revived by her deluded love for her dream acquaintance, was happy for a short while, and completely free from anxiety. A second dream, half a year later, when she had been forced to realize that her love had been "unreal", heralded a new death. Before falling into a deep apathy she dreamt:

> "I am in a classical Roman or Greek landscape. With some students from a university I climb down a long staircase winding between the pillars, arches, and gardens of an ancient and ruined city. They tell me that the famous Stendhal is there and that he is signing autographs. 'That's impossible,' I say, 'the French writer Stendhal lived in the nineteenth century.' 'No, no,' they say, 'it is quite true.' We come to a sort of booth reminiscent of a fair, in which an elderly and very ugly but interesting man signs copies

of his work '*Le Rouge et le Noir*', as they are handed to him. I don't happen to have his book with me but I tell Stendhal that I read it a long time ago. Stendhal replies tactfully, '*Ne vous dérangez pas. J'ai du papier.*' He draws something on a piece of paper and signs it. I am very proud of the fact that he has given me a sketch and not just his autograph, as he did to the others. He seemed to prefer me. On the paper he had drawn a face obviously meant to be my likeness. In place of my mouth he had written my first name in block letters. Scrawled tightly under the drawing I can see the name 'Stendhal'. Then we continue descending the staircase. We come to a very difficult spot. A deep ravine is spanned by a small bridge in bad repair, leading into a garden. A very pleasant, young, silky and jet-black cat is moving about. It has strange paws. Instead of claws it has leaves like daisies turned inside out, but black. On my left side there is a very strange flower-bed. In this bed there are still more black cats. Their entire bodies are leaf-like as well as their paws. They no longer move about, are partly grown together, and hardly look like cats any more. They have already begun to be part of the plant kingdom. Next to the path there are more cats that have turned into white clay or chalk figures. Near by there is a scientific institute for the investigation of this transformation of animals into plants, and from these into inorganic matter. A laboratory assistant shows me an inorganic structure formed out of a cat plant. It looks like a shell necklace."

This dream shows us that our dreamer only exists "with her head". It is for this reason that the situation is hallmarked by students coming out of a university. The town through which she goes is no longer a living community of contemporary men. The ability to co-exist with others has become so lost that she can only wander through the ruins of a time long forgotten, and she finds herself in a decaying world. In particular, she can no longer express her love towards others directly. She can no longer be in love with all her heart. Only indirectly, through Stendhal's book about love, is she receptive to this experience. But even the book is gone. She has left it at home, has read it a very long time ago, and the poet himself actually belongs to a century long past. She has further shut herself off from direct love by having turned it into a mere collection of autographs. To top it all, Stendhal, the poet of love, distorts her mouth in his drawing and turns it into a series of dead block letters on which the patient can read her own name. Such a mouth is naturally closed to all direct communication of love. In this dream, however, unlike her previous one, she no longer falls into a bottomless pit. A fragile bridge carries her over it. But it is a little bridge which only leads into the world of pure scientific knowledge and to laboratory-like observations. With this attitude, which is her only possible one, she notices how the forms of life become more and more regressive, turning from cats into plants and then into mere calcifications and mussel-shells. She is so much involved in this observation of the retrograde process of "the living being" that in her waking life, too, she is only capable of a mere vegetative existence until, finally, all life disappears from her world. When during waking life her apathy had reached rock-bottom she could in fact only exist in this calcified or shell-like manner. Through the eyes of the laboratory assistants in the dream, her reason took note of this complete withering of her potentialities of living.

People suffering from organic psychoses can sense threats to their existence in dreams, long before they or the people of their waking world know anything about it, in the same way as depressives and schizophrenics. We obtain such dreams particularly from people who started suffering from progressive paralysis at a time when their waking consciousness was still deceiving them with feelings of euphoria, or megalomanic ideas of particularly good health. Such a man for instance, gaily reported the following dream:

> "I was sick. Something was wrong with my left foot. It began to fester. I heard somebody say: 'It is doubtful whether this man will ever get better. He will soon have to die. The festering has already gone into his brain.'"

In his dream this man was very much more clear-sighted than in waking life, for in it he became clearly aware of his fatal disease whereas in waking life he was subject to megalomanic ideas, completely unrelated to his past or future. Nevertheless, this sick foot with its festering sore must not be misinterpreted as a diagnostic and symbolic representation or disguise of the terrible paralytic processes of his illness. To start with, progressive paralysis is considered an isolated brain process only in reductive and so-called objective scientific thought. In reality the entire existence of a paralysed person is threatened. Just as our sufferer from cystitis dreamt of a demon of disease and a central-heating pipe, so our paralytic dreamer perceived a festering sore on his foot because he too naturally did not regard his own condition as an isolated state. Nor did he look for a sickness of the mind but experienced himself rather as a relationship to a thing, a peripheral part of his body. Corresponding to his disease which made all progress in life impossible, his dream had to be of just that part of the body which serves "progress".

Finally those dreams must be included amongst the so-called diagnostic ones which not only announce suffering but even the impending death of the dreamer. Many examples can be found in ancient and in recent history. The actor Champmeslé, for instance, suddenly died on the 22nd August, 1701. Two days before his death he met his late mother and his late wife in a dream. The latter beckoned him to follow her. This dream made an extremely vivid impression upon Champmeslé. He related it to his friends. All of them tried in vain to make him forget it. On the following day he appeared as Ulysses in *Iphigenia*. During the interval he walked up and down the foyer and sang continuously, *"Adieu, Panier, vendanges sont faites"*. On Monday, the following day, he went to church and gave the sacristan thirty sous with the request that he say mass for his dead mother and his dead wife. The sacristan wanted to return ten sous to him but Champmeslé told him, "The third mass is meant for me, and I shall be able to hear it myself." After mass Champmeslé met some comrades on the road, chatted with them for a little while, and invited them for lunch. In the middle of the conversation he suddenly fell down dead.[175]

Those so-called diagnostic dreams which are dreamt a few days before the manifest beginning of a disease, or even after its actual inception, are not difficult to understand. We have shown that on many occasions human existence in the dream has a much more concentrated mood than among the distractions of waking life. From this it follows that these dreams must have a greater perceptiveness of the beginning of an illness. Schizophrenics, however, present us with more difficult problems, since from early childhood on, i.e. ten, twenty or even more years before their mental collapse in waking life, some of them have had recurrent dreams of this catastrophic end to their human existence. Amongst all the dreams that have come to our notice, wherever there was the required time for observation, we have never yet heard of any dreams of this very particular sort which were not at some time or another followed by a psychotic disturbance in the waking life of the dreamer. These childhood dreams are distinguished by the fact that they end absolutely hopelessly in catastrophe and inevitable despair. But it is never only the dreamer himself who dies in these dreams. Indeed, many healthy people can experience their own death in their dreams. Sometimes the dying is very easy and sometimes it is associated with the greatest anxiety. Neither the one nor the other kind of dream-death is a fatal indication. From the person of the dream, who happens to be the "ego" of the dreamer at the time, he can only learn of the current structure of his own existence and the way in which he lives it. For this reason people so often dream of death when a new process of maturing is taking place in them. Only when the old form breaks up can the dreamer be re-formed into newer or more mature structures, into new human behaviour patterns. However, in those ominous childhood dreams which we are here discussing it is never the dreamer alone who dies. The dreamer himself often does not die at all. His whole dream world is annihilated.

For instance, one of my patients, who at the age of thirty-two had become a schizophrenic, had twenty-six years previously dreamt that she saw a sphere lying in a plate on a huge round table. As the dreamer went a little way round the table, she could see that the sphere was a death's head grinning at her. Immediately afterwards, table, death's head and dreamer fused into one and dissolved into an indefinite void. This dream was repeated once or twice yearly, and only with the beginning of manifest psychosis did it finally come to an end. The patient told me that she had known from the very start that these dreams foretold her madness. Thus twenty-six years before the death of her mind in waking life, twenty-six years before her mental death, she had learnt of her future state from this death's head, and had become aware that the void of the dream signified the final loss of her existence and of her ecstatic relationships with the things of the world.

Another patient had a dream at the age of eight which from then on she called "The Dream of the Dying Woman at the Bottom of the Sea". She dreamt it altogether seven times, the last time hardly a month before the beginning of her psychosis; she became schizophrenic at the age of twenty-eight. When it first occurred she recounted it to her mother, who at once recorded it in her diary. Her record agrees word for word with the last report of the dream which the patient gave to me. In the dream the patient observed, from a distance, how the body of a grown-up woman fell into the sea. She could very clearly see her blonde hair, parted in the middle and combed backwards. The woman sank quickly to the bottom of the sea and the dreamer could see her lying there without any movement. She was still breathing, and bubbles of air were rising out of her mouth in rhythmical intervals. Then the rhythm of her breathing slowed down, and fewer and fewer bubbles came out of her mouth. Now she was dead. Immediately the sea-weeds on the sea-bottom decayed and disintegrated within a very large radius around the corpse. The corpse sank into a muddy and amorphous slime.

Even when she first had this dream, she had noticed that the age of the female was the age of her mother. At that time her mother was exactly twenty-nine years old, i.e. only one year older than the dreamer at the time of her illness. The hair style of the female figure was exactly that of the patient at the time of the last dream, shortly before the psychosis set in. Then, twenty years after the first dreaming of this dream, the patient had in fact had "the air pumped out of her", and the mental death and decay of her existence started from the very bottom.

But not only the world of unsuspected illness can appear in our dreams. Even a cure can be indicated by the dream events, long before this turn for the better has been noticed in waking life. A patient had been suffering for weeks from the after-effects of influenza with complications of pleurisy. At a time when no improvement of his weak condition could be determined clinically, he dreamt on four subsequent occasions that he was with friends at a restaurant well known for its good food. He was particularly enjoying a special dish called *coppa*. With grim humour he related these dreams to his doctor and asked him whether the dream wished to tell him that *coppa* was perhaps the best form of strength-giving nourishment. The doctor warned him against eating it, particularly since the patient admitted that *coppa* had never agreed with him in waking life, and that it had always given him indigestion. The patient, who was very reasonable, therefore did not satisfy this desire. But there was no mistaking the fact that from the time of these dreams he improved rapidly, to everybody's astonishment. Eight days later he was back at work, whereas the doctor had counted on at least three months' convalescence.

It was this feeling of getting better, this heightened vital mood, which, although hidden from him in waking life, showed itself in his dream as the gay world of the restaurant with the *coppa* meal. This recurrent dream very much resembles a dream sequence of one of C. A. Meier's patients.[176] In this case, however, the doctor had acceded to the patient's request, and had given him his mortadella sausage. Thereupon this patient, too, very soon felt the return of his vitality. It is true that Meier, in accordance with C. G. Jung's theory, immediately imported a pharmacon-archetype into this dream, where it supposedly appeared in the symbolic form of mortadella. Consequently he referred the cure itself to the "extraordinary efficacy" of the archetype. Apart from the fact that the untenable hypothesis of the abstract notion of archetype as an effective agent has here been taken to the point of absurdity, the mere fact that our first patient improved rapidly even when the dream "pharmacon" was withheld from him speaks very strongly against it.

The psychological recovery or growth of a previously infantile neurotic woman of thirty-five years was manifested by the following dream:

> "I saw my little daughter Ursula before me. In my dream I was perfectly certain that she was suffering from incurable cancer. She would only live for a few more days. However, I was not at all sad about this; on the contrary I awoke in a rather glad and pleasant mood, and in the dream I had but the one thought of being as nice to her as possible during her last few days on earth."

This phenomenon, too, in the usual interpretation on the objective level, might appear as expressing the death wish of the dreamer against her seven-year-old child. But this must always remain a completely unprovable hypothesis. Nothing in the dream itself speaks in its favour, nor can any other evidence be adduced. But the arbitrary nature and wilfulness of such an interpretation is clearly shown by the happy mood of the dreamer on waking up, and also by her subsequent remarkable growth in maturity in general, exemplified particularly by her much more genuine, more natural, and more loving attention to her child.

Nor could dream interpretation on the subjective level interpret this dream any better. Strictly speaking, it is not a mere picture into which our dreamer projects her subjective childishness. She experiences an actual meeting with her own child. And she meets her only because of her own childishness at the time of the dream. She was open only to the perception of children and childish things. Nor did the fatal disease of her child "symbolize" merely the collapse of her own childishness and the necessity for its disappearance. Rather she experienced this possibility and certainty for the first time, from the full reality of the dream.

Recovery, in the sense of successful self-discovery, also occurred in the dream of a forty-four-year-old artist, whose fame at the time of the dream had spread far beyond the borders of his country. His decisive dream very much resembled the stereotyped dreams of the poet Peter Rosegger, by means of which A. Maeder attempted to contrast the so-called finalist and prospective function of the dream with Freud's causal and reductive interpretation (*see* page 41). Because of the complete psychoanalysis of our dreamer, which has the invaluable advantage of enabling us to know his condition in the greatest detail, this dream gives us yet another opportunity of showing how artificial are all those interpretations which ascribe to certain dreams either particular intentions due to some psychological factors or else intended effects on the waking consciousness.

Our dreamer had become a painter against the greatest resistance on the part of his parents and relatives. After he had left school his father still insisted on putting him into business. He worked under a completely dried-up and pedantic chief accountant, spending the whole day adding infinitely long sequences of dry figures. After eighteen months of this he could not stand it any longer. He ran away and only got in touch with his family when his paintings had attracted some notice in Paris. For the last twenty years he had had dreams, just like Peter Rosegger, that took him back to the years of his apprenticeship every few weeks. In these dreams, as in the waking life of the years gone by, he had to undergo the torture of these sequences of figures, was incessantly criticized by his superiors, and was constantly reproached for his lack of business acumen. He had to reach the age of forty years and to have had psychoanalysis for two years before this stereotyped dream took a new turn, finally to stop bothering him altogether. In the last of these dreams he saw himself bending over his account books, and having the greatest difficulties with his additions. Again the bookkeeper reproved him and called him an incompetent idiot. This time his superior became louder and louder and more and more enraged. Finally he yelled at our dreamer, telling him to go to the devil, and that he had employed Jacob Blattner in his place. With a kick in the pants the chief accountant threw him outside. Now he stood helplessly in front of the entrance to the business. There was nobody about and he was completely alone. He was terribly ashamed that he had not left long ago of his own free will and, deeply frightened by the events, he woke up. He could smell the coffee that his wife was just preparing next door, his eyes focused on the many precious paintings of famous masters that were the gifts of his admirers. He was filled with an unspeakable feeling of happiness and he was deeply grateful that his present-day life granted him an existence in freedom and fulfilment.

If we keep strictly to the immediate reality of this dream and preserve it in its entirety, then we shall note in it not only the absence of any evidence for Freud's causal theory of wish-fulfilment, but also that there is not the slightest trace of any unconscious psychic factors such as Maeder had introduced into Rosegger's dream, the purpose and aim of which it is to correct the dreamer's pride. Even had our dreamer, like Rosegger, discussed pride and ambition with a friend, there would still be no justification for connecting this discussion with our dream, and for thus confirming an assumption about the dream from events in the waking state. In fact, in the case of this patient, questions of pride and ambition had at no time in his life played a significant role, either in dreams or in waking life. All he learnt from the dream and from the entire atmosphere of the dream was that he still had an immature, unadjusted, much too narrow attitude towards the world, and that he had not yet found himself nor attained his personal freedom. Owing to his being arrested in an apprentice-like and immature behaviour pattern, only a dictatorial chief and a corresponding world could appear in his dream. His emancipation and real self-determination took place at the time of the last dream. In it he had been freed from his childish attitudes in his entire being, and he woke up to the full enjoyment of the independence and freedom of his waking world and completely surrendered to it. True, his fears at the end of the dream, together with very many other dreams and utterances of his, betray that, like many others, he is still considerably afraid of being himself and free, and for this very reason dare not shake off his old, immature and externally imposed ways of living. For this reason, too, in the dream he does not leave the job of his own free will, but has to be thrown out by someone else.

This dream emancipation was soon expressed in his artistic work during waking life. A few weeks after the dream he finally broke through to his own definite style. This is perhaps the best confirmation of our view that dreams are neither the fulfilment of displaced wishes in symbolically disguised hallucinatory form, nor the results of unconscious purposive influences either expressed auto-symbolically or else compensating for some conscious attitude. What did happen in this dream was rather that a man had "merely" been able to develop into the potentialities of real selfhood. As in Rosegger's case, here also it would be quite inexplicable that the dreamer should have woken up so happily into a contemplation of the work of the old masters, had it indeed been the purpose of the dream to punish him for his pride and to humiliate him by means of these paintings. In this case, too, the stereotyped dream of returning into the world of the apprentice only came to an end because he had finally overcome his childish and un-free attitudes on which the dream had been based.

A third, even more obvious and impressive, self-discovery in the true sense of the word happened in the dream of a sixty-year-old patient. She had originally been a mentally and physically healthy woman, intelligent, vivacious and loving. Already during puberty, the severity and violence of her mother had destroyed an essential possibility of the patient's life. Later, still as a young woman, she had married an insensitive and purely materialistic man. Over the years she had increasingly lost her original vitality and her spontaneous enthusiasm and had finally fallen into a chronic, depressed state. Only occasional fits of rage betrayed the presence of a volcano still smouldering slightly. After the brutal destruction of her first great love by her mother, this woman had had a dream which recurred at varying intervals throughout her life. In this dream she met a dark woman dressed in flowing robes who would confront her like a threatening apparition, uncanny in her deadly earnestness. Nothing happened, no words were spoken. As soundlessly as this woman appeared, she disappeared again. Spontaneously, the dreamer called this figure the "Woman of Fate", or her "Norn". At sixty, after medical treatment had been able to give her the courage to be herself, and when her depressive mood had disappeared, this "Norn" appeared in her dream for the last time but now in quite a different way. This was the "self-discovery dream", as the patient herself called it. She prefaced her account of this dream with the following memories from waking life:

"In my home town there was an old guildhall in which three of my favourite playmates were living at the time. They and their generous and affable mothers were well-disposed towards me. The house and its inmates had a very great attraction for me. The adjoining round tower with its broad sandstone spiral staircase, the deep window recesses, the beautiful wooden doors with their brass metal work, the bell-rope that served as a doorbell and that produced silvery sounds, the landings, the bay windows and the paved courtyard at the bottom of the tower were responsible for this mood. There were lovely hiding places for our games and the large loft and the court were full of attractions and surprises. In this dream I found myself in the living-room, in the uppermost room of this very tower. I could hear the silvery sound of the bell which always reminded me of

Christmas bells. I opened the heavy doors which led to a landing and I looked excitedly but without fear to see who it was that might be ascending the staircase. Since it was a spiral staircase, this could only be determined at the last moment. Now the steps came nearer and behold it was my 'Woman of Fate', my 'Norn'. In contrast to our previous meetings she had a knowing and good-natured smile on her face. When she approached me I recognized myself in her and I awoke free of all oppression."

Not only did this dream have a long history in the waking life of this woman, but it was followed by a strange consequence. On the very next day she happened to be looking into the windows of a dress shop in the town. In doing so she sensed that a woman behind her was looking at her. Then she heard her say: "So it's really you." When she turned round she recognized the youngest of the three playmates she had dreamt about and whom she had not seen for forty-five years. The dreamer added that for the last forty years she had never given a single thought to this house and to its inmates, and that she had completely lost touch with it, the three playmates, and their mothers. Only in her dream had she thought of this part of her youth. Our dreamer was therefore completely overwhelmed by this meeting. Her surprise became even greater when her childhood friend asked her, "Are you still as gay and happy as you used to be?" Incredulously she asked her girl-friend, "Was I really?" and she was told: "Yes, indeed! Very much so and always full of new schemes."

Her dream encounter with the house had brought back a world long past. We shall not discuss here whether the surprising fact that a person out of her dream world should happen to meet her soon afterwards in real life can be explained by the improbable yet superficially satisfactory assumption of a so-called accident or not. We are only concerned here with its significant confirmation of the fact that our dreamer had originally been a particularly vivacious, happy, and highly creative person, even though she herself found this hardly credible. In the misery which she had endured after submitting to her mother and after being completely robbed of her selfhood by her husband, she had unquestioningly been arrested in her development. It is this inability to develop his existential potentialities to the full which is the essential guilt of man. For in his essence man is deeply concerned about this ability to be himself completely. In waking life our patient had long ceased to be her own self and a complete being. She had taken refuge in an alien and miserable form of existence impressed upon her by her environment. Although her development was seriously retarded, she nevertheless anticipated her whole life in her dream. True, she did this in the dark disguise of her "Woman of Fate", the "Norn" of her dreams, in which she could not recognize herself. In accordance with her own deep feelings of existential guilt her relationships to the "Norn" were threatening and evil. It was for this reason that the "Norn" had such a reproachful expression. Only at the end of her life did she regain the courage to be herself once more, and the uncanny guilt-laden gap between her factual non-existence and her destined meeting with herself began to close. Thus she could again come to terms with herself, both in her dreams and in her waking life, just as she had been able to do forty-five years before when her true being had not yet surrendered to the pressure of the environment. It is due to this newly regained, yet originally rich, attitude to life that the old and merry world revealed itself anew, and that she found herself once more in the house in which she had played happily in her childhood.

From her meetings with the "Norn", her "Woman of Fate", this woman, even in her girlish dreams, had been able to learn of her own potentialities. True, it had to take four decades to realize them, and to attain that mature selfhood in which she could recognize herself in the "Norn". But already in her very first meeting with the "Norn" she had anticipated her whole future. Is it not a fact that such dreams, and also those dreamt by some schizophrenics, decades before their psychotic break-down in waking life, i.e. specifically catastrophic dreams in general, are only possible because we are not only our past and present, but by way of hidden anticipation our future as well? How else could we ever be aware of what belongs to the future and what will happen in it?

Now, if man is more aware of the future in his dreams than in waking life, is he so only with respect to his own body and soul? Are there not, apart from the so-called diagnostic dreams, telepathic and prophetic dreams of which many contend that they confront us with strange things far beyond the reach of our sense organs?

(b) "Clairvoyant," "Telepathic" and "Prophetic" dreams

Freud, in contrast to most scientific investigators of his time, left open the possibility of the occurrence of clairvoyant and telepathic dreams. He believed that he had every reason to be completely impartial, since he himself was quite indifferent, and knew nothing about it. He even dealt at length with a dream which the dreamer himself considered a clairvoyant one.[177] Unfortunately the dream chosen by Freud is quite unsuited to a study of clairvoyant dream phenomena, for in it nothing was dreamt that corresponded with the dreamer's waking reality, but only with an event which remotely resembled it. Furthermore, in his investigation Freud immediately skipped over the alleged clairvoyant phenomenon itself. He was only concerned with ascribing to it the role of all other latent dream thoughts, i.e. the material used by a displaced drive for obtaining its disguised satisfaction. Although Freud could still just manage to re-interpret his dream example, if only inadequately, in terms of a great number of speculations, he nevertheless granted the impossibility of such an interpretation in those clairvoyant dreams in which an actual event of future waking reality appears as such in a preceding dream. Since such clairvoyant dream phenomena, like traumatic ones, cannot be fitted into his dream theory, he gives them short shrift. In this case he not only carried over the deficiency of his theory of dreams to the phenomenon itself, and spoke of the inadequacy of the dream function, but he simply denied it the character of a dream. For this dictatorial banishment of clairvoyant phenomena out of the realm of dreams, he can give no better justification than that they do not fit into his conception of the dream. His "proof" is so significant for scientific thought in general that it deserves to be cited verbatim. In his work *Dreams and Telepathy*, he writes:

> "Ought we to call such a telepathic experience (in which there is an exact correspondence between dream and event, although the event could not at the time have been perceived with the senses) a 'dream' at all . . . why should we provide a counterpart to the confusion evoked by Maeder who, by refusing to distinguish between the dream work and the latent dream thoughts, has discovered a new function for dreams? Supposing then that we are brought face to face with a pure clairvoyant 'dream', let us call it a merely clairvoyant experience in a state of sleep. A dream without condensation, distortion, dramatization, above all, without wish-fulfilment surely hardly deserves the name."[178]

Much less prejudiced than Freud was the Italian Ermacora's study of telepathic dreams.[179] For three years he studied a boy who was five years old when the investigation started. The investigator himself could never produce telepathic dreams in the boy himself, but only indirectly through an acquaintance. The latter could suggest dreams to the child telepathically as the investigator directed her to do. In order to exclude any direct influence both experimental persons were strictly controlled. Both slept beyond audible reach in different rooms. The doors were locked and bolted to prevent any meeting during the night. One of the many dreams which Ermacora's acquaintance managed to transmit to the child telepathically went as follows:

"The small boy will be a goatsherd and will leave his goats to graze in the mountains. Three goats will be missing. On his return he will meet a lady dressed in blue carrying an umbrella who will tell him that the three goats have fallen into the river."

S.M. (the transmitting person) was told all this while in bed. She could not see the child since he had gone to bed in the other room. Ermacora had placed the child in the care of a nurse who was sleeping in the same room. The room had been locked. The dream, as remembered by the child on the following morning, obeyed Ermacora's instructions almost in every detail. The boy did not say that he had been a goatsherd, simply because goatsherds were outside his experience. In recounting his dream he told Ermacora that he had been walking somewhere very high up with a stick in his hand, and that he had been surrounded by many dogs with horns on their heads. When the nurse, who was kept in the dark as to the nature of the experiment, told him: "Dogs have no horns. They must certainly have been ears," the child insisted, "No, they were real horns." The child was not only ignorant of goatsherds, but had never met any goats. Thus he thought they must have been dogs with horns.

A spontaneous telepathic dream was reported to us by a healthy man in the course of his training analysis. At the time he lived some 900 kilometres away from his mother. On the night between the 4th and the 5th of October he fell ill with pneumonia. That very night he became so feverish that he turned delirious. Throughout his delirium he believed that his mother was with him, and he begged her to place her cool hand on his forehead. In the course of the following morning the mother 'phoned her son's boarding-house. Instead of the usual greeting she anxiously asked the housekeeper, who had answered the telephone, whether her son was seriously ill and whether she ought to come at once. She had dreamt of her son's illness on the previous night, but had had no other information whatsoever. In this dream she had been with her son who had been lying in bed with a high fever. He had been completely delirious and had constantly asked to be cooled. Three years later when he was working in London, and while his mother was on holiday in Chur, he broke his right thigh on the way to his office. The following day he received another telephone call. This time the mother asked if her son's injuries were serious. She had dreamt most vividly that he was lying in a hospital bed, his right leg bandaged from top to bottom.

These two telephone calls were and remained the only long-distance calls that his mother had been able to afford throughout her life. If she had not been completely convinced of the reality of these dreams she would no doubt, on grounds of economy, have made neither of them. Thus there can be no question of an accidental connection between the mother's telephone calls and her son's mishaps.

A further example of a clairvoyant dream is that of Susanna Kubler, a teacher at Heidelberg. This is how she reported it:

> "I am in a hospital ward. In the centre of it my fiancé is lying on a table. His right arm is bare and near his shoulder there is a large wound. Two doctors, a nurse and I are with him. He sees me and he asks, 'Do you still love me?' A few days later I was informed by my bridegroom's mother that he had been shot in the right shoulder on the 18th August near Gravelotte and that he had died on the 23rd August. His nurse had been the first to report his death. Even today I can remember the dream in all its details."

She had dreamt it during the night of the 23rd August, 1870.[180]

The following report comes from Sub.-Lt. V., an intimate friend of Lt. D. who was hit by a bullet on the 3rd September, 1916. The injured man had only just been able to crawl back from the front to have his wound bandaged. Fifteen hours later he was missing during roll call. His comrades looked in vain for him in first-aid stations. He was posted as missing. On the 18th September, the battalion to which both lieutenants belonged returned to the same battle front. On the night between the 18th and 19th September, Lt. V. dreamt that his missing friend was dying in a grenade crater, next to a willow tree at the side of the Chemin Creux. D, reproached the dreamer for having left a friend to die without coming to his aid. V. was the most cold-blooded officer in the world quiet and sceptical. Nevertheless, this dream left him no peace. He approached his C.O., who at first did not take him seriously, but finally gave him permission to look for his friend near the Chemin Creux. V. arrived there and discovered the scene of his dream. At the foot of the willow tree there was a note, "Here lie two French soldiers." Nothing pointed to the fact that D. had been buried there. However they started digging and found D. who had been buried there some fourteen days previously.[181]

However, it is not only *significant* events in the life of the dreamer that are noted clairvoyantly. Very often we dream of very insignificant events or situations. The highly critical Johann Kaspar Lavater, whose extremely strict truthfulness was proverbial, once had two dreams during the same morning. In the first dream he was confronted by a citizen of Zurich whom he had not seen for many years. In the other he dreamt of a letter which he would receive and which would deal with a matter he had considered settled.

"I was awakened," Lavater continues, "and the presence of a client was announced. He was dressed exactly like my dream citizen and had the same posture. On the same day I also received a letter about an old matter that I had considered settled, and which agreed in every detail with the dream letter that I had dismissed as ridiculous on awakening."

On another occasion Lavater dreamt that he had received a quarto letter in hexameters, which he believed he knew almost by heart. The dream letter came from a friend who had not written to him for years. That very morning he was asked if he had not heard from this friend in London. With a smile Lavater replied that if his dream came true, he should receive such a letter that very evening. He went to the post-office, and there a letter was awaiting him, identical with that of the dream.[182]

Charles Dickens once dreamt of a woman in a red shawl who said to him, "I am Miss Napier." "Why Miss Napier?" Dickens asked himself. "I know no Miss Napier." Some hours later two people called on him, and introduced him to a lady in a red shawl. Her name was Miss Napier and she had previously been quite unknown to Dickens.[183]

A psychoanalytic trainee had been told of the possibility of clairvoyant dreams. He had been most critical, for such a possibility threatened to throw his entire previous philosophy out of gear. During his holidays in Ticino he had to give a lecture on C. G. Jung's

"On Psychic Energy" and on Maeder's *"Selbsterhaltung und Selbstheilung"* (Self-Preservation and Self-Cure). By reading these he had again been assailed by the problem of clairvoyant dreams. On the evening of the 16th May, 1951, he discussed this with his wife for a long time. Both came to the conclusion that one would have to experience things oneself before believing in them. He added jokingly that they might perhaps have such an experience that very night. On the following morning his wife told him quite simply and without recalling the discussion of the previous evening that she had had the following dream:

"I could see vicar S. arriving with two boxes. The boxes looked odd to me. I did not dare to open them. Suddenly Anneli A. turned up. The boxes were opened. Anneli A. explained their contents to me. They were children's dresses. In one box there were modern American dresses and in the other box there were older and coloured clothes. I felt that the dresses came from Anneli A. and I was surprised. At the same time it seemed that Anneli A. was somehow related to the vicar, perhaps she was his daughter."

To this dream of his wife, the husband added the following comment:

"This dream appeared extremely strange to both of us, and it seemed to have no real connection either with our everyday lives or with our feelings. We tried to interpret it. All that emerged was that we knew the vicar; that, like us, he was on holiday, and that he owned a summer-house near by. Only the day before we had enquired whether he was there, but had been told that he was not. Anneli A. is in fact a distant relation of mine and as in my wife's dream she happens to be the daughter of a vicar, not, it is true, of the vicar S., but of a cousin of my father's. For years we had lost all touch with her and her husband and, as far as we could remember, we had never visited her, nor received her. We were quite certain that her name had not been mentioned among us for many months. Even after a long search we could remember absolutely nothing which could have brought about her appearance in the dream. Just as little did we know what to think of the children's dresses in the boxes. I concluded our mutual mental search by saying, 'Perhaps it means something which is going to happen in the future.' I only meant this as a joke. An hour later a parcel of two boxes arrived by post. In the one we found white and modern American dresses and in the other, older and coloured dresses for our children. These dresses came from Anneli A. She had sent them to us because she could not use them any longer. The arrival of these parcels was just as unheralded and strange as the appearance of Anneli A. in the dream. The evidence of the inter-relation of dream and subsequent waking experience was so striking, that neither of us had the slightest doubt about the clairvoyant character of this affair."

Another young doctor narrated to an experienced psychotherapist the following clairvoyant dream after having asked him, with only poorly disguised maliciousness, what displaced impulse or instinct could possibly have striven towards fulfilment in this dream. The dreamer had accurately drawn the scene of his dream on a piece of paper. On his sketch there appeared a garden wall some twenty inches high. One side of it adjoined a house, and the other ended twelve inches in front of a little pool. Its top was tiled with reddish sandstone. On the tiles there lay a spirit level and next to it a bunch of dying pink tulips. Behind the little wall there was a small heap of sand. On the sand, and this he saw with special clearness, a little child had left a brass necklace. The dreamer beheld this still-life for quite some time in all its form and colour. Then it simply faded without anything else having taken place. The psychotherapist, thus put to the test, asked his colleague to come for a walk and to tell him all the associations which each dream object brought to mind. They had been walking for well over half an hour. As is the case with all telepathic dreams—although by no means exclusively with such—not even the slightest meaning had emerged. In the meantime they had unexpectedly arrived at a part of the town with which neither had been familiar previously. Some simple family residences were in the process of being completed. Suddenly the dreamer stopped and pointed over a newly planted hedge. There, in the corner of a small garden, both of them could see that the dream sketch had become a reality. Not only was the little wall of the required form and size, not only did one of its ends adjoin the wall of the house and the other almost touch the little pool, but they could also see the dying bunch of pink tulips and the spirit level. They did not have to look far to find a child's brass necklace lying on a sand-heap approximately twelve inches high behind the little wall.

Such dreams can no longer be honestly dismissed as mere

accidents. When we find that the whole constellation of a number of dream things corresponds so exactly to a situation later met during waking life, the belief in a mere "accident" is the most impossible of all hypotheses. This emerges even more clearly from the following dream reported by the Russian doctor Golinsky.

"I usually dine at three o'clock and sleep for one and a half hours afterwards. In July 1888 I was lying on my bed as I usually do, and I fell asleep at about half past three. I dreamt that the bell was ringing and that I was being fetched to a patient. I then entered a small room with dark wallpaper. On the right side of the entrance there was a chest of drawers, and on it a peculiar sort of lamp or candlestick. I was extremely interested in this object. I had never seen anything like it before. On the left side of the door there was a bed in which a woman was bleeding severely. I did not know how I knew that this was the case. Nobody else was present, and I dreamt vaguely that I gave her some drugs. Then I woke up in an odd way. Usually I wake up very slowly, and remain dozing for some time. But this time I suddenly jumped up as if someone had awakened me. Ten minutes after waking up the doorbell rang and I was called to see a patient. When I entered her room I was completely taken aback. It was remarkably similar to that of the room of my dream. An odd little petrol lamp stood on the chest of drawers on the right, and the bed was on the left. As if in a daze I approached the patient and asked her: 'Have you a violent haemorrhage?' 'Yes. How did you know?' she replied. I asked the patient at what time she sent for me. She replied that she had been feeling unwell all the morning. At one o'clock she had had a slight haemorrhage to which she had attached no importance. Only at two o'clock had she begun to be very disturbed and had gone to bed hoping that the bleeding would stop. At four o'clock she had decided to send for me since her bleeding was becoming more and more severe. The distance between the two houses is about twenty minutes' walk."[184]

For clairvoyant and telepathic dreams contemporary thought can find certain analogies in the conquest of large distances by modern technology. Thus scientific thought is no longer forced at all costs to deny the existence of such phenomena. It is conceivable that the objects and people of the dream emit a certain radiation the effects of which are then received and experienced by the dreamer during sleep. This is thought to be implicit in the very name "telepathy". Thus the radiation theory is often illustrated by reference to radio and television. But for what reasons is the name "telepathy" composed of the words "telos" = distance, and "pathos" = suffering? Does not the very idea of telepathy always presuppose a subject shut up in himself, an immanent subjectivity? Only if this were the case would "external objects" have to penetrate into a subjective receiver by means of rays, in order to produce some effect. But if we assume that such an "objective transcendence" must be supposed then we must also grant a "subjective transcendence". A person could have no influence on objects at all if he did not first emerge from and beyond his assumed immanence to reach them. But how could this original immanence be capable of a twofold transcendence, and why should it want to transcend in this way?

On the contrary, the "essence" of a human being, as phenomenological investigations of dream phenomena have shown time after time, is of quite a different kind: man "ex-ists" in the very literal sense of the word. He is always "outside"; he is with the people, animals and things of the world he meets; just as a light can appear as such only through the things it happens to reveal. Insofar as man exists at all, he *is* his relationship to the things of the world; so much so that his possible modes of behaviour towards the things he meets make up his entire actual essence. This basic structure of human existence implies man's dependence on the things around him, and this is precisely what Heidegger denotes by the term "Geworfenheit" which has so frequently been misinterpreted. It is because of it that man is first and foremost absorbed in the objects of the world on which his existence depends. Thus he generally forgets to think of the original event: that all beings *are*. Yet, from this very dependence on things and people there arises man's deepest meaning and highest task. Because of it man always knows from the depths of his heart and conscience that he has been charged by his destiny to care for all that reveals itself to him, and to have a deep concern in helping every being he meets to attain full development.

This structure of man's nature and the significance of his existence arising from it, necessarily imply a quite original openness to, and understanding of, the people he meets and the things he encounters. Were he not essentially like a light shining in the dark— in which light alone all the things of the world can make their appearance—he could not exist in the sense that everywhere and always we can observe him to be from the start "outside", primordially existing *with* all the beings he meets and *as* these very relationships with them. Thus it is not true that things, either of the waking or of the dream world, must first penetrate from the "outside" to the human brain, there to produce perceptions in a most mysterious manner. Quite on the contrary, man's ability to perceive things and other people is grounded in his primary openness. If so, there is no reason why man should not encounter what lies beyond the realm of his sense organs. Eyes, ears, organs of touch, nose and tongue do not perceive anything by themselves, and man does not see, hear, touch, smell or taste because he disposes of the requisite sense organs. On the contrary, he can only have these organs and allow them to function because he is fundamentally a being open to the world to whom the understanding of and perceiving the world is an original property.

Just as man is aware of events from which he is still removed in space, so he can be related to events which are removed in time, events which belong to his future. This relationship is the basis of the occurrence of prophetic dreams, in which things happen that mock all traditional conceptions of space and time. True, there are only a few prophetic dreams that can be satisfactorily verified. But the frequency of their occurrence is quite unimportant for their value in elucidating the structure of human existence. In this respect one single verified prophetic dream could have more importance than a thousand everyday dreams. Of the many prophetic dreams that have come to my notice and that do not deserve to be ignored through mere prejudice, I should like to cite the following:

The very scrupulous Johann Peter Eckermann, the great admirer and friend of Goethe, had a prophetic dream when still a boy. On the 23rd of October, 1827, he related this dream to Goethe as follows:

"I had reared three young linnets to whom I was attached with all my soul and whom I loved very dearly. They fluttered freely through my room, and would settle on my hand as soon as I came through the door. Unfortunately when I came in one afternoon one of the birds flew over my head and out of the house. I searched for it all the afternoon on every roof. I was inconsolable. Sadly, I fell asleep and towards morning I had the following dream: I saw myself walking past our neighbours' houses looking for my bird. Suddenly I heard its voice and I saw it sitting on the roof of a neighbouring house behind our garden-hut. I tried to coax it, it came nearer to me, greedily flapped its wings, but still could not decide to settle on my hand. Then I quickly ran through the garden into my room and brought a cup of soaked rapeseed. I offered the bird its favourite food, it came down on to my hand, and I carried it joyfully back to the other two birds in the room. I then awoke, and since it was full daylight, I quickly dressed and could think of nothing better to do than to rush through our little garden to the house where I had seen the bird in my dream. How great was my surprise when I saw that it was really there! Now everything happened literally as I had seen it in the dream. I coaxed it, it came nearer, but it would not fly on to my hand. I ran back and fetched the food. It flew on to my hand and I brought it back to the others."

Since Eckermann was very surprised at this dream, Goethe told him:

"We all move in mysterious ways. We are surrounded by an atmosphere, which we do not yet fully understand, nor do we appreciate how it impinges on our spirit. This much is certain, that under special conditions the fibres of our soul can reach beyond their physical limits and grant the soul a presentiment, indeed, a real look into the immediate future."[185]

Even A. Lehmann, who was so averse to all so-called occult occurrences, was forced to admit that there were dreams the prophetic character of which satisfied the most careful test, and in which the dreamer could "certainly" not have learnt by natural means of what the dream told him and what subsequently happened in waking life.[186]

This however did not prevent Lehmann from immediately attributing such facts to a "mere accident". But how, for instance, could we attribute to an accident the agreement between dream and subsequent event in the case of the woman from Luneburg who dreamt that both her sons had died in a bicycle collision, and that she herself had died the very same day? In the dream she had asked her sons to sell their bicycles, and the boys had acceded to this maternal request, not so much because they trusted her presentiments but rather in order to put her mind at rest. Then one day her husband, who had previously been in the best of health, was suddenly taken ill. The doctor was quickly called and considered the condition so serious that the patient's wife sent for her two sons.

One was at school, while the other was rehearsing some music for a concert. On being thus summoned both tried to reach their home as quickly as possible. One of them borrowed a bicycle, while the other was taken home in a friend's car. Both happened to be turning into the street from opposite directions, collided with each other, and were instantly killed. When the victims were brought into the parents' house the mother had a stroke. The husband, who had lost both wife and sons on the same day and whose illness was the cause of this fatal series of accidents, quickly recovered, as if nature had merely used him as a figure in a tragic play.[187]

A prophetic dream of world historical significance, and beyond all criticism, was that of Bishop Joseph Lanyi of Grosswardein. The bishop had been the teacher and afterwards a friend of Archduke Franz Ferdinand, assassinated in 1914. In this dream he was informed of the future murder of his previous pupil. He recorded this dream on the morning of the assassination. This is what he wrote:

"On the 28th of June 1914 at a quarter to four in the morning I awakened from a terrible dream. I had dreamt that in the early hours of the morning I had gone to my desk in order to look through my letters. Right on top there was a black-bordered letter bearing a black seal with the coat of arms of the Archduke. I immediately recognized his writing. I opened it and on top of the letter I noticed a light blue picture, like those on a picture postcard, on which there appeared a street and a narrow passage. Their Highnesses were sitting in a motor-car, facing them was a general, and next to the chauffeur there was an officer. On both sides of the street there was a large crowd. Two young fellows suddenly jumped out from the crowd and fired at Their Highnesses. The text of the dream letter itself was, word for word, as follows: 'Dear Dr. Lanyi, I herewith inform you that today my wife and I will fall victims to an assassination. We commend ourselves to your pious prayers. Kindest regards from your Archduke Franz, Serajevo, the 28th of June, 3.45 a.m.' Shivering and in tears I jumped out of bed, and saw from my clock that it was quarter to four. I rushed to my desk immediately, and wrote down all that I had read and seen in the dream. I even copied some of the Archduke's writing as I had seen it in the dream. My servant entered my study at 5.45 a.m. and noticed how pale I was and that I was telling my beads. He asked me if I felt ill. I said: 'Please call my mother and our guest. I wish to say mass for Their Highnesses for I have had a terrible dream.' I then went to our chapel with them. I passed the day in fear and trembling until at 3.30 p.m. a telegram brought news of the assassination."[188]

We owe an important addition to this written record of the Bishop to K., a reporter of the *Wiener Reichspost.* In a personal conversation he had learnt from the Bishop that after the latter had recorded his dream he had also drawn a sketch of the assassination just as he had dreamed it, since he had felt that there had been something peculiar about this particular dream vision. Still on the 28th of June, he had had his drawing certified by two witnesses and had then sent an account of this dream to his brother Edward, a Jesuit Father, to which letter he had appended a sketch of the narrow passage, the motor-car, the crowd, and the murderer at the moment of jumping towards the car and firing the fatal shots. These drawings were in complete agreement with the photographs published in the press some days afterwards.

A further witness for the veracity of the Bishop's report was the well-known editor and writer Bruno Grabinsky. The latter had immediately approached the Bishop's brother, who confirmed all the statements.

There can thus be no doubt either about the authenticity of the report or about the fact that the Bishop had recorded the dream immediately upon waking up and that he had reported it to three people within two hours. It could, indeed, be objected that anyone might have sensed that an assassination was in the air, but this does not explain the exact agreement in time and in so many details. After all, there are an infinite number of ways in which the asassination could have been carried out: for instance on the way to Serajevo, on the steps of the city hall, four people instead of three, one victim instead of two, etc.

In view of this dream Freud might perhaps have admitted, as he did when discussing the general phenomenon of the telepathic dream, that it was a case of prophetic perception. But he would immediately have added that even here the actual dream source itself was nothing but a displaced instinctual wish. The prophetic knowledge was merely more or less accidental and suitable material used by the wish for its disguised hallucinatory satisfaction. For instance it is conceivable that in the prophetic dream vision of the impending assassination there was expressed a displaced death wish of the Bishop directed against the Archduke. But even should this assumption have proved more correct than is usually the case with similar assumptions of dream interpreters, what do we gain by such a proof? Surely not the right to maintain that the Bishop's displaced death wishes were the only essential factors in the dream as a whole.

Among the recently publicized prophetic dreams an example of C. G. Jung's is especially worthy of our attention. He prefaces his report with the following sentence: "The more frequently we find the details of events predicted in dreams the more certain becomes the impression of the existence of pre-cognition and the more improbable becomes the theory of an accident." The author continues:

> "I can remember the story of a fellow student, who had been promised a trip to Spain by his father if he did well in his final examinations. My friend then dreamt that he was walking through a Spanish town. The street led to a square with a Gothic cathedral. Having arrived there he turned to the right into another street. There he encountered an elegant carriage drawn by two dun-coloured horses. Then he woke up. He told us of this dream over a glass of beer. After he had passed his examinations, he went to Spain and there he recognized the street of his dream town. He found the square and the cathedral, which corresponded exactly to the dream vision. At first he wanted to go straight up to the church, but he remembered that he had turned right in the dream, and he therefore turned the corner. He was curious to see whether the rest of his dream would also come true. Hardly had he turned the corner when he saw the carriage with the two dun-coloured horses."[189]

Further on, in the same work, C. G. Jung thinks that he can see the proof that prophetic dreams still continue in such reports as that of Air Vice-Marshal Sir Victor Goddard. Sir Victor tells of the dream of an officer unknown to him in which the subsequent disaster of Goddard's aeroplane was predicted.

CHAPTER 18

"Nonsensical" and "Paradoxical" Dreams

(a) *"Nonsensical" time-and-place relationships in dreams*
IF telepathic and prophetic dreams do not conform to common notions of space and time, there are other dreams which seem to deal even more arbitrarily with these dimensions. The apparently absurd scenes in our dream of the urn suggested strange perceptions of space. Our attempts to interpret it made us suspect that in these very absurdities of the dream there might be revealed a much more primary space and time than can be inferred from the way these are commonly conceived. Perhaps some dreams in which the "nonsensical" and "illogical" treatment of space and time predominate will turn this suspicion into a certainty.

A middle-aged man had never been able to see in people and things anything but the means for satisfying his own selfish ends. He was therefore considered by all and sundry to be utterly insensitive. Up to his thirty-fifth year he had, on his own admission, considered women exclusively as sexual objects. Then for the first time in his life he had fallen in love with a very beautiful and lovable girl. But even towards her his feelings were fickle, and could change from hour to hour. "Why should I burden myself with another human being?" he used to say. "She can only cost me money." At that time he had the following dream:

"My girl-friend and I were in a shabby inn. Like a 3rd class railway waiting-room, it had drab walls and grey, faded furniture. What struck me as most odd was the fact that the whole room was so terribly small, like the room of a doll's house, two yards long, one and a half yards wide, hardly one yard high. We, too, were very small and I very often felt as if I were looking at my girl-friend through the wrong side of opera-glasses, so distant did she appear. Both of us were depressed and bored and seemed to have nothing in common. These feelings were reflected by the atmosphere both of the inn and its surroundings. It was monotonously raining out of a deep grey, cloudy sky, and water was dripping on to the paving in front of the inn. Suddenly the sun broke through. The room became bright. At the same time I felt very attracted to my girl-friend, and found her very pleasant. A wave of warm feelings towards her welled up in me. At that very instant I saw, to my utter astonishment, that the whole room had changed. It had become as gigantically large as the banqueting hall of a magnificent palace and its furnishings had become luxurious and tasteful. We two had also resumed our natural size. Unfortunately this did not last for long. The wave of warm feeling in me quickly ebbed away, and simultaneously the room and our own statures contracted. Again we sat in the doll-like little inn and again we were terribly bored. Then this whole game began anew and was repeated many times. Corresponding to the rhythmical ebb and flow of my feelings of love towards my girl-friend, the room expanded into magnificence only to contract again to the size of a prison cell."

What happened to space in this dream can certainly not be understood by conceptions of space as a given, independent, and homogeneous dimension, measurable with universally valid measuring rods. On the other hand, we can see all the more clearly how space is allotted to the dreamer only in accordance with his existential structure at a given time. When he himself is self-absorbed and restricted by a narrow stinginess, then his world space, too, shrinks to the size of a doll's room. At that moment, however, when he can go "out of himself" his world expands into palatial magnificence.

Even worse things happened to "space" in the dream of another man, more than forty years old.

"At first," the report begins, "the dream dealt with a late friend of mine who was highly narcissistic and homosexual. I have forgotten the exact details. Then I was suddenly concerned about being able to observe the perspective of the room and thus mentally to absorb it into myself. This would then have enabled me to become dimensional in myself, in other words to assimilate space in the form of a physical dimension. While I was concerned with this experiment, the walls of the room began to slant. They arranged themselves in perspective, became foreshortened, and the lines converged towards a vanishing point. By means of this mental operation I managed to remove all distance between the objects and myself. I had the entire distance within me. This mental act suddenly began to have practical consequences, in that other people also experienced this perspective event. One of them looked down from a skyscraper and jumped into the depths. I was terribly frightened. But since the perspective was operating in his case, i.e. since he had absorbed all the perspective foreshortening, depth no longer existed for him. It is for this reason that the jump from the skyscraper was only one of about half a yard. He thus landed quite safely below. Since he had the whole of space to himself no heights presented any danger to him, even though I had thought that it would be a jump into death. Another man who had been unable to execute this philosophical work of annihilating and absorbing space, jumped after him and was instantly killed."

The key to an understanding of this strange dream of space is given by the short meeting with the late narcissistic and homosexual friend. He would not have been admitted at all into the dream world as an intimate friend if the dreamer himself was not involved in the same behaviour. In fact, the dreamer, at the time of this dream, was in a state of extreme solipsism. All his attitudes to things and people had become so shaken, and his self-absorption left so little room for relationships with others, that the whole world appeared to him as a flat projection. Everyday notions of homogeneous space, distinguished by measurable distances, are even less capable of elucidating the spatial arrangement of this dream than that of the previous example. But once more this incorporation of space speaks of the particular way of being in the world of this "narcissistic" man. He had restricted his life to a single relationship—with himself. Significantly the destruction of space in this dream begins with the fact that it is the room in which he finds himself which is first seen in perspective. In this perspective, i.e. seen from the viewpoint of a given subject, there is revealed an intermediary stage of the absorption of total reality into the ego.

The master works of Japanese painting are unaffected by perspective. The spirit of Eastern culture is directed to a bridging of the division between the I and the not-I, and to the interconnection of every individual phenomenon with "life at large". The ancient Greeks did not know of perspective, yet they considered all things to have emerged from a common concealment. Moreover they regarded the revelation of their content as a gesture of the things themselves. It is for this reason only that the ancients considered a thing to be an "ergon", i.e. a work appearing in its completion. Only the Romans began to interpret "ergon" as "opus", and to see in it the result of laborious human operations; till finally through a back translation of the Latin *operare, agere* and *actualitas* into the Greek *energeia*, the concept of energy assumed its contemporary significance of force and efficiency. Together with this change introduced by Roman thought, man increasingly began to believe that it was he who as a thinking and conceiving ego endowed the world with its significance. More and more the essence of things was seen as the result of human activity and of human ideas.

This philosophy culminated finally in the Cartesian conception of a *res cogitans*, that is, a human mental thing or subject, the only indubitable thing. Descartes considered it as the only real thing. Only with this increasing subjectivism, with this enthronement of the human subject above all remaining reality, did perspective make its appearance.

Man's restriction of his being to a single relationship with himself, to an almost total absorption in his own ego, was, in the case of this patient, increased almost to the point of the complete destruction of his existence. Thus he dreamt, some months later:

> "A great crowd, actually the whole of humanity, was following a leader over the whole earth. He was a manly figure in a black cloak. Then the crowd remained behind and soon disappeared out of sight. In front I could only see the black figure marching into the distance by himself. A grandiose and terrible mood pervaded everything and, magnificent in its yellow-grey paleness, it told of the destruction of the world. Now the man was gathering all the objects of the earth: trees, houses and mountains. He put them all into his pocket. This erased and destroyed them, and the world became ever emptier. Only the bare line of the horizon could be dimly recognized in the infinite distance. Then even this was pulled into his pocket. Finally there only remained a diffuse atmosphere into which the leader himself eventually dissolved. At any rate nothing could be seen any more, and the destruction of the world was soon to be completed. But shortly before this happened I woke up. I remained overcome by the impression of this dream for quite some time afterwards."

In this dream the dreamer did not only want to pocket all space and all things into his own body. In this incorporation the things were completely destroyed. But with the loss of all things and of the relationship to them the dreamer was no longer able to be in the world, i.e. to be "there". He was threatened with the immediate and complete destruction of his entire existence, with absolute dissolution. Does not existence in this dream reveal itself as so dependent on things, that the dreamer could only be man as long as there were still things, and as long as he could still be related to them? If then the destruction of world and self are so completely interrelated, is it not true to say, conversely, that human existence and relationships to things are also essentially one and the same?

Whereas in our "strange dream of an urn" the close relationship between loving mother and son produced a sudden proximity, the dream which follows speaks of an infinite distance. The bride of this dreamer had been killed in 1944 by the Russians in East Germany and bestially mutilated. Our patient had discovered her in this state. Shortly afterwards his only sister and his grandmother had died owing to the war. Because of all this he had fallen into the deepest chronic depression which made him completely unfit for work. After the fifth hour of treatment the patient dreamt:

"A number of space rockets have been destroyed while trying to reach Venus. I am the member of the crew of Rocket No. 4 all of whom are volunteers. I hear it rumoured that our ship too, which is already in the stratosphere, is about to be destroyed. The commander of the ship is a Swiss captain. As long as he holds the rudder nothing can go wrong. Suddenly somebody calls: 'We are now leaving the stratosphere!' The acceleration of the ship increases rapidly."

In contrast to the narcissistic world destroyer of the previous dream, this man has a marked desire for, and ability to, love. His despair was only due to the fact that he no longer knew how to satisfy his longing. This was shown by his dream of Venus and his ever new attempts to reach it, irrespective of any possible losses. Yet Venus is at an unapproachable distance. Its distance from him is similar to his distance from the possibility of loving, of which his insurmountable traumatic experiences have robbed him. He had to get above the stratosphere, to leave the envelope of the earth, in order to reach Venus which speaks of love and the heavens. In the dream he found a trustworthy guide, the Swiss captain, just as in waking life he had entrusted himself to the psychotherapeutic guidance of a doctor, whom he had often seen in the uniform of a Swiss captain. This trusting communion between patient and doctor was his first attempt at a new human relationship. At first it was this alone which made it possible for him to be human, and enabled him to be "there" again.

After eight hours of analysis this patient reported the following dream:

> "I was in a dark empty void. I could not even feel any temperature or pull of gravity. Suddenly a large and unending road emerged from the pitch-dark void. I walked along it in extreme exhaustion and suddenly I came to a large empty throne glittering brightly. From the air there appeared two radiant hands which hovered above my head and blessed me. A benign and deep voice spoke to me: 'Go in peace. As you have believed so it will happen.' I felt a tremendous relief, and with a clang something black fell from me, and like a dark mass lay formless at my feet."

From the time of this dream the patient suddenly improved. Within a few weeks he had regained his original vitality and ability for work. Yet this dream too began with the fact that there was nothing at all any more. The tremendous horror of what had happened to him had not only destroyed his capacity to love things and people, but had led to his complete severing of all true relationships with them. For this reason his dream world was also marked by the absence of all things. He had no world at all any more. It seemed to have left him completely. Only he himself remained in the void. Was he at least allowed to exist as himself? Obviously not even that. Time after time he complained bitterly that he could not feel himself any more and that he was no longer alive. Even in the dream he had to lose all his substance, become completely weightless, and finally become lost in the darkness of the void. Again this loss of all relationship to things meant at the same time the collapse of a human existence.

With the dissolution of all things and of himself the great darkness of the void had become completely spaceless too. According to traditional conceptions of space this did not necessarily have to be so, the dreamer need merely have found himself in the empty room of his world. However, in reality there is never an original and independent space, into which things are then placed, thus creating inter-spaces of varied distances. On the contrary, original space is given to our existence only by our actual human relationships to people and things. There never exist positions in an abstract space into which things are put, but on the contrary, things are primary places, and it is our relationships to the things we meet that determine their original distance from us. When, in Rilke's translation of the Seventh Sonnet from the Portuguese, the lover says to his beloved "Nur wo du bist, entsteht ein Ort" (Only where you are does a place arise) he is saying something which holds for all the people and things we encounter.

Heidegger has shown how the modern scientific conception of a homogeneous space arose out of this original space based on our relationship to things. Original space produced by the presence of a thing has, he declares, a number of locations at different distances from it.

"These locations can however be considered as mere points between which there is a measurable distance: a distance—in Greek a *stadion*—is always determined by mere points. What is thus determined by points is a particular space. It is a distance, a stadion, as designated by the Latin word 'spatium': an inter-space. Thus the distances between people and objects become interspatial distances. In this space, considered merely as spatium, an object (e.g. a bridge) now merely appears as something at a point. Each and every point can at any time be occupied by something else or by a mere mark. This is not all: from space considered as spatium, we can isolate mere extensions according to height, breadth and depth. What is thus derived, or 'abstracted' is conceived as the mere multiplicity of the three dimensions. This multiplicity, however, no longer gives distances, is no longer *spatium* but *extensio*—extension. Space as *extensio* can be abstracted further, namely as the relations of analytical algebra. These consist of the possibilities of a purely mathematical construction of quantities with as many dimensions as are desired. We can call this mathematical system "space", but "space" in this sense contains neither room nor places, e.g. things such as a bridge. Conversely, in spaces determined by places space can always be found as inter-space, and in the latter again as pure extension. *Spatium* and *extensio* enable one at all times to fix the position of the objects and points that they determine, by means of distances and directions, and to make the necessary calculations. In no case, however, are the mass numbers, and their dimensions, merely by virtue of the fact that they are applicable to all extensions in general, the *basis* for the essence of spaces and places measurable with the help of mathematics."

Heidegger concludes this section of his work by pointing out that meanwhile modern physics itself has been forced to consider the medium of cosmic space as a field unit, determined by the body as its dynamic centre.[190]

Since the original and real space of our world is based directly on our relationships to things, neither places nor any spatial relationships can exist without them. Since he is unrelated, our dreamer is no longer granted a "staying place" for his existence. It is for this reason that his world is not only an empty void but an inessential nothing. However when the dreamer, thanks to his newly gained relationship to his doctor, began to exist once more, a thing, a glittering throne, made its appearance in this inessential nothing. It was the first and only place. In his relationship, once the dreamer was given the possibility of moving and orientating himself, new spaces revealed themselves within the spaceless and essence-less void. In this world he even discovered a path to fulfilment and deliverance.

Just as we can neither see anything primordial, nor any detached and independent forms, in the space of these dream worlds, so also the time intervals of many dreams do not conform to a generally valid and formal conceptual scheme or to an *a priori* perceptual framework.

The following is the dream of a woman aged thirty-four years:

"I was in a prison cell. On the walls there were many clocks. Suddenly a burglar came in. He tampered with the clocks with a screwdriver and broke them. Although they were still ticking, their hands no longer moved. The ticking warned me that second after second was passing while true time was standing still. This was a terrible crime and at the same time it was terribly uncanny. Time outside went on as usual, but my time in the cell had come to a stop because the hands had been arrested. However I knew that time outside was passing, for my face was becoming lined. Both male and female warders entered and half killed the intruder. They locked me in again, but now my cell was more like one in a lunatic asylum. One warder stayed with me. I complained to him about the clocks. They called for eau-de-Cologne. A green flask came in. The flask had the shape of a man. It smelt wonderfully. Then the flask turned into an elegant young man. This man took me out of the cell to marry me. Now everything was all right again. I really lived once more, and the hands of the clock no longer stood still."

Because I had treated her for three years I was extremely well acquainted with the life history of this woman. So I did not find it difficult to see in this dream a recapitulation of the entire course of her waking life. To this very vivacious and sensuous girl, her prudish and strict parental house had indeed been a prison. In spite of parental supervision, she had been molested, while still a half-grown child, by a man who was attracted by her sensuality. This had been a terrible shock to her, and had truly meant the collapse of her previous world. As a consequence she had fled back into her very childish dependence on her parents, and would not renounce her dependent but well-protected childishness at any price. From then on her life-history, her time, had come to a standstill, and in causing this to happen the man had committed the most heinous crime possible on the girl. The discrepancy between the standstill of her own time and the progress of outer time frightened her by its uncanniness. It was the uncanniness of the deep gulf between her actual existence, arrested in childishness, and the superficial way in which she could still experience the world of grown-ups in its barest outlines. Then, however, a warder arrived to care for her. He appeared because during psychoanalysis she had learnt to accept more mature erotic relationships in an assimilable and bearable form. The dreamer added that the special scent of eau-de-Cologne which appeared in her dream had always excited her senses. Thus she found her way to a man, and could be married in the dream and in waking reality. She took her life into her own hands once more and found a full and proper existence. The clocks again showed the passage of time, since her life-history had restarted.

Another person, a middle-aged woman, had the following dream:

"I left my analyst in a rebellious and masculine-aggressive mood. I went on a long journey. This journey lasted half a life-time. First I went..., that is I didn't actually go but I was guided to my destination by some external force. At first I came to Paris. Here I took lessons in love-making from a blond man. It was purely a question of physical sexuality. I then had my body measured in the way in which beauty queens are measured. I didn't want to have this done to me, for I was beginning to love my teacher very dearly. I was already feeling as if I completely belonged to him as his wife. Finally we went on. We left the town and came to a German village, near my home-town. There we lived together happily for a whole year. Finally

I returned to my analyst in order to have another session. When I came to his house I noticed to my astonishment that only half an hour, and not half a life-time had passed. I then woke up and saw that in fact only half an hour had passed since the time that I had looked at my watch just before falling asleep."

This was the dream of a woman who, from motives to be traced in her life history, had forcefully and successfully suppressed her femininity throughout her life and who had paraded herself behind the façade of a purely masculine attitude. She had become a clever, industrious, and ambitious physician. But on the day before this dream her femininity had emerged quite clearly during the analytic session. She had still rebelled against assuming her inherent existential faculties, and thus against the analyst also, whom she had in fact left in the irate mood of the dream. But after the session she experienced her previously unsuspected wealth of feminine potentialities. At first she only experienced this in the form of a purely physical, sexual, and undirected desire, but soon she also felt herself longing to be able to love one definite man with all her heart and to live completely for him. What had emerged in extraordinary intensity of experience during half an hour did in fact correspond to the usual time of development of half a life-time. This event in waking life was repeated in her dream. But here she experienced it even more fully. For the events of the dream, starting from purely sensual, sexual content and the outwardly frivolous measuring of her erotic charms in Paris, through her falling in love with the blond young man, and finally to her living in a serious, homely and natural German village, did in fact amount to a good half of her existential potentialities. They thus represented a half of her life-time.

Yet the dreamer did not experience the many events in a precipitous rush, as if in the dream half a life-time and all the events in it were compressed into the narrow space of a mere half-hour. Nor may we misinterpret this dream by assuming that she had experienced merely more in half an hour, as if the duration of time had merely been extended, as if what occurred in a so-called objective half an hour had only become long in the dream. This would be a mere mental transposition of quantitatively imagined, so-called objective time, into a fictive dream time. We should in this case simply be neglecting the dreamer's own inner and original temporality, which is historical and corresponds to nothing else but her own life-history, which is herself. Her dream was possible only because her expectations now reached far enough into the future. It was her inner time, her life history, her existential openness, which she inherently lives and is, that revealed themselves to her to so large an extent. The derived and common time of the world receded before the speed of her existential maturing; so much, in fact, that she became conscious of it only at the very end of the dream, and immediately before waking up.

Another woman spent one and a half days in her dream in spite of the fact that, measured by the clock, the dream lasted at most three hours. In her dream this woman went mountaineering with some friends. The party set out long before dawn, and starting out from a close, dark and misty valley, arrived at a mountain hut after a very difficult climb lasting some hours. As the woman looked round the hut carefully, she discovered that the room was full of large mirrors. At the same time she saw a gigantic hair-dressing saloon and a shower bath. The report then continued:

"As it became dark very early, we all went to bed. I fell asleep immediately, but woke up very early next morning and I started to climb on alone for my companions were still asleep. I could see them following me some hours later, as I stood on a peak bathed in radiant sunshine. I woke up before they had arrived."

This was the dream of a woman who had frequently suffered from deep depressions. From the morning after this dream she improved visibly, although another few days had to pass before she could overcome her depression completely. In this dream of mountaineering in which she climbed from the darkness of the sombre valley on to the sunny peak, she had had a glimpse of how she could overcome her sad mood and thus acquire deliberate control over it. True, she still spent a whole night half-way up the mountain, but why did she see mirrors, showers, and beauty salons there? All of these belong to the realm of beauty culture, of which even in dreams, indeed especially in dreams, a woman is only particularly aware when she has rediscovered her true relationship with the world, characterized by a healthy desire to be beautiful and to please. But at the end of this dream the rest of the party had not yet reached the peak. This demonstrates particularly well that the dreamer is only open to such perceptions which in content correspond exactly to the mood of her existence. In fact, on waking she was not completely "together" and at the height of her powers.

Nevertheless her deliverance from depression had reached the point where through her freer and less rigid attitude she could expand her sense of time and make her mountaineering last two days. In her depressive mood of the previous day the patient had still been completely in the grip of her past, and so all relations to her present and future had become repressed. In contrast, the temporality of this dream, in its very essence, led into the open and to a continuously developing "history": her life history. In her depressions she had lived utterly unhistorically, she had been bogged down by the past, without a real future and thus without any historical expectancy. But in the dream her proper time had expanded sufficiently for her to undertake something, to experience it in the present, and to retain it. Once again, she could exist in the unity of future, present and past behaviour. The fact that the mountain tour lasted almost two days, may serve as a measure of her newly won existential breadth and freedom.

The following dream of a single night covered three to four days and nights. It was dreamt by a man who had previously been a pedantic drudge, a man who had counted every working minute and who had been laughed at by everybody around him. He had thus developed a strong inferiority complex. His doctor had finally been able to convince him that he was a rather valuable person who had no need to be ashamed of himself at all, but who ought to be considerably more generous with himself. In his dream, in which he said he had felt extremely well, he was visited by an English royal couple:

> "The royal visitors stayed with me for three days and I felt as if we had known one another for many years. Throughout the whole time not a single false note crept in. Everything was beautiful and harmonious. Nature outside was in full bloom, full of warmth and luminous colours. I dreamt of every detail starting with the sincere and firm handshake of the royal couple on their arrival, and ending with our farewells at the railway station. I can still remember our dinner and how on two occasions we all drove into the country. The security officers were two officials, who relieved each other every few hours. I had to be careful that my wife did not make too much of a fuss. The royal couple were staying with us unofficially, and had refused an official reception in Zurich."

To the dreamer the English royal couple were the **prototype of** decency and humanity. They were exactly what he himself would have liked to become, and what in fact he largely was. During his treatment he had now found the courage to stand by his own individuality, and not to give way to the pressure of the derisive laughter of those around him. To have his behaviour endorsed from the highest quarters, and to be accepted just as he was by a royal couple holding similar views, was so tremendously essential for him, that the very significance of the royal visit produced the large time span of three days. Conversely, from this duration of the royal visit, we can evaluate the significance of this self-acceptance for the dreamer himself. The mere fact that this man, normally so mean with his time, allowed himself three days of relaxation was so extraordinary that it might be considered tantamount to the decision of an average man to take half a year's leave.

Quite a different kind of time is involved in dreams that are "infinitely long", dreams of eternity. In them the dreamers do not experience long spans of time because something significant has happened, or because a great many future possibilities have emerged, but simply because time stands still. We have so far only met such dreams of infinity or of eternity in people who are confirmed drug addicts. Literature too is full of descriptions of the dreams of drug addicts characterized by this sort of time. For instance, S. T. Coleridge, who was an opium addict, told of dreams in which he was kept a prisoner for centuries in secret chambers, or in which he was impaled on the spires of a tower. Then again, for millennia he was buried with mummies and sphinxes in stone coffins, in narrow chambers and inside eternal pyramids, or under soft, indescribably ugly masses of primordial reeds in the slime of the Nile, where Isis and Osiris told him that he had committed so terrible a crime that even the ibis and the crocodile were revolted by it.[191]

A chronic morphinist known to me personally used to dream that he had been buried under a coal mine from time immemorial. In these dreams there was never the slightest possibility of his being saved. What was most horrible, however, was the knowledge that he would never be able to die. Nothing at all happened any more. "The story," according to the dreamer, "neither went forwards nor backwards any longer. All that remained was eternal and constant languishing."

The horrible crime which, in the dream of the English poet, revolted both ibis and crocodile, just as with the burglar in the dream of the arrested clocks, consisted of defrauding existence of its potentialities. With the help of narcotics these addicts had deprived life of its fulfilment by robbing it of any responsible relationships with the environment and with their fellows. Through narcotic paralysis and intoxication they had prevented the development of their own inherent life history. They had brought their own time to a standstill, and their existential time had thus been turned into an empty duration. So the centuries and millennia of being buried, of which they speak when trying to describe their dreams, are not as long a time as the three days in the dream of the royal visit. They are simply a way of expressing the hollow duration of their unhistoric vegetation, of the kind of time that is the essential characteristic and result of their entire existence, degraded into a duration devoid of past and future.

Again, these dreams tell us that the specific duration of the dream event does not belong to an independent and original time structure. However much the conditions of time might have varied in all these dreams, all of them corresponded exactly to the character of the dreamer's total being in the world.

In these dreams we could see again and again that both time and space emerged as mere partial phenomena of the dreamer's whole existence. We should never have been able to understand them from our common conception of time which only knows it as a continuous passage of momentary points, and a corresponding sequence of acts of consciousness happening in them. We add a mere manifold of experiences considered as indifferent, and these are localized in the stream of that consciousness of the present purely objectively. Only in this way can we fill an inherently vacant form of time with any content at all. Yet we have seen that time in dreams is based on the specific quality of the dreamer's human relationships to the things of his dream world. The time of the dream event was always referred to the possibility of occurrence or non-occurrence of dream things and to their significance. For instance, the dreamer did not experience the time of the dream about the royal visit, as a series of momentary points of time lasting for three days in any of which "now" such and such a thing could have occurred. The time of the dream rather dated from the total significant event: the time was as long as the royal visit. Even in waking life we do not stay with friends for five more minutes but just till we have finished smoking one more cigarette and thus date the time from our relationship to a thing. On the other hand the common conception of time consistently ignores both the timing and also the significance of each "now". As the spatial structure is abstracted into a homogeneous extension, so the common idea of time levels it to an equal and countable sequence of "now" points. For this reason so many of the dreams cannot be understood fully through these common abstractions of time and space, but appear as completely senseless and absurd or even as utterly incredible. Thus they force all those who are still bogged down in the common and derived concepts of space and time to employ the most peculiar mental constructions. In the "explanation" of "incomprehensible dreams" it is simply assumed that the sleeper has a disturbed sense of space and time without any evidence that there exists such a sense which could be disturbed in the first place. In other cases, especially in clairvoyant, telepathic and prophetic dreams, one speaks of improbable "accidents of an acausal nature". From this it seems logical to deduce that the psyche can either not be localized in space or time, or that space and time are psychologically relative.[192] All such hypotheses, splitting, as they do, human existence into isolated objects and detached space and time schemata, become completely superfluous as soon as we bethink ourselves of the original and immediately experienced, i.e. existential space and time of man.

(b) *Dreams about a "paradoxical something"*

Dreams, which to everyday thought appear as the most nonsensical and as even much more incomprehensible than the strangest dreams of space and time, are those dealing with a paradoxical something. These dreams can, in one form or another, occur in people ranging from the most educated to the illiterate. In most cases they appear on more than one occasion in the dreamer's life, and are always described by the dreamers as extremely important and striking, despite their apparent "absurdities". Thus, a healthy, very active and highly developed woman first met this kind of dream when she was about eleven years old. It recurred at long intervals right up to the present age of the dreamer, i.e. for more than forty years. She described the dream as follows:

> "There is always something great, and nothing else except this gigantic something. I perceive it with a sense transcending my ordinary senses. I can somehow touch the gigantic something but at the same time I am in it as it is in me. It is gigantic and infinitely small at the same time, and it is just this 'at the same time' that is so magnificent. I am never afraid. All these dreams have always struck me as surprisingly impressive and my astonishment is always mixed with reverence."

This dreamer, as all the other witnesses of this kind of dream experience, had never studied Indian philosophy. But does not the "something" of their dream largely correspond to the Eastern description of the "Over-Self" of man? Is not one of its essential descriptions that it is greater than great and at the same time smaller than small? In any case the great reverence which the appearance of this dream instils in all its dreamers forbids its rejection as mere nonsense. We must at least grant that it is permissible to pose the question, what sort of sense it is that transcends all the "natural" senses? We must admit that it is possible that these dreams are hints of an understanding transcending our everyday knowledge. More precisely perhaps we have here flashes of insight that all phenomena, apart from their objective form or mass normally given to the senses, also have something which far transcends our "usual" experience of spatial extension and objects. Do not these dreams tell us that the human being is part of a nonmaterial something that cannot be sensed, so much so that he is involved in it in a very special way? For do not all these dreamers inform us that they are not so much "inside" this something in the sense of being within a cavity, but rather in the sense of being indissolubly in it and it in them? Does this kind of "being within" perhaps signify that in the dream we have an inkling of what the Eastern sages mean when they consider it the aim of human existence to surmount objective and directed thought, and thus to achieve the complete unification of I and thing?

PART IV *The Dream as a Whole*

CHAPTER 19

The Problem of the Dream as a Whole

OUR discussion of some dozens of individual dreams has merely been able to strengthen our earlier belief that we cannot consider dreaming and waking as two entirely different spheres. In reality there is no such thing as an independent dream on the one hand, and a separate waking condition on the other, which we could distinguish from each other by their characteristics, as for instance the species "fox" is distinguished from the species "eagle". Any such attempt at a distinction is doomed to failure from the very beginning. For it is always the identical human being who awakens from his dreams and who maintains his identity throughout all his waking and dreaming. What we must realize more clearly at the end of our investigation is the fact that we must recognize the dream as a form of human existing in its own right, just as we call the waking state a particular form of man's life.

It is therefore all the more urgent to look for an answer to the question about the difference in the modes of living of waking and dreaming man, for only through an adequate distinction between the two can we appreciate the specific boundaries of dream life and so set this life within them and thus within the sphere of its own proper nature.

We had hoped that man's dreaming mode of being could be distinguished from his waking form of existence either by its smaller number of relationships with things and people or by some particular and specific kind of behaviour to them. But our studies have shown most strikingly that in dreaming—as long as we are within one and the same dream event—we certainly do not have fewer possibilities of behaviour and relationship than in the waking state. On the contrary, we can no longer contradict Aeschylus when, in the 104th and 105th verses of the Eumenides, he even goes so far as to make Clytemnestra say that in his sleep, thanks to the visions of his dream, man's essence reveals itself with great clarity, whereas during the day the fate of mortals is hidden from them. In any case we have now encountered people whose dream worlds indicated an openness which they did not have in everyday life, even though perceptions of such a special clarity are not every-night occurrences. On the other hand, in waking states too, men can from time to time, and with the same certainty of the dream, have so-called telepathic and prophetic visions, and thinkers and poets have occasionally had the experience of original space and then asked questions about the essence underlying all things.

Our investigations have made us look upon dreams as they are themselves, and in their phenomenal state. We have not reinterpreted the dream in terms of a pre-judgment from waking life, alien to the dreams themselves. We regained the ability of seeing in the dream events special ways of being which revealed themselves directly and could thus be directly evaluated. Yet, so far, we have been unable to determine a criterion whereby the essence of our dream life as a whole could be distinguished from waking life. We might be tempted to interpret this as being due to a fundamental impossibility of differentiating the essences of these two ways of living. Has not the wise Chwang-Tse already drawn our attention to this fundamental impossibility? Why else did he confront us with the problem of whether he, as a man, had just dreamt he was a butterfly, or whether now, as a butterfly, he was dreaming that he was a man? Did not Pascal, too, realize that we cannot differentiate dreams from waking reality if in the dream, just as in the waking state, events follow upon one another? Has not Schopenhauer admitted that the only criterion for distinguishing between dreams and reality is in fact nothing else than the empirical fact of waking up? In any event Kant's argument that waking life is different from the dream because of its "interconnection of conceptions according to causal laws" was easily refuted by Schopenhauer when he said that in dreams too "each and every thing depends on the causal law in all its manifestations". But Schopenhauer immediately detracted from the value of his own criterion by concluding: "If we now assume that we must judge both (phenomena) from the outside, then we shall find that there is no particular difference in their essence, and we shall be forced to agree with the poets that life is a long dream."

Perhaps the reason for such a resigned conclusion can be found in the circumstance that waking and dreaming had previously been imagined at most as two spheres of interconnected experiences or ways of conceiving things, separated more or less sharply by awakening. Yet was not this separating, this awakening, taken for granted as an obvious fact and thus left unexplained?

Neither waking nor dreaming can be adequately described as independent interconnections of experiences or conceptions. Whether man is awake or dreaming he always fulfils one and the same existence. Man's existential identity is preserved through all waking and dreaming, since all that is dreamt is nothing but *my* dream, *your* dream, or the dream of a particular individual who remembers what he had dreamed, after he has awakened. But what is the meaning of this awakening, separating dream and waking life? Why do we speak of an awakening into the waking world but never of dreaming into a dream world? "Because," one says, "we always find ourselves in the same world when we wake up, whereas dreams always transport us each time into a different world. In reality both statements are only valid in the reverse sense, in that the essence of awakening is precisely that in it the world always meets us as the same world. This is not the case with the beginning of each new dream. But if awakening is then nothing but a waking into the same world, what do we know about the "sameness" of this waking world?

This "sameness" is the identity and consistency of things and people, and of the form and manner in which they move, and it is characterized by everyday habits, as determined by the everyday historical nature of existence. But are there not enough dreams in which we always return to the same landscape, the same house and the same situation; indeed, in which a very special stress is placed on this character of familiarity? Are there not people who dream very frequently that they wake up in their usual every-day beds, that they get up in the customary every-day way, take their breakfast and get ready to go to work?

Is not perhaps the significant difference the fact that although in the dream we may return to a like situation we can never return to the *same*? For were we to meet the *same* situation in dreams, the dream phenomenon would have to unfold in the identical manner in which waking life unfolds itself, and there would yet have to appear a difference between what was previously dreamt and what is now dreamt once more. At best we only dream of like things. Just as the sound of a church bell heard at eleven o'clock each day is never the same sound but only a repetition of a like one, so in the example of Peter Rosegger's stereotyped dream it is never the same but only a like situation that is being repeated, despite the poet's resistance to its monotonous return when he is awake. We saw that he ended his dream report by saying expressly:

"And then I decided [after each awakening] that if this oppressive dream should appear again I should cast it off with great energy and that I should call out aloud to conjure it away. The next night there I was again in the tailor's workshop."

Similarly, in the many dreams in which a dreamer has to repeat examinations time after time, it is only a *like* event that recurs. If it were a true return into the same world, then every examination, just as a repetition in waking life, would begin where the last dream examination had left off, would be continued somehow in the present and would lead to an expectation of future developments. In fact, however, in these dreams we are occupied with like activities only. Even in the long series of dreams in which a lady dressed in blood red first lay unconscious under the water, and later on danced with the dreamer, the development itself did not take place in the dreams, and was by no means part of their content. In the various dreams the previous phase was never remembered, nor was any future development expected in them. If this man had done nothing else but dream, and if during the day also he had been left to day-dream without distraction, this series of dreams would never have occurred at all. Instead, the stereotype dreams of machinery and worms would have consistently pursued him all his life. For these stereotyped dreams will always return in like form, so long as the life-historical problems they contain are not adequately experienced as such in the dreamer's *waking* life, there to be faced, resolved and matured or at least developed. True, a dream event may have a certain history of its own, since all dreaming too is a form of existing. Thus, the two-day mountain tour of one of our dreamers was unquestionably a continuous historical event. But even in this mountaineering dream the dreamer neither saw any connections with events of previous dreams nor did she historically continue this event in any later dream that has come to our notice.

So the dream life itself nowhere shows the slightest possibility of a return into the same previous dream world. For this reason man, as a mere dreamer, cannot have a continuous development of his life. There is no dreamt life-history running parallel to his waking life-history. Without this historical continuity of his waking life, man would not even be in a position to see the specific discontinuity of his dreaming. A waking life is accordingly presupposed in all dream interpretation. Consequently, all possibilities of determining the essence of the dream in the dimension of waking life must be changed according to our insights into the peculiarities of

THE DREAM AS A WHOLE

the waking state, and all our understanding of the dream must fully depend on our particular understanding of waking existence. Now if our ability to be awake is the most essential condition of all our concern with dreams, then dreams themselves force all future investigators to pay heed to the structure of waking life, instead of taking it for granted.

If, on the basis of such a relationship between dreams and waking, we only speak of dreams in waking life, but never let the question of waking life bother us in the dreams themselves, does this not bear witness to the fact that dreaming is a part of waking life? If, then, waking life on its part belongs to our historical continuity, must it not necessarily include the dream also? Perhaps our life history demands both our waking and our dreaming by revealing itself explicitly and factually in the former, whereas it withholds its inherent development in the latter. If this is the case, then our dreaming also, with all its discontinuity and lack of historical development, might well be based on the mystery of the historical continuity of our existence.

Notes

[1] F. W. HILDEBRANDT: *Der Traum und seine Verwertung fürs Leben*, Leipzig 1875.
[2] Genesis xxxvii, 3–9; xl, 9–19; xli, 1–7.
[3] Genesis xli, 16.
[4] Daniel ii, 28.
[5] *The Iliad*. Book I. Verses 61–3.
[6] PLATO's *Phaedo*. Trans. R. S. Bluck, London. Routledge & Kegan Paul, 1955, p. 42.
[7] JEZOWER: *Das Buch der Träume*, p. 427.
[8] Cf. B. F. MEIER: "Die Welt der Urbilder bei Ali Hamadani", *Eranos Yearbook*, Vol. XVIII, 1950, pp. 115 ff.
[9] After R. WOOD: *The World of Dreams*, New York 1947.
[10] *Opera omnia*, Basle 1585.
[11] CARDANUS: *Somniorum synesiorum, omnis generis in somnia explicantes libri IV*, Bologna 1562.
[12] See also L. BINSWANGER: *Wandlungen in der Auffassung und Deutung des Traumes*, Berlin 1928; and "Traum und Existenz" in *Ausgewählte Vorträge und Aufsätze*, Bern 1947, p. 90.
[13] ARTEMIDORUS: *De somniorum interpretatione libri V*, Basilea 1544; and *Symbolik der Träume* (translated by Fr. S. Krauss, Vienna 1881). Also see S. Freud: *Die Traumdeutung*, Leipzig and Vienna 1922, 7th Edition, p. 3; J. Jacobi in *Ciba-Zeitschrift*, 1945, pp. 3374 ff.; W. Kurth: "Das Traumbuch des Artemidorus im Lichte der Freudschen Traumlehre", *Psyche*, 1951, p. 488.
[14] I. KANT: *Deutlichkeit der Grundsätze der natürlichen, Theologie und Moral*, 2nd contribution.
[15] I. KANT: *Träume eines Geistersehers*, Edition (A), 1766, Leipzig 1880 (K. Kehrbach). Notes on p. 27.
[16] I. KANT: *Reflexionen Kants zur Anthropologie*, edited by B. Erdmann, Leipzig 1882, p. 105.
[17] CICERO: *De divinatione*, II, 71, p. 147.
[18] A. KRAUSS: "Der Sinn im Wahnsinn", *Allg. Zeitschrift für Psychologie*, XV and XVI, 1858–59.
[19] M. SIMON: *Le monde des rêves*, Paris 1888.
[20] S. FREUD: *Die Traumdeutung*, 7th ed., Leipzig and Vienna 1922, p. 29.
[21] S. FREUD: ibid., p. 30.
[22] S. FREUD: ibid., p. 38.
[23] G. H. SCHUBERT: *Die Symbolik des Traumes*, 1814.

[24] BURDACH: *Die Physiologie als Erfahrungswissenschaft*, 1830, Vol. III, p. 486.
[25] NOVALIS: IV, p. 58.
[26] PURKINJE: "Wachen, Schlaf, Traum und verwandte Zustände", Wagner's *Handbook of Physiology*, 1846, p. 456. See also Sante de Sanctis on "Komplementärträume bei Melancholikern" in *Die Träume* (Schmidt), Halle 1901.
[27] S. FREUD: *Die Traumdeutung*, p. 61.
[28] S. FREUD: *Ges. Schr.*, Vol. VII, p. 100.
[29] S. FREUD: *Ges. Schr.*, Vol. VII, p. 98.
[30] S. FREUD: *Ges. Schr.*, Vol. VII, p. 239.
[31] S. FREUD: *Ges. Schr.*, Vol. VII, p. 62.
[32] S. FREUD: *Die Traumdeutung*, p. 94.
[33] S. FREUD: *Vorlesungen zur Einführung in die Psychoanalyse*, p. 229.
[34] S. FREUD: *Die Traumdeutung*, p. 412.
[35] S. FREUD: *Die Traumdeutung*, p. 246.
[36] S. FREUD: *Ges. Schr.*, VII, p. 127.
[37] S. FREUD: *Vorlesungen zur Einf. i.d. Ps.*, VII, pp. 174 ff.
[38] S. FREUD: *Die Traumdeutung*, p. 412.
[39] S. FREUD: *Ges. Schr.*, VII, p. 228.
[40] S. FREUD: *Ges. Schr.*, VII, pp. 124 ff.
[41] S. FREUD: *Die Traumdeutung*, p. 89.
[42] S. FREUD: *Die Traumdeutung*, p. 432.
[43] S. FREUD: *Ges. Schr.*, VII, p. 222.
[44] S. FREUD: *Ges. Schr.*, VII, p. 228.
[45] S. FREUD: *Ges. Schr.*, VII, p. 169.
[46] S. FREUD: *Ges. Schr.*, VII, p. 184.
[47] S. FREUD: *Die Traumdeutung*, p. 94.
[48] S. FREUD: *Die Traumdeutung*, p. 162, and *Ges. Schr.*, VII, p. 223.
[49] A. ADLER: "Traum und Traumdeutung", *Zentralblatt für Psychoanalyse*, 1912–13, p. 174.
[50] W. STEKEL: *Fortschritte und Technik der Traumdeutung*, 1935, Introduction.
[51] A. MAEDER: *Über das Traumproblem*, 1914, p. 2.
[52] A. MAEDER: "Über die Funktion des Traumes", *Psychoanalytische Forschung*, Vol. IV, Vienna 1912, p. 700; and 1913.
[53] A. MAEDER: *Selbsterhaltung und Selbstheilung*, Zurich 1949, pp. 131 ff.
[54] P. ROSEGGER: *Waldheimat*, Vol. II, pp. 321 ff.
[55] A. MAEDER: *Selbsterhaltung und Selbstheilung*, pp. 132 ff.
[56] C. G. JUNG: "Allgemeine Gesichtspunkte zur Psychologie des Traumes" in *Über die Energetik der Seele*, Rascher, Zürich 1928, p. 179.
[57] C. G. JUNG: *Dream Seminary*, 1938–39, and J. Jacobi: *Die Psychologie von C. G. Jung*, Zurich 1949, 3rd ed., p. 145.
[58] C. G. JUNG: *Ciba*, 1945, No. 99, p. 3551.
[59] S. FREUD: *Ges. Schr.*, VII, p. 133.

[60] S. Freud: *Ges. Schr.*, VII, p. 200.
[61] H. Silberer: "Symbolik des Erwachens und Schwellensymbolik überhaupt", *Jahrbuch für psychoanalytische und psychopathologische Forschungen*, Leipzig and Vienna 1912, Vol. III, p. 619.
[62] H. Silberer: "Über die Symbolik", ibid., pp. 710 ff.
[63] W. Stekel: (a) *Zentralblatt für Psychoanalyse*, Vol. III, 1912–13, p. 26. (b) *Fortschritte und Technik der Traumdeutung*, Vienna, Leipzig, Bern 1935, p. 19.
[64] C. G. Jung: *Psychologische Typen*, Zurich 1921, p. 673.
[65] I. Kant: *Erste Einleitung in die Kritik der Urteilskraft*, Leipzig 1927, pp. 24 ff.
[66] A. Teillard: *Traumsymbolik*, Zürich 1945, p. 54.
[67] C. G. Jung: *Das göttliche Kind*, p. 134.
[68] C. G. Jung: "Der Geist der Psychologie", *Eranos Yearbook*, Zurich 1946, p. 477.
[69] J. Jacobi: "Komplex, Archetypus, Symbol", *Schweiz. Zeitschrift für Psychologie*, 1945, p. 299.
[70] C. G. Jung: *Psychologie und Alchemie*, Zürich 1944, p. 32.
[71] See also J. Schwabe: *Archetypus und Tierkreis*, Basel 1951, p. xxxi, and A. Buhler: "Kritische Bemerkungen zur Verwendung ethnographischer Quellen in der Psychologie", *Protokoll der Schweiz. Gesellschaft für Psychiatrie*, 1952, pp. 41 ff., and H. Lommel (Munich): Zarathustra Lecture to Zurich University, Nov. 1952.
[72] C. G. Jung: "Der Geist der Psychologie", *Eranos*, Vol. XIV, 1946, p. 447.
[73] C. G. Jung: *Seelenprobleme der Gegenwart*, Zurich, p. 179.
[74] C. G. Jung: ibid., p. 173.
[75] A. Portmann: "Das Problem der Urbilder in biologischer Sicht", *Eranos*, extra Volume XVIII (1950), pp. 413 ff.
[76] C. G. Jung: *Geist der Psychologie*, p. 479.
[77] C. G. Jung: *Energetik der Seele*, p. 196.
[78] C. G. Jung: *Geist der Psychologie*, p. 448.
[79] C. G. Jung: *Psychologische Typen*, p. 603, and *Tibetanisches Totenbuch*, Zurich 1935, p. 26.
[80] C. G. Jung: *Psychologische Typen*, Zürich 1921, p. 600.
[81] C. G. Jung: *Die Beziehungen zwischen dem Ich und dem Unbewussten*, Zurich 1945, p. 120.
[82] J. Jacobi: *Komplex, Archetypus, Symbol*, p. 229.
[83] C. G. Jung: *Psychologische Typen*, p. 368.
[84] C. G. Jung: *Geist der Psychologie*, p. 460.
[85] C. G. Jung: ibid., pp. 462 ff.
[86] C. G. Jung: ibid., pp. 482 ff.
[87] C. G. Jung: ibid., pp. 483 ff.
[88] C. A. Meier: *Die kulturelle Bedeutung der komplexen Psychologie*, Zurich 1935.
[89] C. G. Jung: *Geist der Psychologie*, p. 484.

[90] For a list of relevant publications the reader is referred to A. Garma, *Psicoanalisis de los sueños*, Buenos Aires 1948.
[91] H. Schultz-Hencke: *Lehrbuch der Traumanalyse*, Stuttgart 1949.
[92] H. Schultz-Hencke: ibid., p. 9.
[93] H. Schultz-Hencke: ibid., p. 69.
[94] H. Schultz-Hencke: ibid., p. 197.
[95] H. Schultz-Hencke: ibid., p. 8.
[96] H. Schultz-Hencke: ibid., p. 62.
[97] H. Schultz-Hencke: ibid., p. 150.
[98] H. Schultz-Hencke: ibid., p. 133.
[99] H. Schultz-Hencke: ibid., p. 20.
[100] H. Schultz-Hencke: ibid., p. 11.
[101] H. Schultz-Hencke: ibid., p. 264.
[102] H. Schultz-Hencke: ibid., p. 85.
[103] H. Schultz-Hencke: ibid., p. 11.
[104] H. Schultz-Hencke: ibid., p. 177.
[105] H. Schultz-Hencke: ibid., p. 178.
[106] H. Schultz-Hencke: ibid., p. 267.
[107] H. Schultz-Hencke: ibid., p. 65.
[108] H. Schultz-Hencke: *Lehrbuch der Traumanalyse*, Stuttgart 1949, p. 82.
[109] H. Schultz-Hencke: ibid., p. 249.
[110] E. Fromm: "The forgotten language". An introduction to the *Understanding of Dreams, Fairy Tales and Myths*, New York 1951, p. 25.
[111] S. Freud: *Ges. Schr.*, Vol. VI, pp. 397 ff.
[112] S. Freud: "Revision der Traumlehre", *Neue Folge der Vorlesungen zur Einführung in die Psychoanalyse*, Vienna 1933, p. 39.
[113] E. Fromm: *The Forgotten Language*, pp. 95–7.
[114] E. Fromm: ibid., p. 7.
[115] E. Fromm: ibid., pp. 175 ff.
[116] C. G. Jung: *Das Unbewusste in normalen und kranken Seelenleben*, Zurich 1926, p. 123.
[117] E. Fromm: *The Forgotten Language*, p. 90.
[118] C. G. Jung: *Die Psychologie der Übertragung*, Zurich 1946, p. 122.
[119] A. Teillard: *Traumsymbolik*, Zurich 1944, p. 88.
[120] E. Fromm: *The Forgotten Language*, p. 97.
[121] K. Leonhard: *Gesetze und Sinn des Träumens*, 2nd ed., Stuttgart 1951.
[122] K. Leonhard: ibid., p. 54.
[123] K. Leonhard, ibid., p. 128.
[124] K. Leonhard: ibid., p. 34.
[125] K. Leonhard: ibid., pp. 49, 78, 133.
[126] K. Leonhard: ibid., p. 120.
[127] K. Leonhard: ibid., p. 14.
[128] K. Leonhard: ibid., p. 139.
[129] G. Siegmund: *Der Traum*, Fulda 1949.
[130] G. Siegmund: ibid., p. 40.
[131] G. Siegmund: ibid., p. 52.

[132] O. J. HARTMANN: *Medizinisch-pastorale Psychologie*, Frankfurt 1952.
[133] R. BOSSARD: *Psychologie des Traumbewusstseins*, Zurich 1951, p. 90.
[134] R. BOSSARD: ibid., pp. 124, 192, 278.
[135] R. BOSSARD: ibid., p. 185
[136] R. BOSSARD: ibid., pp. 82, 85, 87.
[137] R. BOSSARD: ibid., p. 139.
[138] R. BOSSARD: ibid., p. 174.
[139] R. BOSSARD: ibid., p. 174.
[140] L. KLAGES: "Vom Traumbewusstsein", *Zeitschrift für Patho-Psychologie*, Vol. III, Nos. 1 and 4, 1914 and 1919.
[141] G. SIEGMUND: *Der Traum*, p. 39.
[142] J. JEZOWER: *Das Buch der Träume*, Berlin 1928, p. 133.
[143] J. JEZOWER: ibid., p. 273.
[144] A. TEILLARD: *Traumsymbolik*, Zurich 1945, p. 265.
[145] L. BINSWANGER: "Traum und Existenz" in *Ausgewählte Vorträge und Aufsätze*, Bern 1947, pp. 71–81; and "Daseinsanalyse und Psychiatrie" in *Der Nervenarzt*, Vol. 22, 1951, p. 5.
[146] L. BINSWANGER: *Traum und Existenz*, p. 77.
[147] S. FREUD: *Ges. Schr.*, Vol. III, p. 207.
[148] H. KUNZ: *Die anthropologische Bedeutung der Phantasie*, Part I, Basle 1946, p. 19.
[149] L. BINSWANGER: *Traum und Existenz*, pp. 96 ff.
[150] S. FREUD: *Ges. Schr.*, Vol. VII, p. 159.
[151] S. FREUD: *Neue Folge der Vorlesungen zur Einführung in die Psychoanalyse*, Vienna 1933, p. 34.
[152] S. FREUD: *Die Traumdeutung*, p. 262.
[153] C. G. JUNG: *Psychologische Typen*, pp. 675 ff.; and *Aion*, Zurich 1951, p. 107.
[154] H. SILBERER: "Über die Symbolbildung", *Jahrbuch für psychoanalytische und psychopathologische Forschung*, Vol. III, p. 675, Leipzig and Vienna 1912.
[155] C. G. JUNG: *Psychologische Typen*, p. 677.
[156] C. G. JUNG: *Über die psychische Energie und das Wesen der Träume*, Zurich 1948, p. 197.
[157] C. G. JUNG: ibid., p. 199.
[158] C. G. JUNG: *Zur Symbolik des Geistes*, Zurich 1948, pp. 153, 417, 429. See also Martin Buber's criticism in "Religion und modernes Denken", *Merkur*, Vol. VI, 1952, No. 48, Book 2, p. 119.
[159] C. G. JUNG: *Aion*, Zurich 1951, p. 254.
[160] C. G. JUNG: ibid., p. 261.
[161] M. HEIDEGGER: "Bauen, Wohnen, Denken" in the Darmstädter Dialogues: *Mensch und Raum*. Edited by O. Barting, Darmstadt 1952, pp. 77 ff.
[162] PINDAR: *Isthm. Ode V*, verses 1–3.
[163] S. FREUD: *Ges. Schr.*, Vol. VII, p. 119.
[164] S. FREUD: *Ges. Schr.*, Vol. VII, p. 190.

[165] See also E. Blum: "Grundsätzliches zur psychotherapeutischen Situation", *Psyche*, Vol. IV, No. 9 (1952), pp. 536 ff.
[166] S. Freud: *Neue Folge der Vorlesungen zur Einführung in die Psychoanalyse*, p. 39.
[167] See also L. Binswanger: *Traum und Existenz*, pp. 96 ff.
[168] E. Fromm: *The Forgotten Language*, p. 146.
[169] K. L. Reinholdt: *Beiträge zur Berichtigung bisheriger Missverständnisse der Philosophie*, Vol. I, p. 360, Jena 1790.
[170] H. Silberer: *Der Traum*, Stuttgart 1919, p. 101.
[171] R. Anschütz: *A. O. G. Keküle*, II, p. 942, Berlin 1929.
[172] J. Jezower: *Das Buch der Träume*, p. 149.
[173] See also G. Siegmund's examples in *Der Traum*, pp. 99 ff.
[174] Szilasi: *Macht und Ohnmacht des Geistes*, p. 197; and L. Binswanger: "Daseinsanalytik und Psychiatrie", *Der Nervenarzt*, Vol. 22, p. 6, 1951.
[175] J. Jezower: *Das Buch der Träume*, p. 369.
[176] C. A. Meier: *Zeitgemässe Probleme der Traumforschung*, Zurich 1950, pp. 19–20.
[177] S. Freud: *Neue Folge der Vorlesungen zur Einführung in die Psychoanalyse*, Vienna 1933, pp. 51 ff.
[178] S. Freud: *Ges. Schr.*, Vol. III, p. 290.
[179] G. B. Ermacora: *La Telepatia*, Padova 1889, pp. 335 ff.
[180] J. Jezower: *Das Buch der Träume*, p. 376.
[181] J. Jezower: ibid., p. 286.
[182] J. Jezower: ibid., p. 124.
[183] J. Jezower: ibid., p. 178.
[184] J. Jezower: ibid., p. 388.
[185] J. Jezower: ibid., p. 410.
[186] A. Lehmann: *Aberglauben und Zauberei*, 1925, pp. 445 ff.
[187] Based on G. Siegmund's *Der Traum*, p. 91.
[188] F. Moser: *Okkultismus, Tatsachen und Täuschungen*, Vol. II, pp. 465 ff., 1935.
[189] C. G. Jung: "Über Synchronizität", *Eranos*, 1951, Vol. XX, pp. 273 ff., Zürich 1952.
[190] M. Heidegger: *Wohnen, Bauen, Denken*, p. 79.
[191] See K. Birnbaum: *Psychopathologische Dokumente*, Berlin 1920, p. 30.
[192] C. G. Jung: *Über Synchronizität*, p. 283.

INDEX

Aaron, 11
Achaeans, 12
Achilles, 12
Adler, A., ix, 40, 62
Aeschylus, 207
Agamemnon, 12
Agoraphobia, 115
Alchemist, 14
"Anagogic" dream interpretation, 63
"Anima", 61, 117
Anima-archetype, 116
"Animal-dominants", 117
"Animus", 61, 117
Apollo, 15
Aragon, 14
Archduke Franz Ferdinand, assassination of, 186
Archetype, 51, 53, 54, 55, 56, 57, 58, 113, 115, 116, 117, 118, 150, 155, 169, 170
Aristotle, 14, 33, 50
Arnald of Villanova, 14, 159
Artemidorus of Daldis, 15, 33, 159
Asselineau, Charles, 27
Assurbanipal, 11, 12
Assyrian King, 11, 12
Atreus, 12
"Auto-symbolic representations", 49, 120

Babylonian-Assyrian writings, 28
Baudelaire, Charles, 27
Bernheim, H., 27
Binswanger, L., x, 61, 70, 82, 119, 130, 164
Binz, C., 16, 26, 67
Bossard, R., 69, 70, 71, 74, 87
British Museum, 11
Burdach, 23, 24
Byzantine Church, 95

Cardano, Geronimo, 14
Caritas, 146, 149
Cartesian viewpoint, 83, 192

Cebes, 13
Chaldeans, 11
Champmeslé, 167
Chwang-Tse, 11, 83, 208
Cicero, 17
Clairvoyant dreams, 162, 175 ff.
Clytemnestra, 207
Coleridge, S. T., 201
Collective unconscious, 51, 98
Complementariness, 46
"Complex psychology", 58
Condensation (in dream work), 30-1, 32, 112
Conditionalism, 46
Conscious thought in dreams, 133-5
Correggio, 138
Critique of Judgment, 50
Cyrene, 13

Daniel, 12
Dante, 42, 45
Delboeuf, J. R. L., 23
Depression, 113, 144, 147, 193, 199-200
Dêr-el-Medineh, 11
Descartes, 192
Dickens, Charles, 179
Displacement (in dream work), 30, 31, 32
Divine, 146, 149
Dream of:
  Asselineau, Charles, 27
  Chwang-Tse, 11, 83, 208
  Dickens, 179
  Freud, 43
  Freud, Anna, 35
  Herzfelde, Wieland, 73
  Jacob, 12
  Kekulé, 134
  Keller, Gottfried, 80
  Kubler, Susanna, 178
  Lavater, Johann Kaspar, 179
  Leonard, K., 66
  Maury, 23
  Mungo Park, 35
  Nordenskjöld, Otto, 35
  Pharaoh, 12

219

INDEX

Dream of:
  Rosegger, P., 41-2, 44, 45, 171, 172, 209-10
  Silberer, H., 48
  Socrates, 13
  Spemann, Hans, 73
  Varnhagen, Rahel, 73
Dreams:
  Artemidorus's books of, 15
  artistic appreciation in, 138
  clairvoyant, 161-2, 175 ff.
  conscious thought in, 133-4
  danger, warning of, 14
  "diagnostic", 152, 159 ff.
  "endoscopic", 159 ff.
  existence and, 135, 139-40, 146, 148, 149, 150, 155-8, 160, 161-2, 164, 165-7, 174-5, 183, 189-94, 199-200, 202, 207, 209-10, 211
  "extra-sensory" relationships in, 159 ff.
  healing qualities of, 24
  hypermnesic properties of, 23, 86, 153
  imaginary events in, 132-3
  intellectual relationships in, 136-7, 165
  magic and, 154-6
  moral evaluation in, 139-40
  "nonsensical" time-and-place relationships in, 189-203
  personal relationships in, 94, 136-8, 145, 150, 152-3, 162-4, 168, 170, 175, 183, 189, 191, 193-4, 196-7, 202, 207
  prophetic, 175 ff., 203
  reflective behaviour in, 131-2, 134-5
  religious relationships in, 141 ff.
  self-discovery or understanding in, 137, 170-1, 172-3
  telepathic, 175 ff.
  telling lies in, 137
  unconscious mistakes in, 138
  within dreams, 151 ff.
    existing as a dreamer, 151-3
    analysis of dreams, 153-4
    being a thing, 155-8, 160, 162, 167
Dreams about:
  analyses, 43
  animals, 73, 109
  apprentice, 41-2
  assassination at Serajevo, 186-7
  automobiles and aeroplanes, 113
  bees, 147-8, 149
  brother, 163
  burning, 72
  chest, 103
  childhood, 153
  children's dresses, 180-1
  clocks, 196-7
  comrade, 178
  crossing a lake, 35
  crossing a river, 63-4
  crucifix, 148, 149
  Customs officer, 47
  cyclist and the dog, 144
  distorted space, 190-1
  dog bite, 102, 104
  father, 152
  fleeing from pursuers, 110
  flying, 73
  food, 35
  Franciscan monk, 135
  garden god, 141, 149
  girl, 148-9
  goatsherd, 177
  Greek temples, 142-3, 149
  guns, 93
  impending death, 167-8
  incest, 116
  injury, 72
  inn, 189-90
  insects, 114
  letter, 179
  linnets, 184
  magician, 154-5
  "mathematical prison bars", 113
  monastery, 144
  Norn, 173-5
  "paradoxical something", 203-4
  penicillin, 151, 154
  physical petrification, 162-3
  Professor of Physics, 136
  rape, 106
  royal couple, 200-1
  "Run-over Child", 29-30
  shock, 125-8
  sickness, 178
  Stalin, 139-40
  Stendhal, 164
  tigers and panthers, 139
  touch, 72
  tower, 145-6, 149
  urn, 77-9, 98, 100, 189, 193
  visiting a patient, 182
  volition, 129
  vomiting, 71
  work, 108
  Zeus-steer, 143-4, 149
Dream, theories and views of:
  Aristotle, 14
  Binz, C., 16

INDEX

Dream, theories and views of:
  Bossard, R., 69–70
  Burdach, 23
  Cicero, 17
  Fechner, G. Th., 17
  Fichte, J. G., 24
  Freud, ix, 21–31
  Fromm, E., 62–5
  Greeks, 13
  Hartmann, O. J., 68
  Herbart, J. F., 16
  Herder, 25
  Hildebrandt, F. W., 25
  Hobbes, Thomas, 15
  Kant, I., 16
  Klages, L., 71–4
  Leonard, K., 66–8
  Maury, 17
  Novalis, 24
  Petronius, 15
  Purkinje, J. E., 24
  Sante de Sanctis, 68
  Scherner, A., 25–6
  Schubert, Gotthilf Heinrich, 24
  Schultz-Hencke, H., 60–2
  Siegmund, G., 68
  Simon, M., 21
  Voltaire, 15
  "Zurich School", 38–47
Drug induced dreams, 201–2

ECKERMANN, Johann Peter, 184–5
Egyptian dynasty (12th), 11
Elamites, King of, 12
Ellis, Havelock, 77
"Endoscopic" dreams, 159 ff.
Ermacora, G. B., 176–7
Eros, 146, 149
Essential things, 142
Eulaeus, shores of, 12
Eumenides, the, 207
Existence (*see* Dreams)
Existentialist approach, x, 70, 82, 118
Existential identity, 199, 209
Existential structure, 155, 175
"Extra-sensory" relationships, 159 ff.

FECHNER, G. Th., 17
Fichte, J. G., 24
"Finalist" theory of dreams, 38 ff., 50, 51, 104
Franciscan, 135

Freud, ix, 21, 22, 23, 25, 26, 27, 28, 29, 30, 31, 32, 33, 34, 35, 36, 37, 38, 39, 41, 42–4, 45, 46, 47, 52, 53, 54, 58, 59, 60, 61, 62, 63, 64, 65, 66, 84, 91, 92, 94, 95, 96, 97, 98, 102, 103, 104, 105, 112, 118, 119, 120, 125, 158, 171–2, 175–6, 187
Freud, Anna, 35
Freudian school, ix
Freudian theory of dreams, ix, 21–31; critique of, 32–7
Freud's theory of dream symbolism, 91–5
Fromm, E., 62, 63, 64, 65
"Functional dream phenomena", 47

GALEN, 159
Genitalia as symbols, 91, 92, 95, 158
Goddard, Air Vice-Marshal Sir Victor, 188
Goethe, 42, 45, 185
Golinsky (Russian doctor), 182
Graces, 33
Greece, 15
Greeks, 13
Grillparzer, Franz, 82
Gulliver's Travels, 21

HALL, C. S., 89
Hartmann, O. J., 68
Heidegger, M., x, 119, 183, 195–6
Heraclitus, 89
Herbart, J. F., 16
Herder, 25, 33
Herzfelde, Wieland, 73
Hieroglyphics, 27, 28, 40
Hildebrandt, F. W., 25
Hippocrates, 14, 33, 47, 159
Hobbes, Thomas, 15
Hoche, 28
Homer, 42, 45
Horus, 12
Husserl, E. G., 70
Hypermnesia, interpretation of dreams in terms of, 86, 153
Hypnosis:
  dreams during, 93–5

Iliad, 12
Imagination in dreams, 132–3

Interpretation of dreams:
  in terms of symbolism, criticism of, 89–90
  on the objective level, 49, 105, 118, 120, 170
  on the subjective level, 49, 105–6, 170
Ishtar, 12
Isis, 12
Islamic world, 13

JACOB, 11, 12
Jacoby, J., 53, 55
Jessen, 17
Joseph, 11, 12
Jung, C. G., ix, 40, 41, 46, 47, 49, 51, 52, 53, 54, 55, 56, 57, 58, 59, 60, 61, 62, 63, 64, 65, 66, 70, 92, 95, 96, 97, 98, 103, 115, 116, 169, 179–80, 188
Jung's theory of dream symbolism, 95–101
Jupiter, 33

KANT, I., 16, 50, 51, 208
Kekulé, 134
Keller, Gottfried, 80
Klages, L., 71, 72, 73, 74, 82
Krauss, A., 18
Kubler, Susanna, 178

LAMARCK, 54
Language, 53
Lanyi, Bishop Joseph, 186–8
Latent content, 29, 30, 31
Lavater, Johann Kaspar, 179
Lehmann, A., 185
Leonard, K., 66, 67, 68
Luther, 15

MAEDER, A., ix, 40, 41, 44, 46, 49, 62, 63, 171, 172, 176, 180
Magical dream world, 154
Manifest content, 29, 31
Materialism, 16
Materialist, 23
Maury, 17, 18, 23
Mechanistic philosophy, 60
Meier, C. A., 57, 169
Melanchthon, Philipp, 15
Middle Ages, 14

Miriam, 11
Moses, 11
Mountaineering, 147, 149
Mungo Park, 35
Muses, 14
Myths, 53, 63

NAKEDNESS in dreams, 64, 94
Nancy, 27
Natural-scientific view of dreams, 29
Nausicaa, 13
Nebuchadnezzar, 12, 161
"Neo-analytical" dream theories, 60–5
Neo-Babylonian kingdom, 11
Neo-Kantian thought, 56
Nero, 15
Neurosis, 144
Nietzsche, 47
Nineveh, 11
Nordenskjöld, Otto, 35
Novalis, 24, 47
Numen, 149
Numinous experience, 149, 150

"OBJECTIVE" level of dream interpretation, 49, 105, 118, 120, 170
Odysseus, 13
Odyssey, 12
Olympians, 12

PALLAS Athene, 12
Pascal, 208
Pasithea, 33
Perception, 159
Petronius, 15
Phaeacian island, 13
Phaedo, 13
Pharaoh, 11, 12
Phenomenological analysis, 118, 120
Phenomenological interpretations of dreams, 69–74, 82, 121, 130, 150, 183
Philosophy, Socrates' views on, 13
Philosophy, theocentric, 11
"Phylogenetic development", 115
Physics (as complementary to psychology), 57
Pindar, 99
Plato, 13, 33
Plutarch, 14
Portmann, A., 54, 55
Positivist philosophy, 36, 89, 96

INDEX

Pre-cognition, 188
Prophetic dreams, 175 ff., 203
Psychosis, 162, 164, 166, 168-9
Purkinje, J. E., 24

RATIONALISM, 15
Reductive approach, 98
Reflective behaviour in dreams, 131-2, 134-5
Reinhold, K. L., 133
Renaissance, 14
Representation (as form of dream work), 30, 31
Rilke, R. M., 195
Romantic poets, 16
Rosegger, Peter, 41, 44, 45, 171, 172, 209-10
Royal Asiatic Society, 28

SANTE DE SANCTIS, 68
Satan, 138
Scherner, K. A., 25
Schizophrenia, 162, 163, 166, 168
Schopenhauer, 208
Schrötter, 91, 92
Schubert, Gotthilf Heinrich, 24, 27
Schultz-Hencke, H., 60, 61, 62, 84; criticism of, 84-6
Schultz, W., 80
Secondary elaboration (in dreams), 30, 31, 32
"Semiotic" interpretation, 97
Serajevo, 186
"Shadow-archetypes", 117
Shakespeare, 42, 45
Sicily, 14
Siegmund, G., 68, 72
Silberer, H., ix, 40, 47, 48, 49, 63, 92, 95, 133
Simon, M., 21
Socrates (on dreams), 13
Space (in dreams), 189-96
Spemann, Hans, 73
Stalin, 139-40

Statutory law (of Greece), 13
Steiner, R., 68
Stekel, W., ix, 40, 49
Stendhal, 164-5
Strümpel, 18
Subjective level of interpretation, 49, 105-6, 170
"Subjective" meaning of dreams, 47-9, 50, 63, 101, 105, 118, 120
"Symballein", 101
Symbolic disguise, 93, 95
"Symbolic facts", 97
"Symbolic interpretations", 95, 97
"Symbolic representations", 49, 103, 105
Symbolism, 89
Synesius, Bishop of Cyrene, 13
Szilasi, 82, 164

TARTINI, Giuseppe, 138
Technological science, 36
Teillard, A., 64, 73
Teleology, 50, 51
Telepathic dreams, 175 ff.
Telepathy, 182-3
Te-uman, 12
Thea, 99
Tieck, Ludwig, 138
Time (in dreams), 196-203
Troy, 12

VARNHAGEN, Rahel 73
Volitional behaviour in dreams, 129-30
Voltaire, 15

WESTERN metaphysics, 36
Wish-fulfilment theory, criticism of, 42, 84-6, 125, 171-2

ZEUS, 12, 143, 149
Zurich, ix, 45
"Zurich school", 38, 41, 45, 47; critique of, 50-9, 104, 115

3